Power in transition

Power in transition: The peaceful change of international order

Charles A. Kupchan, Emanuel Adler, Jean-Marc Coicaud and Yuen Foong Khong
With the assistance of Jason Davidson and Mira Sucharov

United Nations University Press
TOKYO · NEW YORK · PARIS

JENKS L.R.C.
GORDON COLLEGE
255 GRAPEVINE RD.
WENHAM, MA 01984-1895

© The United Nations University, 2001

The views expressed in this publication are those of the authors and do not necessarily reflect the views of the United Nations University.

United Nations University Press
The United Nations University, 53-70, Jingumae 5-chome,
Shibuya-ku, Tokyo, 150-8925, Japan
Tel: +81-3-3499-2811 Fax: +81-3-3406-7345
E-mail: sales@hq.unu.edu
http://www.unu.edu

United Nations University Office in North America
2 United Nations Plaza, Room DC2-1462-70, New York, NY 10017, USA
Tel: +1-212-963-6387 Fax: +1-212-371-9454
E-mail: unuona@igc.apc.org

United Nations University Press is the publishing division of the United Nations University.

Cover design by Joyce C. Weston

Printed in the United States of America

UNUP-1059
ISBN 92-808-1059-6

Library of Congress Cataloging-in-Publication Data

Power in transition : the peaceful change of international order /
Charles A. Kupchan ... [et al.] ; with the assistance of Jason Davidson and
Mira Sucharov.
    p. cm.
Includes bibliographical references and index.
  ISBN 92-808-1059-6
  1. Peaceful change (International relations)   I. Kupchan, Charles.
II. Davidson, Jason.   III. Sucharov, Mira.
  JZ5538 .P68 2001
  327.1′09′05—dc21

2001004005

Contents

Acknowledgements.. vii

1 Introduction: Explaining peaceful power transition
   Charles A. Kupchan... 1

2 Benign states and peaceful transition
   Charles A. Kupchan... 18

3 Negotiating "order" during power transitions
   Yuen Foong Khong 34

4 Legitimacy, socialization, and international change
   Jean-Marc Coicaud... 68

5 Peaceful power transitions: The historical cases
   Jason Davidson and Mira Sucharov.......................... 101

6 The change of change: Peaceful transitions of power in the multilateral age
   Emanuel Adler 138

7 Conclusion: The shifting nature of power and peaceful systemic change
    Charles A. Kupchan 159

Contributors 174

Index 175

Acknowledgements

This book is the product of a research project conducted under the auspices of the Peace and Governance Programme of the United Nations University in Tokyo. The project was made possible by the generous financial support of the United Nations University. The authors benefited from workshops held at the United Nations University, the Institute of Defence & Strategic Studies in Singapore, the Shanghai Institute for International Studies, and the Carnegie Moscow Center. We thank the participants in these workshops for their insightful and helpful comments on the project. We would also like to express our deep gratitude to Jason Davidson and Mira Sucharov. They not only contributed an excellent case-study chapter to this book and provided research throughout, but also played an important role in the intellectual development of the project. In Tokyo, Yoshie Sawada provided excellent administrative support for the implementation of the project; we thank her for her patience and hard work. We also thank Janet Boileau of the United Nations University Press and the copy editor, Liz Paton.

Charles A. Kupchan
Emanuel Adler
Jean-Marc Coicaud
Yuen Foong Khong

1

Introduction: Explaining peaceful power transition

Charles A. Kupchan

American preponderance provides a remarkable geopolitical stability at the start of the twenty-first century. In virtually every quarter of the globe, American power and purpose are central to the preservation of peace. Even countries with the capability to challenge American leadership, such as Germany and Japan, choose not to do so. Its cultural reach and material preponderance quite possibly endow the United States with greater influence over global affairs than any other power in history has had.

America's unipolar moment will not last indefinitely, however. Economic output in the United States has fallen from one-half to one-quarter of global product over the past five decades, and secular processes of diffusion will continue to redistribute economic and military might in the years ahead. A rising China and a Europe united by a single market and a single currency are emerging counterweights to American power. Assuming the European Union (EU) succeeds in deepening its level of integration and adding new members, it will soon have influence on matters of finance and trade equal to America's. In addition, the American polity may well embrace a more sparing internationalism in coming years. As younger generations rise to positions of influence and constitute a larger share of the electorate, the formative experiences shaping today's internationalism – World War II and the Cold War – will recede into the past.

As the century progresses, America will not be able to sustain the global preponderance that it enjoys today. A unipolar international system will

1

over time give way to a world of multiple centers of power. A more diffuse concentration of power could have quite adverse global consequences. Although scholars disagree about whether bipolar or multipolar systems are more stable, most agree that both are less stable than unipolar systems.[1] A substantial literature also indicates that power transitions are usually accompanied by major war.[2] Furthermore, the absence of a global hegemon could mean turmoil for an international economy characterized by unprecedented flows of capital and goods.[3]

Accordingly, the United States and the broader international community must start to address how to manage this coming transition in the international system. Instead of focusing on how to preserve and wield global primacy, US grand strategy must focus on how to preserve international stability as global power becomes more equally distributed. It is far more prudent to begin preparing for a multipolar world now, while the United States still enjoys preponderance and the influence that comes with it, than to wait until international order has already begun to unravel.

The waning of American hegemony and its geopolitical consequences thus present scholars and policy makers alike with a critical question: Can the impending transition to multipolarity be managed peacefully? In other words, is systemic change possible without war? This query in turn broaches a second question, which is the central focus of this book: Under what conditions and through what causal mechanisms can power transitions occur peacefully?

The importance of addressing how to manage transition in the international distribution of power peacefully does not just stem from the prospect of a near-term shift in the international system. In addition, we seek to fill a major intellectual gap in the field. The existing literature on power transitions is curiously silent on the question of peaceful change. There are two reasons. First, peaceful power transitions are quite rare. Past face-offs between hegemon and rising challenger have, in most cases, led to major war. Second, peaceful transitions have not attracted the attention of scholars precisely because they were non-events (war did not break out). The absence of scholarship on peaceful power transitions, coupled with the prescriptive importance of figuring out how to facilitate them, underscores the value of examining their causes.

This volume thus seeks to fill an important gap in the field of international relations at the same time that it addresses the pressing question of how to facilitate peaceful change. We identify past cases of peaceful transition, seek to understand what variables enable major power shifts to occur without war, and draw lessons for how the international community can best manage the coming transition to multipolarity. In light of the dearth of existing work on this topic, this volume represents a brainstorming effort, not a definitive study. Our aim is to generate an initial set of hypotheses about how and why power transitions can occur without war, to examine these hypotheses through a set of exploratory case studies, and to draw initial lessons for the contemporary era.

The sources of structural change

The intellectual importance of this volume stands on its own: shedding light on the sources of peaceful change will help redress a gap in the literature. The timeliness and policy relevance of the enterprise are more contingent: they rest on the claim that unipolarity will be short-lived and that it is therefore necessary to begin mapping out a strategy for managing systemic change. Many analysts would contest this claim and contend that American primacy will last for decades to come.[4] Accordingly, I begin by explaining why unipolarity is likely to wane in the near term. Understanding the sources of structural change is also important in figuring out how to manage it.

Most scholars of international politics trace change in the distribution of power to two sources: the secular diffusion over time and space of productive capabilities and material resources; and balancing against concentrations of power motivated by the search for security and prestige. Today's great powers will become tomorrow's has-beens as nodes of innovation and efficiency move from the core to the periphery of the international system. In addition, reigning hegemons threaten rising secondary states and thereby provoke the formation of countervailing coalitions. Taken together, these dynamics drive the cyclical pattern of the rise and fall of great powers.[5]

In contrast to this historical pattern, neither the diffusion of power nor balancing against the United States will be important factors driving the coming transition in the international system. It will be decades before any single state can match the United States in terms of either military or economic capability. Current power asymmetries are by historical standards extreme. The United States spends more on defense than all other great powers combined and more on defense research and development (R&D) than the rest of the world combined. Its gross economic output dwarfs that of most other countries and its expenditure on R&D points to a growing qualitative edge in a global economy increasingly dominated by high-technology sectors.[6]

Nor is balancing against American power likely to provoke a countervailing coalition. The United States is separated from both Europe and Asia by large expanses of water, making American power less threatening. Furthermore, it is hard to imagine that the United States would engage in behavior sufficiently aggressive to provoke opposing alliances. Even in the wake of NATO's air campaign against Yugoslavia, US forces are for the most part welcomed by local powers in Europe and East Asia. Despite sporadic comments from French, Russian, and Chinese officials about America's overbearing behavior, the United States is generally viewed as a benign power, not as a predatory hegemon.[7]

The waning of unipolarity is therefore likely to stem from two novel sources: regional amalgamation in Europe and shrinking internationalism in the United States. Europe is in the midst of a long-term process of political and economic integration that is gradually eliminating the importance of borders and centralizing authority and resources. To be sure, the EU is not yet an amalgamated polity with a single center of authority. Nor does Europe have a military capability commensurate with its economic resources. But trend lines do indicate that Europe is heading in the direction of becoming a new pole of power.

A single market and a single currency endow Europe with a collective weight on matters of trade and finance rivaling that of the United States. The aggregate wealth of the EU's 15 members is almost equal to America's, and the coming entry of a host of new members will tilt the balance in Europe's favor. Europe has recently embarked on efforts to forge a common defense policy and to acquire the military wherewithal to operate independently of US forces. The EU has established a policy planning unit, appointed a high representative to oversee security policy, and started to lay the political groundwork for revamping its forces. It will be decades, if ever, before the EU becomes a unitary state, especially in light of its impending enlargement to the east. But, as its resources grow and its decision-making becomes more centralized, power and influence will become more equally distributed between the two sides of the Atlantic.

The continuing rise of Europe and its leveling effect on the global distribution of power will occur gradually. Even more distant will be China's ascent as a major economic and military player, a development that will ultimately have important consequences for both regional and global power balances. Although it may make sense to treat China as one of the world's main powers in order to influence its trajectory, it will be a decade, if not two, before China has a world-class economy and military establishment.

Of more immediate impact will be a diminishing appetite for robust internationalism in the United States. Today's unipolar landscape is a function not just of America's preponderant resources, but also of its willingness to use them to underwrite international order. Accordingly, should the will of the body politic to bear the costs and risks of international leadership decline, so too will America's position of global primacy.

On the face of it, the appetite of the American polity for internationalism has diminished little, if at all, since the collapse of the Soviet Union. Both the Bush (senior) and the Clinton administrations pursued ambitious and activist foreign policies. The United States has taken the lead in building an open international economy and promoting financial stability, and it has repeatedly deployed its forces to trouble spots around the globe. But American internationalism is now at a high-water mark and, for three compelling reasons, it will be dissipating in the years ahead.

First, the internationalism of the 1990s was sustained by a period of unprecedented economic growth in the United States. A booming stock market, an expanding economy, and substantial budget surpluses created a political atmosphere conducive to trade liberalization, expenditure on the military, and repeated engagement in solving problems in less fortunate parts of the globe. Even under these auspicious conditions, the internationalist agenda has shown signs of faltering. Congress, for example, has mustered only a fickle enthusiasm for free trade, approving NAFTA in 1993 and the Uruguay Round in 1994, but then denying President Clinton fast-track negotiating authority in 1997. Congress has also been skeptical of America's interventions in Bosnia and Kosovo, tolerating them, but little more. Now that the stock market has begun to sputter and growth is slowing, these inward-looking currents will grow much stronger. The little support for free trade that still exists will dwindle. And such stinginess is likely to spread into the security realm, intensifying the domestic debate over burden-sharing and calls within Congress for America's regional partners to shoulder increased defense responsibilities.

Second, although the United States pursued a very activist defense policy during the 1990s, it did so on the cheap. Clinton repeatedly authorized the use of force in the Balkans and in the Middle East, but he relied almost exclusively on air power, successfully avoiding the casualties likely to accompany the introduction of ground troops in combat. In Somalia, the one case in which US ground troops suffered significant losses, Clinton ordered the withdrawal of US forces from the operation. In NATO's campaign against Yugoslavia, week after week of bombing only intensified the humanitarian crisis and increased the likelihood of a southward spread of the conflict. Nevertheless, the United States blocked the use of ground forces and insisted that aircraft bomb from 15,000 feet to avoid being shot down.

Congress revolted despite these operational constraints minimizing the risks to US personnel. A month into the campaign, the US House of Representatives voted 249 to 180 to refuse funding for sending US ground troops to Yugoslavia without congressional permission. Even a resolution that merely endorsed the bombing campaign failed to win approval (the vote was 213 to 213). In short, the American polity appears to have near-zero tolerance for accepting casualties. The illusion that internationalism can be maintained with no or minimal loss of life will likely come back to haunt the United States in the years ahead, limiting its ability to use force in the appropriate manner when necessary.

Third, generational change is likely to take a toll on the character and scope of US engagement abroad. The younger Americans already rising to positions of influence in the public and private sectors have not lived through the formative experiences – World War II and the rebuilding of Europe – that serve as historical anchors of internationalism. Individuals schooled in the 1990s and now entering the workforce will not even have first-hand experience of the Cold War. These Americans will not necessarily be isolationist, but they will certainly be less interested in and knowledgeable about foreign affairs than their older colleagues – a pattern already becoming apparent in the Congress. In the absence of a manifest threat to American national security, making the case for engagement and sacrifice abroad thus promises to grow increasingly difficult with time. Trend lines clearly point to a turning inward and a nation tiring of carrying the burdens of global leadership.

This analysis suggests that American primacy will be short lived. The power transition literature and the historical record provide good reason for concern: as unipolarity disappears, so too will the stability it has engendered. At the same time, this structural change will occur through different mechanisms than in the past, suggesting that it may be easier to manage peacefully than previous power transitions. The rising challenger is Europe, not a unitary state with hegemonic ambition. Europe's aspirations will be moderated by the self-checking mechanisms inherent in the EU and by cultural and linguistic barriers to centralization. In addition, the United States is likely to react to a more independent Europe by stepping back and making room for an EU that appears ready to be more self-reliant and more muscular. Unlike reigning hegemons in the past, the United States will not fight to the finish to maintain its primacy and prevent its eclipse by a rising challenger. On the contrary, the United States is likely to cede leadership willingly as its economy slows and it grows weary of being the security guarantor of last resort. The prospect is thus not one of clashing titans, but one of no titans at all.

The challenge for this volume is therefore two-fold. We must shed light on the sorely understudied problem of peaceful systemic change and seek to explain historical cases of power transitions that occurred peacefully. At the same time, we must apply the lessons of the past to the contemporary global arena. As just mentioned, the coming transition in polarity will take place through different pathways than previously. And it will occur in the era of nuclear weapons, economic globalization, and revolutionary changes in information technology – all variables affecting the consequences of systemic change for international order and stability. With a return to multipolarity looming on the horizon, knowing more about how to effect peaceful power transition in the contemporary era takes on a special urgency.

Toward a theory of peaceful systemic change

Power transitions can lead to three outcomes: war, cold peace (stability based on competition and mutual deterrence), or warm peace (stability based on cooperation and mutual reassurance).[8] War is the historical norm; most power transitions lead to violent conflict. Cold peace, because of the advent of nuclear weapons, may become a more frequent result of systemic change. Indeed, the onset of the Cold War was essentially a shift from unipolarity to bipolarity that resulted in a cold peace. Explaining instances of cold peace requires little conceptual innovation. The security competition that usually accompanies power transition is present in a cold peace, but mutual deterrence prevents the outbreak of war.

It is systemic change accompanied by warm peace that poses the most pressing empirical and conceptual puzzle.[9] And it is this puzzle that serves as the central focus of our project. We bring to this inquiry no theoretical predispositions. The aim is to take a step forward in explaining peaceful systemic change, not to advance any single school of thought. At the same time, the authors do share a similar intellectual bent and the problem under study does lend itself to a particular type of argumentation. We share a belief that ideational variables remain sorely understudied in the field of international relations and need to be incorporated much more fully into the mainstream research agenda. The advent of the constructivist school has helped remedy this shortcoming by putting ideas and identity at the center of scholarly inquiry. We do not, however, privilege constructivism. The most fruitful line of inquiry entails examining how power, institutions, and ideas and identity together shape outcomes.

The growing literature on security communities is instructive in this respect.[10] Scholars working on security communities are probing how and in what circumstances states are able to develop stable expectations of peaceful change. Although peaceful transition can occur in the absence of a security community, the process through which zones of stable peace emerge is one clear pathway through which systemic change can take place without war. We also draw on the literature on the democratic peace, a rich and theoretically eclectic body of scholarship that seeks to explain why democratic states have historically not gone to war with one another.[11]

The study of peaceful power transition provides an ideal opportunity to pursue this broad line of inquiry into the relationship between power, institutions, and ideas and identity. Power clearly matters; it is change in its distribution, after all, that triggers contestation over hierarchy. At the same time, the fact that contenders for primacy are able to manage their struggle peacefully suggests the presence of institutional and ideational variables that succeed in moderating security competition. Furthermore, because a rising contender often challenges existing international institutions erected by the hegemon to manage order, considerable explanatory power devolves to ideational variables.

The notion of *ideational contestation* best captures the central analytic focus of this study. Needless to say, power transitions are first and foremost contestations over power. But peaceful transition results from implicit and explicit negotiation over ideas and identity much more than from adjustments to or negotiation of the material balance of power. Potential rivals must first engage in a process of ideational convergence, which then enables them to resolve, or in some cases renders irrelevant, their contest over material power. A shared ideational framework moderates, if not eliminates, the sense of threat posed by countervailing power. In this sense, perceptions of the character of the polities that wield power, not perceptions of the balance of power per se, are the focal point of the inquiry. Explaining peaceful transition thus entails probing under what conditions rival states construct benign images of one another's character and then move on to craft a mutually acceptable and legitimate order.

The central argument is as follows. Ideational contestation gives way to peaceful transition through three related, but distinct, causal mechanisms. First, hegemon and rising challenger must engage in a sustained process of strategic restraint and mutual accommodation that ultimately enables them to view one another as benign polities. Put differently, each party must ascribe to the other a set of characteristics that engenders an abiding, mutual sense of affinity. It is the reciprocal construction of benign images that enables both parties to view the other's material power as non-threatening, if not indeed as a source of mutual security.

Second, peaceful transition emerges from ideational contestation when hegemon and rising challenger succeed in fashioning agreement on the outlines of a new international order. Both parties must be satisfied powers if transition is to occur without war or mutual deterrence. Such mutual satisfaction emerges from a dynamic negotiation over the nature of the emerging order. The key elements of order on which the parties must reach a consensus include: a new hierarchy, basic rules concerning trade and the use of force, procedures for managing territorial change, and mutual recognition of spheres of influence.

Third, peaceful transition depends not just on the ability of hegemon and rising contender to forge agreement on order, but also on their ability to legitimate that order. Order emerges from reaching agreement on behavioral conventions and the institutions of governance. Legitimacy evolves from grounding those conventions and institutions in a broader normative framework. The parties must forge a consensus not just on rules, but on the values that underlie those rules. Legitimacy deepens the durability of peaceful change by protecting it against elite turnover and, during the democratic age, eliciting popular consent in and support for the prevailing international order.

Benign images, order, and legitimacy work together in cumulative fashion. The reciprocal construction of benign images serves as the foundation of our causal chain. But benign images alone are not sufficient to produce peaceful transition. Power and its management still matter, and agreement on order is therefore a second necessary condition. Benign images can persist temporarily in the absence of agreement on order, but they are likely to erode if not eventually embedded in a consensus on ordering principles. In similar fashion, leading states can erect order without sharing benign images of each other, but then order results from deterrence and balancing, not from negotiation and cooperative management. It is the combination of benign images and agreement on order that produces peaceful transition. Legitimacy is the capstone of the process. Peaceful transitions have occurred in the absence of legitimacy. But the resilience and durability that legitimacy grants to benign order make it an important ingredient of a lasting and stable peace. I now elaborate on these three core variables – benign character, order, and legitimacy – which will be explored in further depth in the following three chapters.

Benign character

Realists and institutionalists of various stripes have long appreciated that the quality of power, not just its quantity, matters. In evaluating how to react to a powerful state, nearby states seek to evaluate their neighbor's intentions as well as its capabilities. In Stephen Walt's characterization, states balance against *threatening* power, not just against power alone.[12] And classical realists have long distinguished between aggressor states, which seek to overturn the prevailing system, and status quo states, which seek to preserve it.[13]

Realism and institutionalism, however, both presume that all states have the same essential character and pursue the same interests. Aggressor states and status quo states differ only as to their place in the international hierarchy, their power trajectories, and their need for offensive weapons, not their internal political character and the external behavior it produces. Behavior is a function of relative power and the changing character of power due to shifts in technology, but not of the character of the units that wield power. Institutionalists maintain that power can be tamed by institutions, which ameliorate endemic competition by enabling like states to pursue their own interests through cooperative strategies. But cooperation nevertheless takes place among atomistic, self-regarding states residing in an anarchic environment.

This intellectual template is fundamentally at odds with many observable aspects of contemporary international politics. America's preponderant power is not triggering the formation of opposing coalitions. Indeed, an overt US military presence is welcomed in most quarters of the globe. Relations between the United States and Western Europe are characterized by an abiding sense of trust and commonality, even in the absence of the external threat that initially triggered the formation of the Western alliance. Far from engaging in the security competition consistent with a self-help system, the Western democracies regularly chastise one another for spending *too little* on defense. Not only are these states not threatened by each other's power, but they assign positive value to one another's strength.

The thickening web of international institutions goes part way in explaining these radical departures from realist expectations. But the character of relations among the liberal democracies of North America and Western Europe is based on something far more profound than high levels of transparency and low transaction costs. Members of the Atlantic community are comfortable encouraging one another to acquire more defense capability because it has become virtually unthinkable that one member would ever use such capability against another. In similar fashion, most European and East Asian countries welcome a robust US presence in their respective regions because of a deep-seated comfort with the character of American power and the international intentions they ascribe to the American polity.

The notion of benign character best captures what lies behind this extraordinary level of cooperation. Transformation in the identities that states ascribe to one another produces a radical change in how they react to one another's power, enabling them to escape the competitive dynamics endemic to international politics. The mutual attribution of benign character thus brings about peaceful change by muting, if not eliminating, the security consequences normally associated with shifts in the distribution of power. It is this transformation in the perceived character of states that is at the core of peaceful transition.

Four causal mechanisms appear to be most prominent in enabling and facilitating the mutual construction of benign images. First, the existence of multiple external threats creates incentives for both parties to find ways of reducing the number of potential enemies they face. Hegemon and rising challenger need not face a common external threat. Rather, each must face an array of demanding threats, making reconciliation between them an attractive option for freeing up resources to concentrate against others. The motivation is not power aggregation, as in an alliance. Rather, it is eliminating potential enemies by transforming them into friends.

Second, the exercise of strategic restraint – what I call self-binding – plays an important role in allowing trust and reciprocity to build, in turn enabling an incremental cognitive shift toward the mutual attribution of benign character. Self-binding behavior and institutions communicate benign intentions and a state's willingness to forgo opportunities for individual gain. The assessment of benign intentions over time turns into the attribution of benign character. The process works in a self-reinforcing manner, with each side becoming more willing to engage in self-binding as it attributes benign intentions and character to the other.

Third, the prior existence of an emotive affinity and shared identity facilitates the mutual construction of benign images. A common culture (based on ethnicity, religion, language, or race) can provide a foundation for both parties to assume a special congruence of interest and outlook. So too can similarity in domestic regime breed a certain sense of comfort and affinity. The rational expectation of congruent interest and the emotive draw of cultural similarity work together to encourage the reciprocal attribution of benign character.

Fourth, reconciliation and open dealing with the past facilitate benign imaging, especially when the parties in question have engaged in direct conflict in the past. Even if relevant parties engage in self-binding and exhibit behavior that should engender trust and reciprocity, residual historical animosities block the transformation of the collective images that polities hold of one another. In addition, a state's willingness to engage in open debate about its own past sends a reassuring signal to other states about the nature of its polity. Self-evaluation and accountability reinforce external perceptions of a state's benign character.

Agreement on order

If reigning hegemon and rising challenger are to manage systemic change peacefully, they must reach agreement on how to adapt the prevailing international order to a new distribution of power. Once the rising state has crossed the threshold that enables it credibly to challenge the hegemon, the two parties enter the zone of contestation in which they negotiate over hierarchy and ordering principles and rules. The bargaining may be overt and explicit – both parties seek to resolve their differences through formal negotiation. Or it may take more subtle forms, with each party unilaterally adjusting its objectives and behavior to accommodate the other party. Peaceful transition depends not just on the emergence of a stable order, but also on the manner in which that order takes shape and on how it is sustained. It must emerge through consensual bargaining rather than through one party imposing its will on the other. And it must be sustained through cooperation and mutual satisfaction, not through deterrence and mutual threat.

The dimensions of order on which hegemon and challenger must reach agreement vary across time and space; the constitutive elements of order are not static. Establishing an initial consensus on international hierarchy – a "pecking order" of influence and status – is a starting point. The hegemon tacitly cedes ground, making room at the table for the rising challenger. The challenger accepts its elevated status and influence but, at least at the outset, acknowledges the hegemon's continued primacy. This initial construction of a new hierarchy provides a foundation for negotiation over a host of ordering principles and rules.

Efforts to refashion ordering principles focus on the following issues. Hegemon and challenger must forge a consensus on rules for managing security matters: when, in what circumstances, and against whom the use of force is justified; through what mechanisms to deal with territorial change; what geographic spheres of influence and functional division of labor to establish. Contestation also takes place over the rules and mechanisms that govern international trade and investment. At stake are both organizing principles (such as mercantilism versus free trade) and the more discrete rules and institutions that govern international business.

In chapter 3, Yuen Foong Khong identifies conditions that appear to increase the likelihood that contenders for primacy reach agreement on order. First, the relevant parties need to enjoy an affinity of identity. Second, the rising challenger must be accorded meaningful participation in shaping the new rules of the game. Third, the current hegemon and other status quo powers must perceive this rising challenger as having the necessary resources and resolve to be a serious contender for primacy.

Legitimacy

Peaceful transition depends not just on the emergence of a mutually acceptable international order, but also on the extent to which that order is legitimate. Agreement on order can take shape in the absence of a legitimating framework, but legitimacy facilitates a consensus on order and makes that order more durable and resilient. Legitimacy emerges when hegemon and contender agree not just on hierarchy and a set of core rules on the conduct of foreign policy, but also on a set of deeper normative principles. Rather than being based on causal assumptions and followed because of their practical appeal, normative principles are based on values and followed because of their moral appeal. States abide by them because they *ought* to, not because it is in their material interest to do so.

The legitimation of order facilitates peaceful transition and makes it more durable for three main reasons. First, legitimacy engenders a shared identity and sense of we-ness. In this sense, hegemon and rising contender do not just live comfortably alongside each other, but they construct a common political space. Second, embedding order in a legitimating framework makes that order more able to accommodate change. If continuing power shifts or exogenous shock threaten the new order erected by hegemon and rising contender, both parties can fall back on a shared set of values as they seek to find a new equilibrium. Third, legitimacy ensures greater continuity by broadening the social base that supports reconciliation and accommodation. At a minimum, the existence of a legitimating framework means that the entire elite community, not just those at the top, share the values on which peaceful transition is based. Regime change then becomes less destabilizing. And, in the era of democracy, legitimacy ensures that peaceful transition rests on broader popular support, making it even more durable.

Legitimacy most readily emerges when the polities in question share a common religion or other normative framework prior to the time they enter the zone of contestation. Shared moral values then provide a ready foundation for the reciprocal construction of benign images, agreement on order, and the legitimation of that order. It is possible, however, for polities deliberately to engage in practices aimed at embedding international order in a legitimating framework. The European Union, for example, has established a European Parliament and a host of other supranational institutions and practices in order to erect a legitimate realm of politics at the supranational level.

In chapter 4, Jean-Marc Coicaud identifies a number of important conditions that can help build international legitimacy. He notes that status quo powers should not be too beholden to maintaining the status quo. Embracing normative change and making room for rising contenders are essential to legitimating new conceptions of order. In this respect, and somewhat paradoxically, contenders for primacy that enjoy healthy levels of national integration, strong state structures, and clear national values are more likely than their weaker counterparts to embrace normative change. Strong states have the domestic conditions that facilitate compromise and reciprocity. National integration and legitimacy at home thus strengthen a state's ability to promote socialization and legitimacy at the international level. Coicaud goes on to develop the notion of democratic hegemony as he maps out how the United States might go about promoting international legitimacy as its material preponderance wanes.

The historical cases

The historical cases on which we draw fall into two categories. The first is classic overtake, in which a rising challenger approaches parity with and then surpasses the reigning hegemon, but a new order emerges without war. Classic overtake represents the standard version of power transition within the existing literature. Within this category, we focus primarily on one case study: the peaceful transition that took place between the United States and Great Britain during the late 1800s and early 1900s. The United States emerged as a great power toward the end of the nineteenth century and threatened British positions in the Americas as well as British naval supremacy in the Atlantic. Nevertheless, the United States and Britain did not engage in a hegemonic war. On the contrary, they resolved their differences through negotiation and forged a strategic partnership that has lasted to this day. We will examine how and why. Other illustrative cases of overtake are also studied, particularly in Khong's chapter.

The second set of cases involves what we label regulatory conventions for power management. These cases do not entail the explicit overtake of the hegemon by the rising challenger. Instead, contenders for primacy generate institutions and rules to regulate ongoing shifts in the distribution of power so as to avoid the security competition and rivalry that usually accompany such shifts. This broadening of the notion of power transition is the product of two considerations. First, instances of classic overtake that occur peacefully are exceedingly rare. Indeed, the US–British transition appears to be the only clear case.[14] Second, the generic class of events under examination here is consequential change in the distribution of power that does not trigger security competition. Classic overtake, because primacy passes from one state to another, is only the most pronounced form. Conventions for power management that succeed in regulating the consequences of ongoing power shifts also shed light on how states go about escaping competition and building order based on cooperation rather than deterrence.

We examine two cases involving regulatory conventions for power management: the Concert of Europe and the Association of South East

Asian Nations (ASEAN). The Concert succeeded in preserving peace in Europe from the end of the Napoleonic Wars (1815) until the Crimean War (1854). During this period, Europe's five major powers (Britain, France, Prussia, Austria, and Russia) worked within the framework of the Concert to mute balancing and regulate relations among themselves – despite successive crises and shifts in the strategic landscape. The Concert unraveled after the revolutions of 1848.

ASEAN emerged in South-East Asia in 1967 and has succeeded in preserving peace among its members ever since. Its initial members were Indonesia, Malaysia, Thailand, Singapore, and the Philippines. Vietnam, Cambodia, Brunei, and Myanmar have since joined. Examining ASEAN helps broaden the conceptual range of the cases because it involves non-European states and cultures and because its members are small and middle powers rather than great powers.

Although these cases are quite disparate, they are united by the light they shed on how polities escape endemic competition with each other and thereby enable power transitions to occur peacefully. Rapprochement between Britain and the United States, the formation and operation of the Concert of Europe, the ability of ASEAN to preserve peace in an unstable neighborhood – these all illuminate how to eliminate strategic rivalry among proximate states.

Furthermore, the different types of historical cases parallel the different types of challenges facing the international community. The rise of China will confront the United States with economic and geopolitical dilemmas similar to those that America's rise posed to Britain. The United States and the European Union will need to erect regulatory conventions, such as a concert, to manage their economic and strategic relations, especially as Europe becomes a more influential global actor. And ASEAN sheds light on how countries in the midst of economic and political transition can nevertheless build a lasting peace with one another. This achievement is especially important in light of the finding that democratization and economic change can often be sources of instability and conflict.[15]

In the next chapter, I develop the notion of benign character and examine the role it plays in facilitating peaceful transition. In the third chapter, Yuen Foong Khong examines the concept of international order and the conditions under which states are able to reach agreement on the basic dimensions of order. Jean-Marc Coicaud then follows with a chapter on international legitimacy and socialization, examining the role that they play in facilitating peaceful transition and making it durable. Each of these chapters uses the three case studies to explore the three key elements of the argument – benign character, order, and legitimacy. Jason Davidson and Mira Sucharov then follow with a chapter that provides a detailed examination of the volume's three cases and demonstrates the importance of benign character, agreement on order, and legitimacy in explaining outcomes. In chapter 6, Emanuel Adler reflects on the changing nature of power transition in the contemporary era of multilateralism, seeking to put the volume in a broader historical perspective. In chapter 7, I offer further reflections on how changes in the nature of power are likely to affect systemic change in the present era. I then lay out the main policy recommendations that arise from our analysis, addressing what steps the international community can take to facilitate peaceful change.

Notes

1. On the greater stability of bipolarity, see Kenneth N. Waltz, "The Stability of a Bipolar World," *Daedalus*, Vol. 93, No. 3 (Summer 1964), pp. 881–909; and John J. Mearsheimer, "Back to the Future: Instability in Europe after the Cold War," in Sean M. Lynn-Jones and Steven Miller, eds., *The Cold War and After: Prospects for Peace* (Cambridge, MA: MIT Press, 1993), pp. 141–192. For arguments in favor of multipolarity, see Karl Deutsch and J. David Singer, "Multipolar Power Systems and International Stability," *World Politics*, Vol. 16, No. 3 (April 1964), pp. 390–406. For general discussion of polarity and stability, see Stephen Van Evera, "Primed for Peace: Europe after the Cold War," *International Security*, Vol. 15, No. 3 (Winter 1990/91), pp. 7–57; and Michael Mastanduno, "Preserving the Unipolar Moment: Realist Theories and U.S. Grand Strategy after the Cold War," *International Security*, Vol. 21, No. 4 (Spring 1997), pp. 49–88. On the stability of unipolarity, see William Wohlforth, "The Stability of a Unipolar World," *International Security*, Vol. 24, No. 1 (Summer 1999), pp. 5–41; and Charles Kupchan, "After Pax Americana: Benign Power, Regional Integration, and the Sources of a Stable Multipolarity," *International Security*, Vol. 23, No. 2 (Fall 1998), pp. 40–79.
2. See A. F. K. Organski, *World Politics* (New York: Knopf, 1958); and A. F. K. Organski and Jacek Kugler, *The War Ledger* (Chicago: University of Chicago Press, 1980).
3. This is a central insight of hegemonic stability theory. See Charles Kindleberger, *The World in Depression, 1929–1939* (Berkeley: University of California Press, 1973).
4. See Wohlforth, "The Stability of a Unipolar World."
5. See Robert Gilpin, *War and Change in World Politics* (Cambridge: Cambridge University Press, 1981); Paul Kennedy, *The Rise and Fall of the Great Powers* (New York: Random House, 1987); and Christopher Layne, "The Unipolar Illusion: Why New Great Powers Will Rise," *International Security*, Vol. 17, No. 4 (Spring 1993), pp. 5–51.
6. Wohlforth, "The Stability of a Unipolar World," pp. 10–22.
7. On the concept of benign power, see Kupchan, "After Pax Americana."
8. I will use the notion of peaceful power transition to refer only to warm peace. For a categorization of different types of peace, including those based on deterrence, see Kenneth Boulding, *Stable Peace* (Austin: University of Texas Press, 1978); Alexander George, "From Conflict to Peace: Stages along the Road," *United States Institute of Peace Journal*, Vol. 5, No. 6 (December 1992); and Arie Kacowicz, "From Theory to Historical Lessons: The Relevance of Stable Peace," unpublished manuscript, Hebrew University, July 1998.

9. We presume that a consequential power transition can take either of two forms: a change of the hegemon from one state to another while polarity remains unchanged, or a change in polarity.
10. See Emanuel Adler and Michael Barnett, *Security Communities* (Cambridge: Cambridge University Press, 1998).
11. A good anthology of the relevant literature is Michael Brown, ed., *Debating the Democratic Peace* (Cambridge, MA: MIT Press, 1996).
12. Stephen Walt, *The Origins of Alliances* (Ithaca, NY: Cornell University Press, 1987).
13. See, for example, Arnold Wolfers, "The Balance of Power in Theory and Practice," in Wolfers, ed., *Discord and Collaboration: Essays on International Politics* (Baltimore, MD: Johns Hopkins University Press, 1962), pp. 117–133; Randall Schweller, "Tripolarity and the Second World War," *International Studies Quarterly*, Vol. 37, No. 1 (March 1993), pp. 73–103; Schweller, "Neorealism's Status-Quo Bias: What Security Dilemma?" in *Security Studies*, Vol. 5, No. 3 (Spring 1996), pp. 90–121; and Mastanduno, "Preserving the Unipolar Moment."
14. Other potential case studies include relations between the Byzantine Empire and the Holy Roman Empire from the ninth until the eleventh century and the peaceful end of the Cold War. These cases will be examined in a future study.
15. See Edward Mansfield and Jack Snyder, "Democratization and the Danger of War," *International Security*, Vol. 20. No. 2 (Summer 1995), pp. 5–38.

2

Benign states and peaceful transition

Charles A. Kupchan

The twentieth century witnessed the emergence of several "pockets of nonanarchic space" – groupings of states that have escaped the security dilemma and behave toward one another without fear of predatory intent. Scholars across different theoretical traditions acknowledge that the United States and Canada, the Nordic countries, the states of Western Europe, and the Atlantic democracies taken collectively enjoy a quality of stable peace that defies traditional notions of anarchic competition. Just as citizens in most liberal democracies go about their business without police escort or guns at their waists, so do these states interact with one another with their guard down and their fear of armed conflict almost nonexistent.

I argue in this chapter that this anomalous behavior stems from a profound and deep-seated belief among the states in question that they will not do one another harm. This deep-seated belief in turn arises from a reciprocal process in which the parties engage in the mutual attribution of benign character. They come to see one another as benign polities with benign intent, enabling them to escape the competitive imperatives of the international system. The central task of the chapter is to flesh out the concept of benign character, theorize about how and when it emerges, and through the case studies demonstrate its importance in facilitating peaceful transition.

Benign states

The existing literature on state type regularly distinguishes between revisionist and status quo states.[1] Revisionist states are rising powers that seek to overturn the existing international order. Status quo states are reigning powers that seek to preserve the existing order. A state's type is a function solely of its power trajectory – whether it is rising or declining – and the objectives that follow from its position.[2]

In contrast, I propose three state types: aggressor, status quo, and benign. Aggressor states are polities that seek power as opposed to security and that rely on acquisitive and predatory strategies to do so. They see competition and conflict as necessary to attain their objectives. Status quo states seek to preserve the existing order and hierarchy primarily by meeting challenges to that order. They see competition as necessary for turning back challengers, but otherwise do not initiate security competition or engage in predatory behavior. Benign states seek security rather than power and do so primarily through deepening the stability and cooperative character of international order. They pursue competitive security strategies only when necessary to meet challengers, and otherwise pursue cooperative strategies and seek to foster consensual forms of international governance.

Benign character manifests itself in quantitative, qualitative, and procedural dimensions. In quantitative terms, benign states engage in self-binding by withholding power and refraining from fully exercising their resources and influence. This strategic restraint may be codified, as in the cases of contemporary Germany and Japan, or it may be embodied only in practice.[3] The qualitative dimension of benign character concerns the ends to which power is exercised. Benign states seek to manage rather than maximize power, to promote joint gains rather than to behave in an extractive and exploitative manner, and to erect orders based upon the notion that international community and the spread of shared norms and identities can overcome competitive relations among atomistic state units. The procedural dimensions of benignity entail a preference for multilateral over unilateral initiative. Benign states favor consensual governance, and resort to unilateral decision-making only when multilateralism fails to produce an acceptable outcome.

The key difference between a status quo state and a benign state stems from their diverging conceptions of the sources of order and stability. Stability in a world of status quo states stems from the absence of strategic rivalry among satisfied – but atomistic and self-regarding – state units still residing in an anarchic environment. The security dilemma is in abeyance because no aggressor state triggers it. Stability in a world of benign states stems from successful efforts to carve out nonanarchic space through promoting cooperation, trust, and shared values and identities. The security dilemma is eliminated because states no longer reside in an anarchic, self-help setting.

Benign behavior is a necessary but not a sufficient condition for the mutual attribution of benign character. For perceptions of benign character to follow from instances of benign behavior, a political process within the observing state must generate the construction of a new corporate identity of the target state. Furthermore, this process must work in a reciprocal fashion. Each party must see the other as benign for the process of rapprochement to be sustained and lead to peaceful transition, and for peaceful transition to lead to a durable and stable peace.

The attribution of benign character: Causal mechanisms

What causal engines drive the political and social processes through which the mutual attribution of benign character takes place? Strategic necessity provides the initial impetus. Each of the states in question faces multiple threats, saddling them with a range of commitments that strains available resources. Mutual accommodation at first emerges as a means of easing these burdens and improving the strategic environment for both states.[4] The parties in question are not forming an alliance to aggregate capabilities against a common threat. Instead, they are removing one another from their respective lists of potential enemies. A number of factors determine why these states choose one another – as opposed to other adversaries – for rapprochement. Proximity, the nature of the threats they pose to each other, and the relative importance of the interests at stake are key variables. Interestingly, emotive affinity plays perhaps its most potent role at this point in the story by serving as a source of social selection. Everything else being equal, states will select like states as partners for rapprochement, rather than states with which they do not share cultural ties.[5]

Once strategic necessity provides the initial opening, the mutual attribution of benign character proceeds through three causal mechanisms. First, the parties begin to exercise strategic restraint. Reciprocal self-binding is less a driving force behind rapprochement than a practice that makes room for the process to move forward. Passing up opportunities for individual advantage plays a critical role in signaling benign intent. In so doing, it in turn creates further opportunities for instances of mutual accommodation. Both parties reap material benefits because they are able to focus attention and military resources on remaining threats. Lasting rapprochement gains a stable foothold when a pattern of reciprocal accommodation has been established, with both sides enjoying payoffs and looking to the next round.

Second, social and economic interaction between parties breeds more knowledge of and familiarity with the other. In some cases, interaction actually increases as a result of initial rapprochement, fostering new social links. In other cases, interaction that already existed has a more potent impact because it takes place within a new political context. Agents within the state that stand to benefit from better relations begin to play a role in furthering rapprochement. Military establishments, for example, see a way to reduce overcommitment and begin to develop closer ties. And traders and bankers begin to see economic opportunities in rapprochement. Material incentive thus provides impetus behind ideational change.

Third, political elites in both parties capitalize on clear instances of cooperative behavior to begin constructing a new domestic narrative about the other – a key step in moving toward the mutual attribution of benign character. At the early stages of this process of identity construction, elites focus primarily on tearing down preexisting enemy images. They do so in large part to disarm critics of their accommodating policies and to provide political cover for rapprochement. But they are also laying the groundwork, even if unwittingly, for a deeper and more durable transformation of the corporate identities that the parties hold of each other. In part through the conscious and deliberate efforts of elites, and in part through processes of social construction that eventually run on their own steam (interaction and the spread and deepening of social networks), the tearing down of enemy images gives way to the building up of benign images. The agents of social construction range from discrete actors within both states (political elites, bureaucracies, journalists and writers, economic interest groups, political action groups) to transnational institutions and networks that begin to constitute a collective realm of political and social activity.

The historical cases

The purpose of this section is two-fold. I will use the notion of benign character to shed new light on the case studies and, in doing so, demonstrate the analytic value of the concept. At the same time, examination of the cases will help refine and provide a more nuanced understanding of when and how polities come to see each other as benign. Discussion of the cases is necessarily selective and aimed primarily at conceptual development. Readers not familiar with the broad outlines of the cases may want to read the historical overviews in chapter 5 before proceeding.

Rapprochement between the United States and Great Britain

The rapprochement that emerged between the United States and Great Britain at the turn of the twentieth century represents not just a remarkable instance of peaceful power transition, but also an excellent case for studying transformation in the identities that states hold of each other. The United States and Britain started the nineteenth century at war with one another. They then spent decades eyeing each other suspiciously and maintaining fortifications and garrisons along the Canadian border, fearful that any number of territorial or trade issues could again lead to hostilities. By the beginning of the twentieth century, however, the two countries had not just settled their disputes, but become lasting partners. Indeed, elites on both sides of the Atlantic were proclaiming that war between their two countries had become unthinkable.

Many scholars of the period attribute this dramatic shift in US–British relations to the rise of Germany and the threat that it posed to Great Britain.[6] The German naval buildup, the argument goes, left Britain with no choice but to reduce its commitments in the western Atlantic so that it could concentrate its resources in Europe. The problem with this argument is that rapprochement began far earlier than did Germany's armaments program. Both Britain and the United States started leaving the Canadian border undefended in the 1870s.[7] The crisis over borders in Venezuela, which many historians identify as a watershed event in recasting relations between the two powers, occurred in 1895, well before the first German Naval Law of 1898. Balancing against Germany, although it did come to play a role in consolidating US–British links, was not the engine behind Anglo-American rapprochement.[8]

The temporal turning point in the relationship appears to have been the US Civil War. Determined to demobilize much of the army and dramatically reduce defense spending, the United States decided to leave most of its border with Canada undefended. Canada meanwhile formed a confederation and became relatively autonomous from Britain in 1867. Britain subsequently lost interest in picking up the cost of fortifying and patrolling the Canadian border with the United States. From roughly 1871 onwards, both the US and Canadian territory were vulnerable to attack. Nonetheless, neither side took advantage of the resultant opportunities for territorial gain. This reciprocal strategic restraint set in motion a process through which both parties began to assume that the other had benign intentions.[9] There was no dramatic or immediate warming up of relations, but there was a gradual erosion of the sense on both sides that the United States and Britain were destined to be implacable enemies.

The crisis over Venezuela helped crystallize the emerging sense of affinity that was growing between the two countries.[10] In response to vociferous American objections to Britain's stance on Venezuela's borders, Britain backed down. The two countries then agreed to submit all future disputes to neutral arbitration. Public officials and journalists on both sides of the Atlantic acclaimed the resolution of the matter and the new amity in the relationship. It is important to keep in mind that this episode of strategic restraint and rapprochement took place years before Germany embarked on building its high seas fleet.

During the following years, rapprochement at the elite level began to give way to a sense of broader social affinity and, over time, to the reciprocal attribution of benign character. Rapprochement was taking place not just at the level of high politics and diplomacy; a broader societal transformation was taking place. This shift in the images the two polities held of each other proceeded as social groups in both states began to reap the benefits of rapprochement and sought to further it and make it more durable. Politicians needed to justify their accommodating policies by portraying the other party as a friend that could be trusted. Military planners found resources freed up as they no longer had to plan for war with each other. Traders saw the prospect of increased profits. Through speeches in Parliament or Congress, articles in magazines and newspapers, and educational outlets these agents played an important role in altering the identities that the two polities held of each other.[11]

The depth of these changes in mutual perception was reflected in the extent to which the two sides saw one another not just as not threatening, but as contributors to one another's security. American elites came to see British concessions not just as isolated instances of accommodation, but as a sign of British acceptance of a new division of labor in building security in the Atlantic. In turn, the British came not just to tolerate, but also to welcome, America's increasing power and appetite for expansion. The British broke with their European counterparts in supporting the United States in the Spanish–American War. And they reacted positively to America's annexation of the Philippines, arguing that Britain would much prefer to have America in control of the islands than any other great power. *The Times* of London reacted to America's move into the western Pacific with "equanimity and indeed with satisfaction. We can only say that while we would welcome the Americans in the Philippines as kinfolks and allies united with us in the Far East by the most powerful bonds of interest, we should regard very differently the acquisition of the archipelago by any other power."[12]

The extent to which common ethnicity and language facilitated the mutual attribution of benign character is difficult to assess. Once reciprocal restraint had given way to rapprochement, individuals on both sides of the Atlantic began to refer to war between the United States and Great Britain as fratricide. As Lionel Gelber notes, by the end of the nineteenth century, the British sensed that war with the United States would bring with it "some of the unnatural horror of a civil war."[13] American commentators shared this sentiment. Such statements made clear that the two parties shared a sense of cultural affinity. At the same time, decades of hostility made evident that racial ties were not a sufficient condition for the emergence of benign images. Strategic necessity and the desire of both Britain and the United States to reduce defense commitments were driving rapprochement. These drivers created the environment in which racial affinity then kicked in as an important variable.

Once in play, cultural affinity appears to have facilitated a peaceful power transition between the United States and Britain through two discrete pathways. First, a process of social selection may well have been at work in determining which of several rising powers Britain ultimately chose to appease. Germany's proximity to Britain clearly played a role in London's decision to challenge the rise of German power while, in contrast, it sought to accommodate the rise of the United States. But British strategy was also shaped by a certain comfort with the United States, which derived from a common heritage and a similar political culture.[14] The British believed that these similarities made it less likely that the United States would seek unilateral advantage and exploit their willingness to make concessions. As mentioned, British officials welcomed America's imperial push into the Philippines, preferring that the United States, rather than its European rivals, establish a strong presence in the Pacific. Britain's elites thus developed a deep-seated belief that the United States had benign intentions and that its rise would not ultimately threaten British security.

Second, cultural similarities made it easier for elites in both the United States and Britain to sell mutual accommodation to their respective publics. After years of antagonism, giving ground and making concessions entailed considerable political risk. Elected officials on both sides of the Atlantic faced criticism from hardliners and from interest groups that felt threatened by the scaling back of defense commitments. Cultural ties provided elites with ready ammunition against these critics, and offered elected representatives and journalists a panoply of arguments that they could use in propagating benign images of the other. In this sense, cultural affinity closed the distance between the two polities and thereby facilitated the mutual attribution of benign character.

The Concert of Europe

The Concert of Europe emerged in 1815 from the remnants of the alliance formed to defeat Napoleonic France. Nonetheless, the four victorious powers moved quickly to transform an alliance used to aggregate power into a concert used primarily to restrain power. And, instead of imposing a punitive peace on France, they invited their defeated adversary to join the Concert and embraced it in their great power councils.

The self-binding and strategic restraint that muted competitive balancing among Europe's major powers emerged through explicit negotiation. The statesmen of the day gathered face-to-face to map out the rules of the road to which all five states agreed to adhere. Although opportunities soon emerged for individual members to pursue individual advantage, they refrained from doing so in order to preserve trust and reciprocity within the Concert framework. When crises emerged, such as over the Spanish revolution of 1820 or the military uprising in Naples during the same year, the Concert did recognize spheres of influence related to the geographic and historical interests of particular parties. But intervention and settlement of borders took place only after consultation. The guiding principle, aptly stated by a French diplomat of the time, was that "the concurrence of the great powers is necessary in order to preserve that unanimity of views which is the fundamental character of the alliance, and which it is of the utmost importance to maintain and emphasize as a guarantee for the repose of Europe."[15] In many instances, the Concert coordinated inaction in order to avoid potential rivalry and the clash of interests. By withholding their power and refraining from intervention, the great powers preempted the competition that would have otherwise emerged.[16]

Building on the momentum provided by the alliance against Napoleon, the Concert did succeed in promoting a nascent sense of benignity among its members. The mutual attribution of benign character emerged from the sense of common purpose, the face-to-face contact among leaders and their diplomats, and the practice of strategic restraint. The personal contacts that developed among leaders during the war against Napoleon and through the concert system appear to have been crucial in building a sense of community and affinity. Metternich and other key participants in the Concert explicitly noted how crucial were the personal relationships that developed through direct contact.[17] In this sense, the leaders of Europe's great powers were able to cultivate a feeling of commonality and a shared identity.

The Concert could, however, go only so far in propagating a sense of benign character among its members. Several factors limited the extent to which the Concert was able to advance self-binding and reciprocity to the more profound stage of transforming social identities. First, the Concert preserved an undercurrent of competitive balancing as a deterrent to members contemplating defection; the prospect of facing a preponderant opposing coalition helped keep the great powers in line.[18] As a consequence, the members did not completely drop their guard. They saw each other as partners for now, but the return of militarized rivalry was not out of the question. In this sense, elites neither believed nor propagated the idea that their partners in the Concert were benign polities that could be permanently trusted.

Second, the Concert was split between two liberalizing states (Britain and France) and three monarchies (Russia, Prussia, and Austria). This difference in the domestic structure of member states not only produced a divergence about how to react to liberal uprisings in Europe, but also limited the extent to which a sentiment of affinity emerged among Concert members. Indeed, Russia, Prussia, and Austria participated in the Holy Alliance at the same time that they were members of the Concert, formalizing their separate status as monarchies. Britain and France did not form a liberal counterpart, but they tended to find themselves in the same camp when the Concert was confronted with responding to the emergence of liberal movements in Europe's smaller countries. So too did strains emerge within the Holy Alliance, with nationalistic ambitions causing tension between Prussia and Russia, and Prussia and Austria jockeying for position within Germanic Europe. These divides stood in the way of the emergence of a shared identity and mutual sense of benign character.

Finally, the limited degree of popular participation in foreign affairs stymied the processes of social construction through which new identities emerge. The leaders and top diplomats of Europe's five major powers developed close personal ties and nurtured an atmosphere of reciprocity and trust. But the Concert operated in the realm of high politics; the bonds developed among top officials did not trickle down and serve as the basis for either a new domestic narrative or new social contacts among the five parties. As a result, the Concert was extremely vulnerable to leadership change. Indeed, the revolutions of 1848 effectively brought the Concert to an end by giving power to a new cadre of elites, who operated without the personal contacts and expectations of reciprocity enjoyed by their predecessors. Had the polities at large, and not just elites, been party to the processes of strategic restraint and community-building that were at the heart of the Concert, it might well have survived the domestic upheavals of 1848.

ASEAN

The formation of ASEAN followed Indonesia's decision to end its policy of *"konfrontasi"* ("confrontation") with its immediate neighbors. As the dominant power in South-East Asia, Indonesia set the tone for the region. When flexing its muscles and demonstrating aggressive intent, Indonesia stood in the way of a region-wide security regime. Once Indonesia began to practice strategic restraint, however, the stage was set for basing regional stability on cooperation and integration rather than on deterrence and balancing.[19]

As in the other cases, strategic necessity drove reconsideration of Indonesia's policy of confrontation: the costs of strategic competition to economic development and the burden on the region as a whole were too high.[20] Early initiatives within ASEAN focused on resolving territorial disputes and coordinating efforts to counter the domestic threats posed by communist insurgencies throughout the region. Over time, the members began to focus more explicitly on nurturing a collective regional identity and using ASEAN not just to resolve disputes and counter threats, but also to promote a durable sense of community that would reduce, if not eliminate, security competition among member states. The notions of "ASEAN spirit" and "ASEAN way" were propagated as a means of both developing shared norms and practices and promoting a shared identity.[21]

Dispute resolution and more regular contacts among ASEAN members have fallen short of producing the mutual attribution of benign character; ASEAN states still do not have complete confidence in the intentions of their neighbors. Indeed, Singapore maintains a robust air force largely as a deterrent in reserve against its much larger neighbors. At the same time, ASEAN has succeeded in nurturing a collective regional identity or "we-ness" that has dramatically reduced inter-state tensions and the likelihood of armed conflict. With the exception of Singapore, members do not maintain robust military forces capable of sustained offensive operations. Border patrols focus on interdicting drugs far more than on territorial protection. As Acharya notes, "no ASEAN country seriously envisages war against another at present."[22] Especially in light of the region's domestic challenges and complicated ethnic politics, the absence of inter-state security competition is quite striking.

The ASEAN case differs from the two cases discussed above in several important respects. First, all of ASEAN's members, including Indonesia, are regional powers, not great powers. And they live in a neighborhood into which outside great powers often extend their reach. As a result, collective balancing against the United States, Japan, and China (in differing degrees and at different times) has figured in the form and substance of regional cooperation. The goal has been not to aggregate capability against outside powers or to project ASEAN's influence externally, but to resolve South-East Asia's problems internally as a means of preempting great power intervention. This outside "other" has helped ASEAN build a collective regional identity.

Second, ASEAN members, with the exception of Singapore, have tended to view domestic threats as far more serious than external threats. Even with the decline of communist movements in the region, managing regime change, dealing with multi-ethnic societies, and responding to pressures for political liberalization have focused the attention of elites on internal threats. Somewhat paradoxically, this inward focus has facilitated regional security cooperation. Military forces have been trained and used to deal primarily with internal security, not territorial defense or acquisition. As a consequence, ASEAN members have neither the capability nor the inclination to threaten each other. In addition, elites interested in remaining in power and countering domestic opponents help one another prevent cross-border flows of personnel and arms, providing momentum behind security cooperation. Domestic instability has therefore served the interests of regional cooperation and integration.

Third, ASEAN has worked through far more informal and ad hoc mechanisms than most other multilateral organizations. Cultural factors have played an important role in this respect; East Asians in general are uncomfortable with the legalism and institutionalization of Anglo-Saxon and European diplomacy. Disputes are resolved by working through informal networks, not by making deals at the negotiating table. Decisions emerge through building a consensus, not through codified procedures. Again, its distinctive style of negotiation and dispute resolution has helped ASEAN promote a collective identity.

The financial crisis in South-East Asia in 1998 put ASEAN's peace-preserving capabilities to the test. Its broader security agenda was put on hold as governments focused on recovering economic stability and growth. The Indonesian government fell; political instability, accompanied by sporadic bouts of violence, ensued. Malaysia was spared the same scope of turmoil, but fell prey to considerable domestic unrest.

ASEAN and the regional security order it has promoted demonstrated remarkable resilience throughout the economic crisis. Despite conditions that gave elites strong incentives to seek to export domestic challenges by triggering external conflict, relations among ASEAN members remained stable. Malaysian leader Mohamed Mahathir did play the foreign confrontation card to bolster his popularity, but the targets were the United States, George Soros, and Israel, not Malaysia's neighbors. Indeed, no signs of regional security competition emerged throughout the crisis. ASEAN appears to have fostered a security order and regional identity sufficiently robust to weather major economic dislocation and political turmoil.

Cultural and racial affinities have both aided and hindered regional rapprochement and the cultivation of a shared regional identity and sense of benign character. Malay language and ethnicity have furthered cultural affinity among Indonesia, Malaysia, and Singapore. At the same time, the substantial Chinese populations in these countries (and their disproportionate wealth) have complicated both domestic politics and inter-state ties, especially between Singapore and its immediate neighbors. Nonetheless, the concept of the "ASEAN way" emerges from an inclusive understanding of Asian culture that cuts across the many different ethnic groups represented in the member countries. That Australia and New Zealand are not welcomed into the group despite their proximity and prominent role in shaping the regional security environment makes clear, however, that such cultural inclusivity does not extend to Anglo-Saxon or European cultures.

Benign character and managing contemporary power transition

A common identity and shared sense of benign character, even if only nascent, have played an important role in creating the pockets of stable peace examined above. As already mentioned, state identity and the mutual attribution of benign character are also critical in understanding the formation of the stable zone of peace that today exists among the Atlantic democracies. Accordingly, these variables must be taken into consideration in looking ahead to the coming return to multipolarity. If emerging centers of power see each other as benign, the return to multipolarity will be far easier to manage peacefully than systemic transitions in the past. Indeed, a key goal of policy makers should be to consolidate and gradually expand the pockets of stable peace that exist today.[23]

The importance of consolidating existing zones of peace raises the critical question of what will happen to Atlantic relations as a more equal distribution of power emerges between the United States and Europe. As mentioned in chapter 1, Europe, not Asia, represents the near-term challenger to American predominance. Is the mutual sense of benignity that has emerged between North America and Western Europe irreversible, or will it be overwhelmed by the competitive incentives that will accompany parity? History suggests that a more equal distribution of power and influence between Europe and the United States will bring with it renewed geopolitical competition. The emergence of rivalry among poles of power is, after all, one of the few recurring truths of international politics.

Whether relative parity will indeed trigger rivalry between Europe and the United States depends in large part on what it is that now keeps the Atlantic relationship in such good shape. If it is American preponderance that now holds competition in abeyance, then the rise of Europe promises to trigger geopolitical competition. From this perspective, Europe is following America's lead because it does not have the power to do otherwise. When the power asymmetry comes to an end, so will European acquiescence. If, on the other hand, the mutual attribution of benign character and a shared commitment to democratic values and an open, multilateral order are the foundation of the transatlantic community, then the West should easily weather a more equal distribution of power across the Atlantic. From this perspective, benignity, democratic norms, and multilateral institutions will overwhelm the incentives on both sides of the Atlantic to engage in power balancing.[24]

My own assessment is that power asymmetry and benign character are working together to produce the current durability and cohesiveness of the transatlantic community. Europe has been following America's lead in part because of US preponderance, but also because it welcomes the particular brand of international order that the United States has crafted.[25] As Europe matures and its aspirations broaden, more competition with the United States will follow. But this competition is likely to be muted and restricted largely to the economic realm. Such optimism that geopolitical rivalry between North America and Europe is not on the horizon stems from the following considerations.

The Atlantic democracies are far more than allies of convenience. They have succeeded in carving out a unique political space in which the rules of anarchic competition no longer apply. These states enjoy unprecedented levels of trust and reciprocity. It is hard to imagine that their interests would diverge sufficiently to trigger strategic rivalry. Indeed, armed conflict among the members of the Atlantic community has become unthinkable. These attributes of the Atlantic community are deeply rooted in the democratic character of its members and in the thick network of institutions they have erected to regulate their relations. The benign quality of the relationship between North America and Europe is very unlikely to be threatened even by a quantitative shift in the balance of power.

The character of the emerging European polity also minimizes the potential for security competition between Europe and the United States. The European Union is primarily an instrument for managing the power of its member states, not for amassing and projecting it. Furthermore, even as integration proceeds, cultural and linguistic barriers are likely to prevent Europe from amalgamating into a single pole of power under a central authority. The decentralized nature of the emerging Europe will limit its willingness and ability to project power externally, further diminishing the risk of geopolitical competition with the United States.[26]

Despite the low probability that Europe's rise will lead to estrangement from the United States, some preventive measures are in order. Washington should ensure that it makes room for and encourages a stronger and more independent Europe. American efforts to resist Europe's ascent as a power center would only alienate Europeans and increase the chances of balancing and geopolitical rivalry. The United States and its European partners should also strengthen multilateral practices and institutions. When Washington is no longer able to call the shots, it will have no choice but to rely more heavily on consensual governance and multilateral institutions to manage international order.

Expanding the existing zone of peace will for several reasons be far more difficult than simply preserving it. First, strategic necessity played an important role in binding together North America and Europe. So too did an external threat facilitate Franco-German rapprochement and the enterprise of European integration. Europe is now sustained by its own internal logic, and the process of deepening and widening the EU continues even in the absence of an external threat. But EU integration is likely to proceed slowly and extend only so far. For countries outside the Atlantic community, it is not apparent what will serve as the driving force behind rapprochement either with the Atlantic democracies or with each other.

Second, cultural affinity does seem to matter in the formation of stable zones of peace. The historical record suggests that benign images most readily form among polities that share a common culture, language, or ethnicity: USA–Britain, USA–Canada, the Nordic states, and Western Europe. Efforts to expand the Atlantic zone of peace to include Asian states may therefore run up against cultural barriers. Indeed, talk of an Asian way and the exclusion of Australia and New Zealand from ASEAN suggest that it may be difficult to foster the mutual attribution of benign character among European and Asian polities. It is perhaps more likely that the ASEAN process will spread northward, serving as a model for security integration throughout East Asia. That prospect raises the issue of what type of relations would emerge between a more integrated and collective East Asia and regional collectives in North America or Europe. Such relations may ultimately depend more on the ability of regional groupings to reach agreement on the basic features of international order than on their ability to promote benign images. It is just this issue of negotiating order that Yuen Foong Khong takes up in the following chapter.

Notes

1. See, for example, Arnold Wolfers, "The Balance of Power in Theory and Practice," in Wolfers, ed., *Discord and Collaboration: Essays on International Politics* (Baltimore, MD: Johns Hopkins University Press, 1962), pp. 117–133; Randall Schweller, "Tripolarity and the Second World War," *International Studies Quarterly*, Vol. 37, No. 1 (March 1993), pp. 73–103; Schweller, "Neorealism's Status-Quo Bias: What Security Dilemma?" in *Security Studies*, Vol. 5, No. 3 (Spring 1996), pp. 90–121; and Michael Mastanduno, "Preserving the Unipolar Moment: Realist Theories and U.S. Grand Strategy after the Cold War," *International Security*, Vol. 21, No. 4 (Spring 1997), pp. 49–88.
2. Inquiry into state type and its relationship to state role appears to be enjoying a resurgence. For earlier work on role theory, see K. J. Holsti, "National Role Conceptions in the Study of Foreign Policy," *International Studies Quarterly*, Vol. 14, No. 3 (September 1970), pp. 233–309. Recent literature on type and role includes: Randall Schweller, *Deadly Imbalances: Tripolarity and Hitler's Strategy of World Conquest* (New York: Columbia University Press, 1998); Gideon Rose, "Neoclassical Realism and Theories of Foreign Policy," *World Politics*, Vol. 51 (October 1998), pp. 144–172; James Fearon, "What Is Identity (As We Now Use the Word)?" unpublished manuscript, University of Chicago (1997); Mira Sucharov, "Types and Roles in International Relations: Beyond the Green Room," unpublished paper, Georgetown University.

3. For further discussion of self-binding and strategic restraint, see Charles Kupchan, "After Pax Americana: Benign Power, Regional Integration, and the Sources of a Stable Multipolarity," *International Security*, Vol. 23, No. 2 (Fall 1998), pp. 40–79; and John Ikenberry, "Institutions, Strategic Restraint, and the Persistence of American Postwar Order," *International Security*, Vol. 23, No. 3 (Winter 1998/99), pp. 43–78.
4. To simplify the analysis, this discussion assumes rapprochement is taking place between only two states. The same logic would apply were three or more involved.
5. In stressing the importance of emotive affinity, I am not directly arguing against Stephen Walt's conclusion in *The Origins of Alliances* (Ithaca, NY: Cornell University Press, 1987) that ideology is a weak determinant of a state's choice of alliance partner. Alliance and rapprochement are quite different animals. Alliances provide convenient, instrumental means of aggregating capability against a common external threat. Rapprochement entails a far more profound and durable transformation of relations, not just a marriage of convenience. In addition, I believe that Walt underestimates the extent to which ideational factors color threat perception. Emotive affinity drops out as an independent variable for Walt because his definition of threat is not sufficiently nuanced or disaggregated.
6. Aaron Friedberg, *The Weary Titan* (Princeton, NJ: Princeton University Press, 1988).
7. See Sean Shore, "No Fences Make Good Neighbors: The Development of the Canadian–US Security Community, 1871–1940," in Emanuel Adler and Michael Barnett, eds., *Security Communities* (Cambridge: Cambridge University Press, 1998), pp. 333–367.
8. For further support of this position, see Stephen Rock, *Why Peace Breaks out* (Chapel Hill: University of North Carolina Press, 1989), p. 8.
9. Shore, "No Fences Make Good Neighbors," pp. 344–347.
10. See Rock, *Why Peace Breaks out*, pp. 25–27.
11. For documentation of this period, see A. E. Campbell, *Great Britain and the United States, 1895–1903* (London: Longman, 1960); and R. G. Neale, *Great Britain and United States Expansion: 1898–1900* (East Lansing, MI: Michigan State University Press, 1966).
12. Cited in Neale, *Great Britain and United States Expansion*, p. 90.
13. Lionel Gelber, *The Rise of Anglo-American Friendship* (London: Oxford University Press, 1938).
14. See Campbell, *Great Britain and the United States*, pp. 195–207.
15. Montmorency cited in Bruce Cronin, *Community under Anarchy* (New York: Columbia University Press, 1999), p. 72.
16. For example, when the Spanish revolution first broke out in 1820, the Russians wanted to intervene to restore the monarchy. The lack of a consensus prevented intervention. The following year, changed circumstances led to a consensus in favor of intervention, with France authorized to send forces to Spain by the Concert as a whole. See Ibid., pp. 68–72.
17. See Ibid., p. 58.
18. Charles Kupchan and Clifford Kupchan, "Concerts, Collective Security, and the Future of Europe," *International Security*, Vol. 16, No. 1 (Summer 1991), pp. 114–161.
19. On the evolution of ASEAN, see Yuen Foong Khong, "Evolving Regional Security and Economic Institutions," *Southeast Asian Affairs 1995* (Singapore: Institute of Southeast Asian Studies, 1995).
20. Amitav Acharya, "Collective Identity and Conflict Management in Southeast Asia," in Adler and Barnett, *Security Communities*, p. 203.
21. Amitav Acharya, "Ideas, Identity, and Institution-Building: From the 'ASEAN Way' to the 'Asia-Pacific Way'," *Pacific Review*, Vol. 10, No. 3 (1997), pp. 319–346.
22. Acharya, "Collective Identity and Conflict Management in Southeast Asia," p. 214.
23. On this point, see Adler and Barnett, *Security Communities*, and Adler's chapter in this volume (chap. 6).

24. See Ikenberry, "Institutions, Strategic Restraint, and the Persistence of American Postwar Order."
25. I acknowledge that benignity is in the eye of the beholder and that not all European states, and certainly not all states of the world, consistently view the United States as a benign power. At the same time, for reasons of both history and cultural and political similarity, the United States and Western Europe have forged a particularly strong and mutual sense of affinity. The French, for example, may complain about America's *hyperpuissance*, but they are questioning Washington's way of doing business, not America's basic intentions.
26. Fareed Zakaria has shown that centralization and a strong state were necessary conditions for ambitious external policies in the United States. See *From Wealth to Power: The Unusual Origins of America's World Role* (Princeton, NJ: Princeton University Press, 1998).

3
Negotiating "order" during power transitions

Yuen Foong Khong

War between the rising power and the declining power is the historical norm during power transitions. Power transition theorists also argue that such wars occur when the power differential between the existing hegemon and the rising challenger narrows. More precise studies have suggested that war is unlikely when the existing hegemon enjoys an overwhelming power advantage (say, 10:1); war becomes much more likely when the preponderance of the hegemon declines substantially (to, say, 3:1).[1] If these findings are accepted, the relative shift in power between the hegemon and the challenger must be seen as the *underlying cause of transition wars*.

Yet, as the case of the United States' overtake of Britain and other less well-known cases of peaceful transitions indicate, the existence of an underlying cause of war does not mean war will always be the result. For war to occur, there need to be proximate causes as well.[2] The authors of this book assume that the clash of ideas and convictions – ideational contestation – about order in the international system is one such proximate cause. As the rising power closes in on the declining power, the rising power expects its ideas about how the system ought to be organized and governed to be taken seriously. If these notions about order are fundamentally at odds with those of the declining power and if neither side is willing to give way, the proximate cause of war will obtain, and a conflict is very likely. On the other hand, if agreement on the principles of order is successfully negotiated, an important proximate cause of war will be removed, and the chances for a peaceful transition will be increased.

This chapter will examine four cases of rising powers in the Asian Pacific system – Japan's rise in East Asia in the late nineteenth century, the United States at the turn of the twentieth century, Indonesia's bid for hegemony in South-East Asia in the 1960s and its aftermath, and the rise of China since the 1980s – to tease out how the elements of "order" were negotiated. In the analysis that follows, I elaborate on the notion of order and suggest why it becomes such an important issue of contention during power transitions. Following Gilpin, I assume that the elements of order that are most in need of negotiation during power transitions are: the hierarchy of prestige; rules about trade and the use of force; procedures for managing territorial change; and mutual recognition of spheres of influence.[3] If the rising power or challenger (A) and declining power or existing hegemon (B) can come to agreement on most or all of these elements, order is likely to be obtained (see table 3.1).

Agreement on the hierarchy of prestige means acknowledgement by A and B about their relative status and power (A and B agree on who is the top dog and the kind of influence that each deserves to exercise in the international community). Agreement on the rules of trade means A and B are favorably disposed toward, or have signed, pacts – such as the General Agreement on Tariffs and Trade and the World Trade Organization – that regulate their trading relationship. Consensus on the use of force refers to a common understanding on the conditions under which military force may be used. For example, A and B may consider it legitimate to use force (in the nineteenth century) to obtain colonies or (in the twenty-first century) to prevent any state from pursuing a policy of ethnic cleansing. Agreement on procedures for managing territorial change means sharing common views on issues such as the right to self-determination, the legitimacy of using military force, and the role of the United Nations in effecting territorial revisions. Mutual recognition of spheres of influence refers to A's understanding that B has a special interest in some portion of the globe (say the Western hemisphere) and refraining from interfering, in the expectation that B would show similar restraint and understanding for A's areas of interest.

The analysis suggests that in two of the cases – Japan and Indonesia – there was no agreement on the above elements of order with the declining powers. Despite their growing power, neither Japan nor Indonesia succeeded in moving up the international hierarchy of prestige; nor were their spheres of influence or attempts at territorial change recognized by the West. Not surprisingly, the rise of both Japan and Indonesia in the Asian Pacific subsystem resulted in conflict with the declining or retreating powers. In contrast, in our third case study, Britain was quick to recognize the United States' great power status in 1895 and to reaffirm America's sphere of influence in the Western hemisphere. Both countries also had common understandings on trade and the role of arbitration in

Table 3.1 **Outcomes of negotiations between rising and declining powers**

Rising power	Japan	USA	Indonesia[a]	China, 1989–
Existing/declining power	"West"[b]	Britain	"Malaysia"[c]	USA
Elements of order to be negotiated	AGREEMENT?			
New hierarchy	No	Yes	No	No
Rules on trade	No	Yes	No	Yes
Use of force, rules	No	Yes	No	No
Managing territorial change	No	Yes	No	No
Spheres of influence	No	Yes	No	No

Notes: For explanations of outcomes, see table 3.2.
a. 1963–1967.
b. Britain, France, Germany.
c. Backed by Britain.

managing territorial change; these common understandings facilitated the peaceful overtake of Britain by the United States. The outcome of the fourth case study – China's rise since 1989 – is too soon to tell, although, if our indicators are anything to go by, it would seem that to date there is greater disagreement than agreement between China and the United States (the existing hegemon or assumed declining power over time).

In addition to analyzing the relationship between agreement on order and peaceful transition, this chapter also explores, in a more tentative way, the issue of what makes agreement (on order) more likely. All in all, the cases suggest that negotiations about order between the declining power and the rising power are more likely to succeed if (a) there exists some affinity of identity between the powers concerned; (b) the declining power allows real participatory negotiation by the rising power; (c) the rising power is perceived to "have what it takes," i.e. strong current and potential capabilities (see table 3.2).

Conceptualizing international order

"Order" in the most general sense refers to a condition or state of affairs, but more specifically "order" describes a pattern or method that signifies the lack of chaos.[4] At the international level, order is most widely construed in terms of its normative *substance*, as the condition of "peace" or the absence of general war. As an introductory textbook on international relations put it, "Order is when relationships between states are stable, predictable, controlled and not characterised by violence, turbulence or chaos."[5]

Table 3.2 **Power transitions, ideational contestations, and outcomes in the Asia Pacific**

Rising power/ challenger	Declining power/ hegemon	Explanatory variables			Agreement on order?
		Affinity?	Participatory equality?	Non-pushover?	
Japan	"West"	No	No	No	No
USA	Britain	Yes	Yes	Yes	Yes
Indonesia	Malaysia (backed by UK)	No	No	No	No
China	USA	No–Yes	No	No	Depends

When, and more importantly how, such predictability, stability, and non-violence can come to characterize inter-state relations are the key questions and the key points of contention between rising and declining powers. Lenin addressed the "when" by arguing that the international system would be conflict prone as capitalism reaches its highest stage and ushers in an era of imperialistic rivalry and wars; only a socialist revolution would short-circuit this logic of capitalism and bring about peace and stability.[6] Evan Luard took an important stab at the "how" in his study of the Principles of International Order when he argued that "to secure order in international society... a more hopeful course was... to develop the kind of conventions and understandings which are the underlying basis of order in less advanced [domestic] societies." Moreover, for Luard, these conventions and understandings change with time: "each generation of states... requires its own code to meet its own conditions and needs"[7]

Agreeing with Luard, Hedley Bull has also addressed the "how" of international order in his work, *The Anarchical Society*.[8] Bull focuses on the importance of *institutions* in engendering order. Institutions, for Bull, are the habitual practices, or norms, or rules of the game which define social practices, assign roles, and guide interactions among actors in the system.[9] Institutions are the means by which order is achieved, sustained, and maintained, and can thus be expected to be the main focus of contention about international order, where negotiations and agreement are crucial.

Bull and Luard's focus on habitual practices, norms, and the rules of the game points us in the right direction. To use these notions to illuminate ideational contestation during power transitions, however, we need to be more specific about the "objects" or "issues" around which states will want to construct the rules of the game. Bull himself identifies the need for three kinds of rules of the game relevant to international order:

the fundamental normative principle of world politics, the rules of coexistence, and rules regulating cooperation.[10] As indicated earlier, these "rules" will be operationalized along the lines suggested by Gilpin, namely, the kinds of rules and understandings that the rising and declining powers would need to agree upon are the new hierarchy, rules concerning the use of force and trade, spheres of influence, and procedures for managing territorial change.[11] Agreement on these issues means agreement on the principles of international order. It also means the removal of a potential proximate cause of war.

Order and peaceful power transition

Attempts to reconceptualize the form and substance of international order can be expected in times of structural change: when there is a shift in the distribution of power among the major states; with the ascension of large numbers of new members; or when states develop new capabilities with systemic impacts. The focus of this book is on the first instance of change, particularly the transition from one leading great power to another. Changes in relative power at the great power level are associated with competition over positions within the hierarchy, often accompanied by contestation over the relative importance of the various basic goals of international society.

Realist and neorealist theorists are pessimistic about prospects for peaceful power transitions. Notably, Robert Gilpin's "hegemonic instability" theory asserts that the incongruity between a rising power's capabilities and its continued subordinate position in an international system dominated by an erstwhile hegemon triggers a security dilemma that can be resolved only by major war.[12] His is a stark realist view that regards states as driven by zero-sum power concerns which make negotiation on hierarchy, rules, and values impossible. Empirically, it would seem that neorealists are correct: a large majority of power transitions are accompanied by war, with the modifications to the international order made by the victors on the basis of victorious military contestation rather than ideational negotiation. Yet the existence of historical examples of peaceful power transitions – though rare – suggests that there are specific conditions under which the incongruity between capabilities and status felt by the rising power does not necessarily lead it to war. In particular, I am interested in the cases in which the rising and declining powers do not fight each other, but try to negotiate a new international order.[13]

Indications of these conditions may be found within the broad range of liberal arguments emphasizing the *congruence* of state interests that help reduce threat perception and thus overcome the security dilemma. Interdependence theorists, for instance, assert that mutual dependence acts as an incentive for states to negotiate and agree on changes in the international order, by rendering war unacceptably costly.[14] The condition of congruence suggests not just commonality but complementarity of state interests and goals; it is this quality of mutually reinforcing needs that may help to overcome conflicts resulting from changes in relative power.[15] Liberal approaches highlight a second condition that contributes to the propensity for peaceful transitions: *affinity*, which refers to the recognition of common identity, be it ethnic, historical, or ideological, and thus a shared understanding and acceptance of a certain order which relative power changes are not allowed to affect. Democratic peace theory, for example, emphasizes an affinity based on democratic norms and structures.[16]

Congruence of interests and affinity of identity that allow states to reduce their perceptions of threat from changes in relative power are thus the conditions that may contribute to peaceful power transitions. However, there still remains the question of how this may be achieved. As seen from the previous discussion of institutions and rules, the concept of order turns on *management*, which encompasses the whole range of procedures and subtleties that constitute diplomacy and what may be called ideational engagement and contestation in the context of change to bring about peaceful outcomes. Concert diplomacy is a prime example of regulatory conventions that seek to manage and contain the process of change to preempt violent overtake and rivalry.[17] The idea of managing conflicts is also very strong in more recent institutional theories of regimes and governance.[18] On the other hand, peaceful resolution of rivalries associated with great power overtake may be managed through bilateral negotiations and arrangements between the declining and rising power.

Having explored the reasons why agreement might be possible between the contending powers, it is now possible to delve into the four case studies to examine whether and to what extent the contending powers were able to agree on the principal elements of international order.

The rise of Japan in the late nineteenth century

Between 1895 and 1915, Japan "emerged as one of the world's great powers."[19] Japan's meteoric rise to great power status was, typically, studded by war: making its debut with victory in the Sino-Japanese War of 1894–1895, Japan signaled its "arrival" by defeating Russia in 1905. Yet, given our interest in the potential of agreed norms in effecting peaceful change, it is worth noting that Japan's conscientious conformity to the agreed norms of international society at the time did not prevent violent power transition in the Far East. In the 50 years following its forced opening to the outside world in 1853, Japan proved an example *par excellence* in conforming its government institutions, legal system, and general international practices to the interests, rules, and values of "civilized" international society, as prescribed by Western nations. The Meiji government declared Japan's intention of joining international society by formally abandoning Japan's 200-year seclusion in 1868.[20] This was followed by the 1871–1873 Iwakura Mission to the West, which marked the beginning of earnest learning about the institutions of Western international society.[21] For the first time, Tokyo sent permanent resident diplomatic missions abroad to reciprocate those established in Japan as a result of "unequal" treaties.

Japan successfully applied the European model in its diplomatic relations with Korea and China: in an imitation of Western relations with "uncivilized" Japan, Japan imposed a series of "unequal" treaties on Korea in 1876, ending the latter's seclusion. In 1896, Japan also gained most-favored-nation (MFN) status with China.[22] Japan's acceptance and learning of international law were also impressive – the Meiji government used the law of nations to defend Japan against unequal treaties and Western interference in its domestic affairs, employing concepts such as sovereign equality, independence, and non-intervention.[23] Its success is indicated by Britain's 1894 agreement to terminate consular jurisdiction in Japan, and the removal of all restrictions on tariff autonomy by 1911. Even in war, Japan tried to impress the West by its meticulous observation of international law: eminent Japanese jurists were involved in the conduct of both the Sino-Japanese and Russo-Japanese wars as legal advisers.[24]

This should have been an "easy" example of norms agreement – the rising power willingly subscribed to the rules of the game played by existing powers in return for the right to play. Yet the power competition that ensued was marked by three major wars within 50 years. The impediments to peaceful transition in this case appear to lie in the process of negotiation for membership, associated with understandings about the nature of the prevailing order itself. Some writers contend that Japanese frustration and humiliation at the perceived double standards employed against them by the Western powers during their rise to international society contributed to greater subsequent Japanese aggression.[25] In this vein, most writers highlight the censure of the 1895 Triple Intervention after the Sino-Japanese War.

As was pointed out earlier, Japan's victory over China in the Sino-Japanese War of 1894–1895 marked its "debut" as a great power in Asia.

This had been the first Far Eastern war in which the Western powers agreed to non-intervention, yet Russia, Germany, and France subsequently threatened collective military action if Japan did not return the Liaotung peninsular to China.[26] Japanese humiliation and anger were further exacerbated when these powers proceeded to claim ports in the very territory that Japan had been forced to return. From the point of view of the Japanese, their careful conformity to the spirit and letter of international law and diplomacy had been rewarded by a display of superior coercive force. This drove home Japan's inferior status as well as the hollowness of the principle of sovereign equality amongst members of the international society. Richard Storry writes that "[n]o understanding of twentieth century Japanese nationalism is possible without some comprehension of the bitterness and sense of humiliation that swept the country in the wake of the Triple Intervention"; "Western nations had been feared usually; and disliked very often. But on the whole they had been respected by Japan. Now they were distrusted, despised even, as hypocrites."[27]

Japan's hopes of being recognized as a great power via its success in the first Sino-Japanese War were dashed by the Triple Intervention. Despite its victory, Japan was relegated to its old position in the (international) hierarchy of prestige. From Japan's perspective, "the rules of the game" were also inconsistently applied. Understandings on the use of force, territorial change, and spheres of influence meant one thing when used by the Western powers (to their advantage); they meant another thing when applied to Japan (to its disadvantage).

The Triple Intervention had a significant impact on Japanese nationalism because of the change in self-perception it engendered. The feeling that Japan had been something of a naïve pushover was widely expressed in the media and by politicians. It seemed that, having adopted and abided by the established diplomatic and legal norms of international society, Japan still did not gain the respect of the other "civilized" powers. Thus Japan came to see superior military force as the way to earn the equal treatment and security it desired.[28] In this context, the deputy foreign minister at the time wrote that Japan had now to bide its time and concentrate on building up the forces to consolidate its national power, and particularly to pursue an alliance with a stronger power.[29] In the run-up to the war with Russia in 1905, broad-based pressure groups argued strongly for war on the basis that, because of Japan's weak stance in 1895, Russia did not accord it sufficient respect to give in on their disputes over Korea and Manchuria.[30] The importance of overcoming their humiliation at being perceived as a pushover can be seen in the way the Japanese deliberately phrased their diplomatic correspondence to the Russians concerning the 1905 Treaty of Portsmouth after their victory in the Russo-Japanese War, and the ultimatum issued to the Germans in 1914, in language very similar to that of the Triple Intervention.[31]

The failure of the great powers to engage with a rising Japan in facilitating a smooth power transition or at least peaceful accommodation may be attributed to the inability to arrive at any agreement on the five elements highlighted in table 3.1. There was no recognition of Japan's status in the hierarchy of the great power club, and this prevented the possibility of arriving at any agreement on the four other elements. It was not that Japan's demands were not heard at the negotiating table; rather, its very existence at the table was denied. In its zeal to be considered a "modern" state, Japan had to accept the double-edged sword of nationalism – the principal imperative of nationalist doctrine being the attainment of congruity between the nation and the state."[32] Although nationalism allowed for the state to use its propaganda machine in order to mobilize its people when it was under threat, the constructions of "self" and "other" generated by nationalist discourse made territorial integrity and security of the utmost importance in any government's maintenance of legitimacy.

The failure of the great powers to accept Japan into their ranks, coupled with their encroachments into areas contiguous to Japan (i.e. China, Manchuria, and Korea), made it almost inevitable that Japan would force its way in – removing all possibility of either accommodation or peaceful power transition. Aritomo Yamagata, Japanese prime minister in 1898, expressed this point succinctly by predicting that "within ten years, we shall be at war. At that time, our enemy will be neither China nor Korea, but Britain, France and Russia."[33]

Failure to achieve agreement on the four other elements may be seen in the significant length of time Japan took to unchain itself from the burden of extraterritoriality and the attainment of tariff autonomy. As early as 1869, the Japanese were aware that extraterritoriality was a violation of its independence, and by 1876 Foreign Minister Terashima Munenori expressed the importance of the restoration of tariff autonomy.[34] This burden was eased in 1899 with the coming into force of Japan's civil code, which allowed for treaty revisions that leveled the economic playing field between Britain and Japan. The recognition of Japan as a sovereign state and an equal trading partner consequently was established with all the other powers, though not immediately.[35] The difficulty in removing the unequal treaties clearly illustrates two main points: first, Japan's rise to great power status was not recognized and its location in the hierarchy of states was unclear; and, secondly, there was no agreement on the rules of trade – one of the elements of a peaceful power transition.

With regard to the final three elements of a peaceful transition (agreement on the rules regarding the use of force, managing territorial claims, and the allocation of respective spheres of influence), their closely related nature makes it difficult to discuss them separately. In general, the norm established for all three elements was that of imperialism. This was distinguished by colonialism for economic gain and the practice of *realpolitik* in the form of power politics in order to create a sphere of influence for oneself.[36] In the management of territorial claims and the allocation of spheres of influence, there was agreement between Russia and Japan over the exchange of Sakhalin for the Kurils in 1875, whereby Russia was to control Sakhalin and Japan would obtain the Kurils.[37] This agreement was, however, a break from the norm. As mentioned above, the failure to arrive at an agreement on the three final elements of a peaceful transition between existing/declining powers and rising powers culminated in the Triple Intervention.

The late nineteenth century saw the height of Western imperialism, and Japan in its modernization streak merely took on board the available *modus operandi* of the period. Therefore, it seemed "normal" for it to compete with the other powers through colonial expansion for its own benefits.[38] The moral of the story is that it would seem that a necessary but perhaps not a sufficient condition requires that there be real participatory negotiation with even the most acquiescent of rising powers. In the case of Japan, this was certainly missing, in large part because of the perception that it was indeed not an equal member of the great power club. Despite Japan's military prowess, there was no recognition of its place in the new hierarchy of states in Asia.

There was a marked lack of perceived affinity on the part of the Western powers towards Japan, stemming from the fact that Japan was an anomaly in the nineteenth-century international system centered on Europe and European imperial rivalries (see table 3.2). Japan's rapid economic, social, and political development along Western lines and its military capability portended the rise of the first Oriental great power, at once a member of "civilized" international society and irascibly foreign. Because of its late start in a region peripheral to Europe however, Japan was seen as an impudent second-rate power, constituting a "yellow peril" but unable to defeat China or Russia. Britain and Germany hoped at the best that Japan would act as a side-show to keep Russia occupied in the Far East for some time, distracting its attention from Europe.[39] However, even after its victory over Russia, Japan saw itself as continually singled out for discrimination despite being recognized as a "civilized" great power. Japanese immigrants to the United States were discriminated against in Immigration Acts in 1913, 1917, and 1924. More significantly, Japan's attempt to secure clauses on "racial equality" or even a simple endorsement of the principle of the equality of nations in the League of Nations Covenant failed at the Paris Peace Conference, even though a majority of 11 out of 17 states voted in favor.[40] Such real discrimination on the part of the Western great powers alienated Japan and convinced the Japanese that they would not be accorded respect by adhering to international norms selectively applied by biased Western powers.

The United States and Britain in the early twentieth century

The United States, in contrast to Japan, rose from being a new great power in 1865 to becoming the new hegemon in 1945. Here, we consider the salient elements of the first phase of US ascension prior to World War I to compare the different experiences of the United States and Japan. Based on its size and resources, the United States was recognized from the aftermath of its Civil War as a formidable potential great power. However, it only really "arrived" after the Spanish–American War in 1898: after its victory and seizure of the Philippines, the United States began its steady "backyard expansion" into the Caribbean, Latin America, and the Pacific islands.

The initial phase of US ascension and expansion was – apart from the Philippines – confined to the Western hemisphere, its natural sphere of influence and where its preponderant power prevented serious challenges from other great powers with limited power projection capabilities. A declining Britain found its interests in the Western hemisphere exposed and, in the wake of the Boer War, chose to cede dominance of this region to the United States as it focused on Europe and limited commitments elsewhere.[41] Initially, US expansion occurred in much the same way as that of other great powers: buying and leasing ports, acquiring protectorates, making commercial treaties, and annexing territory. However, the United States also began to apply its own particular rules to the "game." For instance, in its intervention in the Venezuelan crisis of 1895, the Cleveland administration extended the Monroe Doctrine espousing principles of non-intervention and non-colonization, and used it as a basis for American opposition to European expansion in Latin America. It incurred Lord Salisbury's caustic reminder that the Monroe Doctrine was not international law and "no nation, however powerful, [is] competent to insert into the code of international law a novel principle which was never recognized before, and which has not since been accepted by the government of any country."[42] Even in the Far East, where all the great powers had their fingers in the Chinese pie, the United States tried to impose its own open door doctrine – an ingenious policy ostensibly promoting free trade, but in fact seeking to protect commercial interests for the United States, which had no formal sphere of influence with which to compete.[43]

Much has been written about the rise of the United States and the ceding of British preeminence at the turn of the twentieth century. The relevant question for us is how the two powers "negotiated" the rules of the game such that it avoided war. As the above suggests, the United States and Britain came close to war over the Venezuelan crisis in 1895. The British–American negotiations during the crisis provide fascinating insights into their ability to agree on the various elements of order and on the domestic forces and affinities that nudge them in the direction of agreement.

What is incontrovertible is that the crisis was resolved when Britain appeased the United States: Prime Minister Salisbury's cabinet voted, over his lone objection, to accept adjudication by a US Commission on the Venezuelan–British Guiana border. This action by Britain would be the first of several signals that the old hegemon was ceding its place to the upcoming hegemon, and of course that the upcoming hegemon – the United States – was rising to the top of the prestige hierarchy.[44] In short, Britain and the United States were able to agree on the new hierarchy.

But why did the Salisbury cabinet choose to cede ground to the Americans? Realists argue that Britain was militarily weaker than the United States and that threats emanating from Germany and Russia persuaded its policy makers to appease the United States.[45] The British concession was further motivated by London's recognition of the limits of its own military ability to protect its far-flung interests on so many fronts. As Paul Kennedy has argued, "the Royal Navy, although superior to any American fleet, could only be superior in the western hemisphere by abandoning the Mediterranean." Britain was indeed alarmed by German pretensions in South Africa, which the British regarded as a vital piece of real estate, when Wilhelm II expressed his support of the Boer leader, Kruger, for repelling the Jameson raid. Britain viewed the Germans rather than the Americans as a relatively more serious threat to its interests. Therefore, "it was not difficult for the Cabinet to agree to American arbitration to the Venezuelan issue" while it recognized American predominance in the Western hemisphere.[46]

Liberals, however, place greater emphasis on the political affinity between Britain and the United States: the two countries identified with, and had greater trust in, one another because they see themselves as democracies. It was that democratic affinity that persuaded Britain to choose to appease the United States, instead of, say, Germany.[47] Liberals also point to the pacifying effects of economic interdependence: economic interests on both sides of the Atlantic were keen to ensure nothing untoward would jeopardize the relations between the two countries. When the war scare precipitated by the 1895 Venezuela dispute triggered panic selling on the New York stock exchange by the British unloading of American securities, business communities pressured their governments to resolve the squabble amicably.[48] Whether the realists or the liberals are right will not affect the fact that Britain ceded ground and the United States came out on top; but if perceptions of mutual "democraticness" influenced Britain to choose the United States, the emphasis we place on the role of identity and affinity in negotiating the new international order would be fully justified.

As far as agreement on the rules of trade is concerned, the strengthening of the federal government under the constitution and the Jay Treaty of 1794 placed the economic relations of the United States and Britain on the basis of "reciprocal and perfect liberty." This essentially allowed Washington to expand its economic relations with London on an equal basis of competition and trade and freed British economic interests from many of the obstructive controls applicable under the mercantilist colonial system.[49] The United States consequently became a chief source of raw materials for British producers while British manufactured goods, textiles, and investment capital were sought across the Atlantic.

After the American Civil War, the Industrial Revolution profoundly affected the economies of both countries. Although the United States continued to export products such as cotton and wheat to Britain, such exports were now accompanied by manufactured goods. The United States also refrained from reciprocating Britain's unilateral lowering of barriers to international trade from 1860 as it continued to exploit the opportunity afforded by British free trade policies to flood that market with steel, iron, and wheat.[50] The deficits created by that exchange were huge. In 1893, US$421 million worth of American products went to Britain whereas US$183 million worth of British products were imported into the United States. In 1899, the respective figures were US$512 million and US$118 million.[51] As Paul Kennedy aptly noted, "[b]ecause it [the United States] had such a vast surplus in its trade with Europe, the latter's deficit had to be met by capital transfers – joining the enormous stream of direct European investments into US industry, utilities, and services."[52] British capital invested in areas like the American range-cattle, mining, milling and agriculture industries and the stock exchange contributed substantially to the economic development of the United States and bound both economies closely to each other.[53]

The process by which the British reconciled themselves to the right of the Americans to wield a preponderant influence in the Western hemisphere was undoubtedly also helped by American reciprocity in its Chinese economic interests. Dominating 70 percent of China's trade (equaling one-sixth of the total British commerce), the British were keen to maintain their access to the Chinese market. British officials valued American support and this came about in 1894 when the Chinese government ventured to restrict the import of foreign machinery. The State Department consequently endorsed the Foreign Office's remonstrances against China's policy, illustrating both countries' commitment to keeping the Far Eastern markets open to economic penetration. This indubitably stocked up much goodwill between the two countries to smooth over future difficulties.[54]

The British decision to accept adjudication by the US Commission on the Venezuela–British Guiana border dispute affirmed the Monroe Doctrine: the Western hemisphere would remain under the jurisdiction of the United States and even British possessions there would need the assent of the United States for territorial changes. As Salisbury's biographer noted, "British Governments had for long accepted the Monroe Doctrine. Salisbury was also ready to recognize it, not it is true as a binding international treaty but as expressing the wishes of the United States."[55] In his initial refusal to subject areas along the Venezuela–British Guiana border long settled by British citizens to arbitration, the Prime Minister merely wished to ensure the protection of British settlers' rights and interests against Venezuelan pretensions. "We are contending for men not for land," Salisbury wrote to Colonial Secretary Joseph Chamberlain.[56] Notably, when the Prime Minister maintained to his cabinet that he would resign rather than accede unreservedly to "American threats," Salisbury was willing nonetheless to accept the arbitration of unsettled territories east of the Schomburgk line.[57] At any rate, the consensus reached within the British government as a result of the whole Venezuela affair was that the Western hemisphere was undeniably Washington's domain. The American ambassador to Britain, Thomas Bayard, noted that, with the resolution of the territorial squabble, "'the doctrine of European abstention' from colonialism in Latin America [had become] 'a fixed fact.'"[58] This was affirmed in the public discourse of leading British officials and opinion-makers. Colonial Secretary Joseph Chamberlain and the Leader of the House of Commons, Arthur Balfour (Salisbury's nephew), publicly expressed their recognition of the Monroe Doctrine, as did Queen Victoria, Liberal Opposition leader Sir William Harcourt, and the Earl of Rosebery.[59]

That acquiescent British disposition toward the United States regarding the Monroe Doctrine would be reaffirmed during the 1898 Spanish–American War. In August 1895 an editorial in the London *Times* commenting on Spanish–American squabbles in the Caribbean had stated that "the annexation of Cuba to the United States would be regarded with little favour by British statesmen." Yet when the United States fought Spain and annexed Cuba in 1898, British officials would lend their endorsement to American imperialism.[60]

Parenthetically, while Washington sought to establish its claim to primacy in Latin American affairs, it reaffirmed to London its diplomatic principles of non-interference in European affairs. Since London had recognized American rights, it would be incumbent upon the United States to assure it would show similar restraint and conciliation in relation to Britain's interests in Europe and elsewhere. India, for example, was regarded as a British preserve. Olney's missive to Chamberlain was understandably conciliatory: although the Monroe Doctrine "enjoins certain duties upon the United States as regards the States of the Western Hemisphere, it forbids any interference in the political affairs of European States or any alliance with European States looking to such interference."[61] That mutual recognition of each power's sphere of influence went far toward assuaging whatever tensions might have spilled over from the Venezuelan dispute.

The recourse to arbitration in the Venezuelan affair and the signing of a general arbitration treaty (despite its non-ratification by Congress) marked the culmination of an Anglo-American practice that proved to be an effective diplomatic instrument in managing territorial change as well as alleviating the resultant strains between the two Anglo-Saxon nations. Arbitration had its ideological roots in nineteenth-century liberalism when the general aversion to war moved many Western nations to formulate agreements among themselves that difficult issues would be resolved before a stipulated arbitral body. Washington and London were advocates of that liberal initiative and both governments endorsed the arbitration principle in 1873 (House of Commons) and 1874 (Congress).[62] In the period between the end of the American Civil War and the Venezuela crisis, both countries submitted no fewer than six disputes for arbitration. These included the *Alabama* claims, the San Juan border disagreements, the Civil War claims, the contentious fishery articles in the Treaty of Washington, and quarrels over pelagic sealing in the Bering Sea.[63] Meanwhile, there were moves by interested elements from both sides of the Atlantic for the United States and Britain to conclude a general arbitration treaty. It was within this historical context that the Venezuela crisis flared up.

Understandably, the American demand for the Salisbury government to submit its territorial claims along the Venezuela–British Guiana border for arbitration was not a novel idea. The existence and legitimacy of such a procedure between the two countries for managing territorial change and the historical precedents that had been established over the years arguably helped to defuse the prospects for further diplomatic misunderstanding over the American challenge to British territorial claims. For that matter, the talk of war spontaneously led to the mobilization of journalists, the clergy, liberals, lawyers, business interests, academia, and politicians in both countries to push for arbitration on the territorial issue. These groups also gave fresh impetus to the movement toward the negotiation of a general arbitration treaty between Britain and the United States.[64]

Although Congress later refused to ratify a general arbitration treaty that had come out of Olney's and Pauncefote's negotiations, London's assent to arbitration and the subsequent Anglo-American submission to the rulings of an arbitral commission over the disputed Venezuela–British Guiana territories in effect staved off conflict between the two countries. Of course, the effectiveness of these arbitral bodies in preventing conflict had depended to a large extent on the two countries' acknowledgement of their legitimacy and impartiality. The composition of the Arbitration Tribunal (two Americans, two British members, and one non-Anglo-American) facilitated acceptance of its rulings by Washington and London in October 1899.[65]

The above analysis suggests that the ability of Britain and the United States to agree on the new hierarchy, reciprocity in trade, spheres of influence, and management of territorial change appears to have been conducive to the peaceful overtaking of the former by the latter (see table 3.1). On a more comparative note, the cases of Japan and the United States illustrate opposing power transition scenarios: a relatively weak new power with limited regional ambitions conforming to a set of norms already agreed upon and held by others, compared with a strong new great power candidate with a well-defined regional dominance, increasingly trying to establish its own rules in competition with others, and to play its own game beyond its regional sphere. Ironically, the first case led to war whereas the second did not. This paradoxical pair of cases serves to highlight some of the critical conditions under which the negotiation of hierarchy and norms may be successful. The degree of affinity between rising and incumbent power, the extent to which the rising power is allowed to participate in constructing the new order (Japan was denied that role), and the perceived potential and current capabilities of the rising power all seem to influence the success of the negotiations (table 3.2).

Indonesia's bid for regional hegemony and its aftermath

It is possible to view the international relations of peninsular South-East Asia in the 1950s and 1960s in terms of an abortive Indonesian bid for regional hegemony in the wake of decolonization by the Western powers. The United States in the Philippines, Britain in Malaya, Singapore, and Burma, France in Indo-China, and the Netherlands in Indonesia either were retreating willingly or were engaged in losing battles to hold on to their colonies. What was unmistakable to all in South-East Asia was that the force of nationalism was unstoppable and that the days of formal empire were over. It was in this context that Indonesian President Sukarno made a bid for leadership of the region.

Indonesia loomed large in peninsular South-East Asia by virtue of its territorial expanse and population. It was also the first South-East Asian nation to declare independence from its colonial masters – the Dutch in this case – in the aftermath of World War II. Unlike its closest neighbors (the Philippines, Malaya, and Singapore), Indonesia had to fight a bloody war of independence against the Dutch and it was not until 1949 that it defeated the Dutch and achieved true independence.

Success in wresting independence and "recovering" Irian Jaya from the Netherlands brought Indonesia and President Sukarno enormous prestige and self-confidence. Many third world leaders looked up to President Sukarno as a spokesperson for the developing world. Moreover, Sukarno and some (though not all) of his closest associates believed in a "Greater Indonesia," with Indonesia as the natural leader of the Malay archipelago, an area they defined as stretching beyond Java and Sumatra to Malaya and the Philippines.[66]

Sukarno and his colleagues also articulated an approach to regional order that positioned Indonesia as the vanguard of the new and progressive forces. According to this approach, the world could be divided into two groups: the New Emerging Forces (NEFOS) and the Old Established Forces (OLDEFOS). Indonesia was a natural leader of the NEFOS and it saw itself at the top of the hierarchy of NEFOS, especially within peninsular South-East Asia. As the leading NEFO in South-East Asia, Indonesia's assent was to be expected for any changes to the regional system. Sukarno was also skeptical about the rules of the capitalist trading system, and he reserved the right to use force to manage territorial change or maintain Indonesia's sphere of influence.

Indonesia's notion of regional order suffered a rude jolt when the departing British mooted the creation of a Federation of Malaysia in 1963. Malaya, a former British colony, had been independent since 1957. As Britain prepared to let go of its remaining colonies in South-East Asia in the early 1960s – Singapore, North Borneo (Sabah), and South Borneo (Sarawak) – it saw fit to link them with Malaya to form the Federation of Malaysia. Geography "dictated" that Malaya was Singapore's natural hinterland; ideology made it unthinkable (to British and Malayan officials) to risk an independent Singapore vulnerable to communist influence. A Singapore that was a part of Malaysia was assumed to be more economically and politically resilient. But the inclusion of Chinese-dominated Singapore threatened to upset the ethnic balance in Malaya. To restore the ethnic balance, Sabah and Sarawak were then appended to the Federation of Malaysia. This detach-and-combine approach to decolonization, whereby Malaya, Singapore, Sabah, and Sarawak were to form Malaysia, would have been hailed by historians as an ingenious way of managing territorial change had it not triggered a violent reaction from the aspiring regional hegemon, Indonesia.

Neither Britain nor Malaya consulted Indonesia about the impending formation of Malaysia. President Sukarno saw the latter as an affront to Indonesia and its conception of regional order. The departing powers appeared not to recognize the position of Indonesia in the post-colonial hierarchy in South-East Asia. Moreover, the integration of resource-rich Sabah and Sarawak, two states that share a border with Kalimantan Indonesia, would almost double Malaya's geographic land mass and, by implication, its power. Indonesia was not consulted on this neocolonial attempt to effect territorial change; moreover, the intended territorial revision (in Malaysia's favor) not only occurred within what Indonesia perceived as its sphere of influence, but actually involved territory contiguous to Indonesia's borders.

Equally ominous for Sukarno, the formation of Malaysia represented a restoration of the OLDEFOS – Malayans did not fight for their independence, it was "given" to them by Britain; despite formal independence, Malaya remained very much a neocolony. For Sukarno, authentic states such as Indonesia, which achieved their independence through the baptism of fire, could not countenance the emergence of OLDEFOS since they represented the reinsertion of the old colonial order and its unjust and exploitative ways.[67] In short, from Indonesia's perspective, the formation of Malaysia threatened to alter the very nature of the regional order in a direction opposed to the vision and interests of Indonesia.

Thus it is unsurprising that, when the British and Malayans went ahead to create Malaysia despite Indonesia's objections, Sukarno launched a military campaign known as *konfrontasi* (confrontation) to "crush" Malaysia. *Konfrontasi* has been analyzed extensively elsewhere and its details need not be recounted here.[68] What is relevant is that the military campaign failed, and Indonesia's bid to become the arbiter of regional order faltered. Indeed, Indonesia's bid for regional hegemony was not the only victim; the failure of *konfrontasi* was also a factor in the Indonesian military's decision to depose Sukarno in 1965. With Sukarno and his closest associates out of power, Indonesia under General Suharto embarked on a process of reconciliation with Malaysia and Singapore. Instead of aspiring to be the regional hegemon, Indonesia focused on being a good neighbor. A major outcome of this process of regional reconciliation was the creation of the Association of South East Asian Nations (ASEAN) in 1967.

The advent of ASEAN was a critical milestone in the negotiation of regional order among the peninsular South-East Asian countries. After all, it was disagreement between Indonesia and Britain/Malaysia about who was sovereign over what – Indonesia felt that Sabah and Sarawak could not be part of Malaysia – that led Sukarno down the war path. With Sukarno gone, Indonesia, together with Thailand and Malaysia, was able to co-found ASEAN, in effect recognizing Malaysia (with Sabah and Sarawak in it) and Singapore (which separated from Malaysia in 1965 for reasons not relevant to this chapter) as sovereign states. It was precisely the ideational contestation over the relevant units or the players who qualified that was responsible for the turmoil of 1963–1965. Indonesia, the rising power, saw itself as being at the top of the regional hierarchy and assumed the prerogative of determining the relevant players and the territory over which they could be sovereign. The departing power (Britain) and the leaders of newly formed Malaysia contested this bid for regional hegemony and Indonesia decided to use force. The formation of ASEAN brought an end to this contestation because it signaled agreement on the relevant players and the territory over which they were sovereign. It also signaled that Indonesia was distancing itself from aspiring to be at the top of the hierarchy of South-East Asian states. In short, ASEAN, a regional organization constituted by states, affirmed the sovereign status and equality of its members.

While ASEAN's formation resolved the issue of who can play, the rules of the game were codified less by formal agreement than by years of practice. It was not until 1976 – spurred mainly by the altered strategic circumstances in Indo-China – that ASEAN spelt out a regional code for the conduct of inter-state relations. Enshrined in the ASEAN Treaty of Amity and Cooperation (TAC) are norms and principles which are to guide signatories in their conduct of relations with one another. These norms include "mutual respect for the independence, sovereignty ... territorial integrity of all nations"; "non-interference in the internal affairs of one another"; "settlement of differences or disputes by peaceful means"; and "renunciation of the threat or use of force."[69] Although these norms have a universal ring to them, they were considered especially relevant to the ASEAN states. One reason for codifying them in 1976 was the hope that a victorious Vietnam – perceived as a potential hegemon by some – would recognize these norms and abide by them in the conduct of its relations with other states. In a sense, it was Sukarno's disavowal of these norms and his preference for the NEFOS norms that made military conflict an option.

Sukarno's replacement by Suharto, the advent of ASEAN, as well as the subsequent codification of the TAC norms facilitated the emergence of a more tranquil South-East Asia. The adventurism and rivalry of the early 1960s were gradually replaced by the exercise of "self-restraint" and cooperation. Some analysts believe that ASEAN has already become a "security community"; elsewhere I have argued that, at best, ASEAN is a nascent security community, and a very fragile one at that.[70] However, between 1967 and 1997, the institution of ASEAN became a focal point around which member states in general, and Indonesia in particular, found it convenient to "bind" themselves in most senses of the term: voluntary and reciprocal self-restraint, identity building, and also binding oneself (with the other ASEAN members) when arguing against domestic pressure groups.[77] Suharto and the other pro-status quo elites of South-East Asia saw fit to emphasize the importance of ASEAN solidarity and cooperation, thus erecting a formidable obstacle for domestic forces in Indonesia and elsewhere who might otherwise have been more insistent about their aspirations for regional leadership, if not hegemony.

In the late 1990s, Indonesia was plagued by economic, political, and ethnic convulsions generated by the Asian financial crisis, and Suharto himself was ousted from power by a popular uprising. Many Indonesians felt that, although the Suharto years had brought impressive economic growth, this had benefited Suharto's family, cronies, and friends disproportionately. Suharto's successors seem to place less of a premium on ASEAN and regional solidarity, and the continued ability of ASEAN's norms and modalities to bind Indonesia will be subjected to exacting tests in the years ahead. When Indonesia finally recovers from its economic crisis, it is likely to take on a more assertive regional role than in the heyday of ASEAN and Suharto, but it is likely to remain well below the domineering and militaristic thresholds established during the Sukarno years.

The analyses of Indonesia in the 1960s and the formation of ASEAN are instructive because they suggest that a rising regional power with aspirations to replace the declining power(s) is likely to engage in some form of ideational contestation. When events threaten to undermine this attempt at creating a new normative order (as when Britain announced the formation of Malaysia), the rising power may resort to force (as Sukarno did in 1963–1965). The absence of a consensus on the requirements of order is thus a proximate cause of *konfrontasi*. In contrast, ASEAN's success in arriving at a consensus on hierarchy (no formal hierarchy will be tolerated) and the governing norms (as stipulated in the TAC) seems to have gone a long way toward creating a warm peace between its members. Since the mid-1960s, Indonesia's population and geographic land mass have expanded; it has seen substantial economic progress, but it has not deemed it vital or necessary to assume the top spot or call all the shots in South-East Asia.

China as a rising power

The rise of China in the twenty-first century represents for many the beginning of the next major global power transition. Like the United States, China falls within the category of "natural" great powers: historically, the "Middle Kingdom" dominated the North-East Asian region by virtue of its geographical size and its material, political, and moral superiority. However, in modern times China has never been accorded international great power status, because of first the intrinsic introspection of the Chinese Empire, then the "century of humiliation" that followed its opening and defeat by Western powers, followed by the severe constraints placed upon communist China during the Cold War. The period of change and transition following the end of the Cold War is regarded with a strong sense of inevitability as China's golden opportunity to develop and assert its great potential capabilities, but the regional context of its rise portends severe power competition.

East Asia today is probably one of the most inauspicious regions in which to rise as a new great power, given the range of international interests in it. East Asia contains one of the world's economic superpowers and many of the most dynamic economies, and is a crucial part of the world economy. More importantly, it is of enduring interest to the world's remaining superpower. It was the major theater for the "hot" elements of the Cold War fought as a part of the American ideological crusade; the United States built up a system of bilateral alliances that cemented its hegemonic position in the region. The United States has signaled its determination to keep a position of strength in the region beyond the Cold War context because of remaining communist regimes in China, North Korea, and Vietnam, because of the region's economic importance, and because of its security commitments in the region.

China in the post–Cold War hierarchy

The rise of a "natural" great power such as China in this context poses direct hierarchical contestation with the United States as superpower, in spite of their current power differentials. Furthermore, the contrasting ideologies and historical experience of regional leadership of the two powers up the stakes of this power challenge so that it has become about the clash of different versions of regional order altogether. This underlies the way in which the two powers have tried from the start to clearly articulate their relative hierarchical positions.

A 1990 Pentagon review of the strategic future of the Asia Pacific specifically stated that the United States would maintain a military presence to check the "expansionist regional aspirations" of "second-tier" states – a term that demotes China from its Cold War international position between the two superpowers to that of a regional power on par with potential powers such as Japan, Korea, or Indonesia.[72] China, on the other hand, is making a quiet claim to rightful regional leadership, and official Chinese rhetoric repeatedly brands the United States as a superpower in decline in a now multipolar world and is scathing about the United States' continued "hegemonism" and imperialist ambitions to dominate East Asia.

A new incongruity has arisen within the "junior partner" status China acquired from the Sino-American rapprochement in the 1970s, because the binding power of a common enemy has been lost with the collapse of the Soviet Union. As the notion of "second-tier" states implies, from the viewpoint of the United States China has yet to qualify as a "peer" state of the United States in the post–Cold War hierarchy. Moreover, although a member of the "Perm-Five" (Permanent Member of the United Nations Security Council), China has not so far been invited to the G-8 meetings – of which Russia is a member – despite its being a recognized economic power. As far as the United States and the G-8 are concerned, China has potential, but has yet to make it to the big league.

Without the previous congruence of strategic interests, domestic politics have come to the fore in determining both Chinese and American foreign policies. In China, the diminished need to maintain good ties with Washington coincided with a heightened focus on maintaining regime stability following the collapse of communism in Eastern Europe and the challenge of pro-democracy movements at home. The regime's suppression of pro-democracy protesters in Tiananmen Square in 1989 highlighted Beijing's concern for suppressing domestic dissent, and American support for the democracy movement was a sharp reminder of the fundamental ideological rivalry with the United States, which had been ignored for more than a decade because of strategic partnership.[73] The domestic determinants of China's foreign policy can be expected to remain strong because China is in a process of economic and political transition usually associated with aggressive external policies.[74] Succession politics, regime and general political stability in the face of liberalization and development, and the fear of external subversion make it difficult for Chinese leaders to demonstrate conciliatory attitudes to the West for fear of being seen as capitulating to Western "hegemony" and selling out the national interest.[75]

In the United States, the 1980s consensus between the executive and the legislature on American China policy has similarly been eroded, especially with the Tiananmen episode, which fueled diverse interest groups ranging from the Hollywood entertainment industry championing Tibetan human rights, to various American–Chinese constituencies concerned about the repercussions for Hong Kong and Taiwan. Congressional activism on China policy has been on the rise since then, with a wide spectrum of Congressmen and Congresswomen finding it beneficial to adopt stances strongly critical of Beijing.[76] The uproar over human rights spilled over into a range of conflictual issues in Sino-American relations – the trade deficit, arms control, Taiwan, and now National and Theater Missile Defense – and fueled general charges that China was investing in a huge military buildup, developing a muscular foreign policy, and swiftly becoming the next "rogue" revisionist superpower. In the 1992 Presidential election, Bill Clinton was tough on China; he criticized Bush's "coddling of dictators" and promised to use trade relations as a lever to force China to improve its human rights record.[77] Although electoral rhetoric, including that emanating from the 2000 Presidential election, ought not to be accepted at face value, it does point to an underlying reservoir of sentiment in the American polity that is doubtful about how benign and legitimate a great power China is likely to be. In the post-Cold War era, the granting or withholding of "peer status" to China is undoubtedly linked to images about China's benignness and moral legitimacy.

The lack of agreement on the new hierarchy does not mean that the United States and China are destined to clash. The desire for the peaceful assimilation of China as an emerging power, along with the recognition of a new congruence in interests, has led the United States to engage more positively in negotiations with China on the "rules of the game." At times, it still appears to US policy makers that China consistently takes an opposite stance on every issue that the administration regards as an international norm or principle. The discussion that follows will examine the negotiations over four main international norms under contention, and evaluate the prospects for a peaceful transition. It suggests that agreement on the rules of trade has been possible whereas agreement on the use of force, territorial change, and spheres of influence remains difficult.

Trade rules

The international order under American leadership has been characterized by the promotion of the liberal values of democracy and human rights, and market economies. Engagement with China over these liberal norms has resulted in significant compromises, but the issue of bilateral trade shows most clearly the opportunities provided by asymmetrical power for the United States to influence China's acceptance of some international norms.

The conflict between China and the United States on human rights turns on Beijing's insistence that issues such as Tibet, China's population planning program, the treatment of prisoners, and the way it deals with internal subversion are internal affairs of a sovereign state, with a right to non-interference from foreign states, organizations, or individuals. The United States, on the other hand, has sought to assert the existence of universal human rights norms by expressing its concern over Beijing's violations in their bilateral relations, notably through the linkage of human rights with trade issues.

However, as discussed above, Clinton backed down on the attempted linkage to MFN status for China in 1994, realizing that revoking China's trading status would not only abandon American interests in the world's largest emerging market, but lose the opportunity for the contacts with a broad spectrum of Chinese society that will come with interdependence and the spread of technology.[78] MFN has moved from being associated with a tool of containment to being a part of the crucial need to bring China into international society and the norms of more open trading regimes.[79] This move towards a more flexible approach that disentangles the various "games" is an essential first step towards negotiating a post–Cold War East Asian order.[80]

However, there remain issues of contention inherent in Sino-American bilateral trade relations. The United States registers a large and growing trade deficit with China, which grew from US$68 million in 1983 to almost US$40 billion in 1996, and is now second only to that of Japan.[81] Although indications are that the causes for this lie in the trend of newly industrializing economies transferring production to China, the administration exerted pressure on China to open up its markets, as part of what was seen as Clinton's economic brinkmanship in a conscious attempt to link the domestic economy and jobs with foreign policy.[82] Beijing has made significant compromises on this front, lowering trade barriers (such as in the 1997 textile agreement), and also in the agreement to protect US intellectual property rights from piracy in China. The latter has become the main issue of contention; the inadequate implementation of the agreement led to the threat of 100 percent tariffs on a range of China exports to the United States in 1997.[83] China's concessions on bilateral trade issues reflect the current superior bargaining power of the United States, which is the main supplier of the advanced technology – high-technology consumer goods, agricultural and industrial equipment, as well as some defense technology – crucial to further Chinese economic and defense development. The United States has also been one of China's largest markets for its low-technology consumer goods.[84] In contrast, in spite of the estimated 170,000 jobs dependent upon US$12 billion worth of exports to China each year, this represents only a small portion of US foreign trade.[85]

This points to the potential in more general economic tools that may be used to induce China to negotiate on a broad range of norms. The main source of limitations for China lies in economic exigencies: Beijing has placed priority on participating in the international economic arena, and on securing crucial trade links and investments in Chinese industrial development. China has excellent chances of becoming an economic superpower in the medium term, and interdependence arguments may yet prove persuasive in favor of peaceful negotiations for a new order that will allow this to happen.[86] In East Asia, economic ties may forge a sure route to agreement on regional security and order. Japan and China, despite mutual strategic fears, have actively cultivated their economic relationship since the 1970s. China recognizes Japan's invaluable role as a trading partner and source of advanced technology, and Japan thus has an important role in using its present economic and technological superiority to steer China into a constructive and cooperative engagement in regional politics.[87]

An examination of US–Chinese negotiations on China's entry into the World Trade Organization (WTO) is instructive. WTO membership has been linked by the United States to the condition of China making credible commitments to lowering its trade barriers; the wrangles continued to the last minute in part because China was acutely conscious of the domestic costs of making those commitments. China already enjoyed substantial access to the markets of the advanced industrialized countries and, although joining the WTO would improve and formalize such access, it would also place overall limits on its protectionist policies and special treatment of national enterprises, which currently violate the rules.[88] However, from the point of view of upholding a liberal global economy, China's participation is crucial because of its size and the degree to which other states have a stake in its economic health.[89] The key to this apparent dilemma is to couple the realization of China's power with a recognition of its desire to shape its international milieu as befits a great power.

We have seen with the case of Japan that a new power that simply accepts given norms may undermine its own international image by appearing to be a pushover – this logic is multiplied in the context of a rising China acutely aware of its past humiliations and its rising power, and above all concerned with trying to consolidate regime stability partly through foreign policy that is seen to protect the national interest. This to some extent explains why the WTO negotiations were so protracted and contentious, and also suggests why negotiations over the other elements of order are also likely to be long and acrimonious, with no assured outcomes.

But the ultimately successful WTO negotiations between the United States and China signal broad agreement between the two countries on the rules of international trade, and that is conducive to order. China did its calculations and concluded that, despite the domestic costs, it was better to be part of the WTO rather than outside of it. A China that is part and parcel of, and that partakes in making the new rules for, critical international institutions such as the WTO, is less likely to view itself and to be viewed by others as a pushover. Analysts do not see China's entry into the WTO as merely benefiting world trade; they also see it as advantageous to international order.

Use of force, territorial change, and spheres of influence

A key element in ensuring a peaceful power transition is to arrive at a consensus on the norm of peaceful conflict resolution. This is particularly pertinent to China, which, according to some analysts, has been one of the states most ready to employ force in the past 50 years.[90] The most urgent areas of current concern about China's use of force are Taiwan and the islands in the South China Sea, over which it claims sovereignty. This discussion will focus on Taiwan, because it is the most important of China's claims as well as the most dangerous flash-point in Sino-American relations. The acrimonious debate between China and the United States over Taiwan illustrates the lack of agreement on norms regarding the use of force and managing territorial change.

For China, Taiwan has always been a domestic issue, the product of an unfinished civil war; it asserts a sovereign claim over Taiwan as a renegade province in a similar position to Xinjiang, Inner Mongolia, or Tibet, for which self-determination is not an option. The main problem with Taiwan is the United States' role in ensuring the perpetuation of its separation from the mainland. As of Sino-American rapprochement in 1972, the United States has recognized the principle of "one China," that is, that Taiwan is part of China. However, it has continued to maintain a strong defense relationship with Taiwan, to deter China from imposing reunification by force. Thus the United States has held up the norm of peaceful conflict resolution against China's claims of sovereign equality and non-interference.[91]

The United States has to tread a fine line between the two Chinas, and constructive engagement with China on this issue must be accompanied by pressure on Taiwan for restraint while waiting for a peaceful solution.[92] The United States must assure Taiwanese security but also accommodate China's interest in preventing international recognition of Taiwan as a sovereign state. China has not so far attempted an invasion of Taiwan, but Washington's handling of the sensitive issue in the post–Cold War period was careless up to 1996, reflecting the general tendency on the part of the United States to dictate the rules of the game to China.

George Bush's 1992 decision to sell F-16 aircraft to Taiwan was followed in 1994 by a policy review that responded to the development of Taiwanese democracy by upgrading Taiwan's protocol status and receiving Taiwanese cabinet-level officials in US government offices, and finally in 1995 by issuing a visa to Taiwan President Lee Teng-hui to visit Cornell University. The last provoked the 1996 Taiwan Straits crisis, in which Beijing carried out military exercises and live-fire missile tests near Taiwan, and the United States sent two carriers to the region in response. Washington had failed to exercise its "balancing" influence and had instead taken steps unilaterally to alter the rules of US–Taiwan relations, which could have encouraged Taiwan to declare independence – a move that Beijing has stated would lead to war.[93]

Since then Washington has handled the issue defined by Chinese leaders as core to national sovereignty more adroitly. This coincided with the gradual consolidation of the domestic leadership of both presidents. As President Jiang Zemin consolidated his leadership position in the past few years, there are indications that the Chinese government is coming to a greater acceptance of the international rules of the foreign policy game – President Jiang attempts to justify the actions of his government to Western media rather than simply dismissing criticism in the manner of his predecessors. Also, he has made cautious assurances about the place of democracy and the rule of law within China and in Hong Kong.[94]

President Clinton, on his part, was able to adopt a new policy of "strategic dialogue" with China in 1996, involving summit meetings between the two leaders. These meetings were important in signaling the perceived equality of status between the two states, and led to positive improvements in relations. The 1998 Clinton–Jiang summit was an opportunity for Clinton to assure his Chinese hosts that "we do not seek to impose our vision on others," and later in effect to agree to disagree with the Chinese over Tiananmen, urging Americans to "acknowledge the painful moments in our own history when fundamental human rights were denied ... [and the fact that] we still have to continue to work to advance the dignity and freedom and equality of our own people." This implied that the United States had to be patient and sensitive to the Chinese, and in the meantime, having expressed their disagreements, move on in "partnership and honest friendship."[95]

Clinton also took the significant step of reiterating US policy on Taiwan by enunciating the "3 No's": the United States does not support Taiwanese independence, or one China, one Taiwan, or Taiwan's membership in international organizations that require statehood. The administration has also reiterated that its alliance with Taiwan is purely defensive, and that Taiwan can expect no support if it declares independence.

The worry is that both China and Taiwan may perceive their respective time horizons to be narrowing – China fears that Taiwan may gain more international sympathy and supporters with time and Taiwan fears that China's military might turn decisively against Taiwan in the medium term. Disagreement between China and the United States on the legitimacy of using force in managing territorial change in the case of Taiwan reveals a potential flash-point and issue of military contention between the rising and existing powers. The initial moves of the George W. Bush administration have been far from reassuring to the Chinese. In contrast to the Clinton administration, which portrayed China as a "strategic partner," Bush and his advisers prefer to see China as a "competitor." The Bush administration also appears to be distancing itself from China and moving closer to Taiwan, if its willingness to consider selling major armaments to Taiwan is any indication. Still, only time will tell whether the new Republican administration really intends to move down the route of containment and confrontation.

What the above account of the various issues suggests is that the United States and China seem to be able to arrive at a common understanding on trade; the United States does not, however, consider China a peer power, nor does it recognize a Chinese sphere of influence in East Asia or China's right to use force to effect territorial change with respect to Taiwan or the South China Sea. These partial agreements and major differences indicate that the ideological contestation associated with power transitions is already discernible in the US–China relationship and that the two powers have much work to do if they are to narrow their differences through negotiations in the years to come.

Conclusion

This chapter has explored the preconditions of peaceful transitions. I have argued that if the rising and existing/declining powers share a similar notion of or are able to negotiate and come to a consensus on "international order," the chances for a peaceful transition will be substantially increased. International order was defined as a condition where relationships between states are stable and predictable and not characterized by violence and chaos. Following the literature, I assumed that to attain that stability and predictability it is necessary for the relevant powers to come to an agreement on hierarchy, trade rules, rules on the use of force, rules on managing territorial change, and spheres of influence. The analysis of four cases of rising powers in the Asian subsystem along these lines confirmed the expectation that the ability to come to an agreement on most of these elements of order – as in the case of the United States and Britain in the 1890s – was correlated with peaceful transition, whereas failure to agree on most of these elements – as in the case of Japan and Indonesia – was associated with violent transitions.

As far as the next transition in most analysts' minds is concerned – the case of a rising China challenging the United States, the existing hegemon – there is more disagreement than agreement between the two powers at this early stage. Although the chapter has focused on whether or not there was agreement between the relevant powers on the various issues, it also broached the question of why agreement was possible in some cases and not possible in others, albeit in a more tentative manner. Agreement between the contending powers is more likely if there exists some affinity of identity between them; if the rising power is afforded serious participation in the shaping of the rules of the game; and if the rising power is perceived to have what it takes. If these findings are not totally off the mark, they could provide analysts with crude indicators of how close or far apart future contending powers are, and of the chances of their coming to an eventual agreement, given their identities and their mutual perceptions.

Acknowledgements

I would like to acknowledge the invaluable research assistance provided by Evelyn Goh at Nuffield College, Oxford, by Norman Vasu, and by Joey Long at the Institute of Defence & Strategic Studies, Singapore.

Notes

1. See Erich Weede, "Overwhelming Preponderance as a Pacifying Condition among Contiguous Asian Dyads, 1950–1969," *Journal of Conflict Resolution*, Vol. 20, No. 3 (September 1976); and Jonathan DiCicco, "Power Transitions, Parity, and War Onset: A Critical Review," unpublished paper presented at the 39th Annual Meeting of the International Studies Association, Minneapolis, Minnesota, March 1998, p. 8.
2. The distinction between underlying and proximate causes parallels that made by Kenneth Waltz, *Man, the State, and War* (New York: Columbia University Press, 1954), pp. 232–234, who wrote about "permissive" and "efficient" causes of war.
3. Robert Gilpin, *War and Change in World Politics* (New York: Cambridge University Press, 1981), chap. 5, and Kupchan, this volume, chap. 1.
4. Definitions from *The Oxford Modern Dictionary* (Oxford: Oxford University Press, 1994).
5. John Baylis and Steve Smith, *The Globalization of World Politics* (Oxford: Oxford University Press, 1997), p. 270.
6. V. I. Lenin, *Imperialism, the Highest Stage of Capitalism* (New York: International Publishers, 1939).

7. Evan Luard, *Conflict and Peace in the Modern International System: A Study of the Principles of International Order* (London: Macmillan, 1988), pp. xi–xii.
8. Hedley Bull, *The Anarchical Society: A Study of Order in World Politics* (New York: Columbia University Press, 1977).
9. For a discussion of governance and institutions, see for instance Oran R. Young, *International Governance: Protecting the Environment in a Stateless Society* (Ithaca, NY: Cornell University Press, 1994), p. 15.
10. Bull, *The Anarchical Society*, pp. 67–74.
11. Gilpin, *War and Change in World Politics*, chap. 5; see also chap. 1 in this volume.
12. Gilpin, *War and Change in World Politics*.
13. The relationship between the incidence of war and power transitions is not clear-cut. Some wars, such as the Thirty Years War, between rising and declining powers do not result in power transition; in other cases, such as the end of the Cold War, peaceful power transitions are achieved when the contending power acknowledges defeat and gives in to a new international order; in yet other cases, the major war occurs after a power transition has taken place, as will be discussed later.
14. Wars are costly in an era of economic interdependence because they may alienate trading partners, and they are ineffective because modern economic power depends less on conquerable assets such as land than on skills such as knowledge and technology. See Robert O. Keohane and Joseph S. Nye, *Power and Interdependence: World Politics in Transition* (Boston: Little, Brown, 1989). Realists argue in turn that interdependence tends to be uneven, and thus generates more insecurity for dependent states, which multiplies potential conflicts. See Kenneth N. Waltz, *Theory of International Politics* (New York: McGraw-Hill, 1979), pp. 138–146.
15. On the difference between complementarity and cooperation forged from common interests, see Charles F. Doran, *The Politics of Assimilation: Hegemony and Its Aftermath* (Baltimore, MD: Johns Hopkins Press, 1971), pp. 9–10.
16. Michael W. Doyle, "Kant, Liberal Legacies, and Foreign Affairs," *Philosophy and Public Affairs*, Vol. 12 (Fall 1983), pp. 323–353. For a flavor of the intense debate surrounding this theory, see Christopher Layne, "Kant or Cant: The Myth of Democratic Peace," *International Security*, Vol. 19 (Fall 1994), pp. 5–49.
17. See chap. 2 in this volume, pp. 24–26.
18. See Stephen D. Krasner, ed., *International Regimes* (Ithaca, NY: Cornell University Press, 1983), and Young, *International Governance*.
19. Kenneth Pyle, *The Making of Modern Japan* (Lexington, MA: D.C. Heath, 1996), p. 133.
20. See W. G. Beasley, *The Meiji Restoration* (Stanford, CA: Stanford University Press, 1973), p. 323.
21. Gerritt W. Gong, *The Standard of "Civilization" in International Society* (Oxford: Oxford University Press, 1984), pp. 179–180.
22. Ibid., pp. 183–184.
23. Ibid., pp. 190–195. For a discussion on legal modernization in Japan, see Dan Fenno Henderson, "Law and Political Modernization in Japan," in Robert E. Ward, ed., *Political Development in Modern Japan* (Princeton, NJ: Princeton University Press, 1968).
24. See Sakuye Takahashi, *Cases on International Law during the Chino-Japanese War* (Cambridge: Cambridge University Press, 1899).
25. See, for instance, Gong, *The Standard of "Civilization"*, chap. VI.
26. Richard Storry, *Japan and the Decline of the West in Asia, 1894–1943* (London: Macmillan, 1979), pp. 20–21.
27. Ibid., p. 29; Storry, *A History of Modern Japan* (Harmondsworth: Penguin, 1968), p. 127.

28. Marius B. Jensen, "Modernization and Foreign Policy," in Ward, *Political Development in Modern Japan*, p. 184; Gong, *The Standard of "Civilization"*, p. 196.
29. Hayashi Tadasu, writing in the Japanese journal *Jiji Shimpo*, 21 June 1895, quoted in Storry, *Japan and the Decline of the West*, p. 30. As a result of Japan's naval buildup, the Anglo-Japanese alliance was forged in 1902 – this is regarded as one of the key events signaling Japan's great power status.
30. Ian Nish, *Japanese Foreign Policy 1862–1942: Kasumigaseki to Miyakezaki* (London: Routledge & Kegan Paul, 1977), p. 67.
31. Gong, *The Standard of "Civilization"*, p. 197; Storry, *Japan and the Decline of the West*, p. 104.
32. Ernest Gellner, *Nations and Nationalism* (Ithaca, NY: Cornell University Press, 1983), p. 1.
33. Quoted from George Friedman and Meredith Lebard, *The Coming War with Japan* (New York: St. Martin's Press, 1919), p. 30.
34. Akira Iriye, "Japan's Drive to Great Power Status," in Marius B. Jansen, ed., *The Emergence of Meiji Japan* (Cambridge: Cambridge University Press, 1995), pp. 283 and 285.
35. Sydney Giffard, *Japan among the Powers: 1890–1990* (New Haven, CT: Yale University Press, 1994), p. 15.
36. Akira Iriye, *Japan and the Wider World: From the Mid-Nineteenth Century to the Present* (London: Longman, 1997), pp. 11–15.
37. Akira Iriye, "Japan's Drive to Great Power Status," p. 288.
38. P. W. Preston, *Understanding Modern Japan* (Sage, 2000), p. 154.
39. Storry, *Japan and the Decline of the West*, pp. 31–32, 68–70.
40. Viscount Kikujiro Ishii, "The Permanent Bases of Japanese Foreign Policy," *Foreign Affairs*, Vol. 2 (January 1933), pp. 220–224.
41. Ibid., pp. 161–190. On the subject of British decline and accommodation with the United States in this period, see also Kenneth Bourne, *Britain and the Balance of Power in North America, 1815–1908* (Berkeley: University of California Press, 1967); Bradford Perkins, *The Great Rapprochement: England and the United States, 1895–1914* (New York: Atheneum, 1968).
42. *Foreign Relations of the United States, 1895* (Washington DC: US Government Printing Office), Vol. 1, p. 575. For the way the Monroe Doctrine was reinterpreted and employed during the rise of American power, see Dexter Perkins, *The Monroe Doctrine, 1867–1907* (Baltimore, MD: Johns Hopkins University Press, 1937); and Zakaria, *From Wealth to Power*, pp. 148–171.
43. See George F. Kennan, *American Diplomacy*, expanded edn (Chicago: University of Chicago Press, 1984), chap. 2.
44. The final signals could be either 1947, when Britain handed over the Greece–Turkey problem to the United States, or 1956, when Britain retreated from enforcing its military solution to the Suez crisis in the wake of stern American objections.
45. Layne, "Kant or Cant," pp. 22–28.
46. Paul Kennedy, *The Realities behind Diplomacy: Background Influences on British External Policy, 1865–1980* (London: Fontana Press, 1985), pp. 107–108.
47. John Owen, "How Liberalism Produces Democratic Peace," *International Security*, Vol. 19, No. 2 (Fall 1994), pp. 114–119.
48. Charles C. Campbell, *The Transformation of American Foreign Relations: 1865–1900* (New York: Harper & Row, 1976), p. 211.
49. Crane Brinton, *The United States and Britain* (London: Oxford University Press, 1945), pp. 123–124.

50. Morton Rothstein, "America in the International Rivalry for the British Wheat Market, 1860–1914," *Mississippi Valley Historical Review*, Vol. 47, No. 3 (December 1960), pp. 401–418; Paul Kennedy, *The Rise and Fall of the Great Powers: Economic Change and Military Conflict from 1500 to 2000* (London: Fontana Press, 1988), pp. 315–316; and Arthur A. Stein, "The Hegemon's Dilemma: Great Britain, the United States, and the International Economic Order," *International Organization*, Vol. 38, No. 2 (Spring 1984), pp. 360–373, where he points out that the United States, like Russia, was never a part of the "liberal order of the 1860s."
51. Campbell, *The Transformation of American Foreign Relations*, pp. 334–335.
52. Kennedy, *The Rise and Fall of the Great Powers*, p. 316.
53. Herbert O. Brayer, "The Influence of British Capital on the Western Range-Cattle Industry," *Journal of Economic History*, Vol. 9, Issue Supplement: *The Tasks of Economic History* (1949), pp. 85–98.
54. Walter LaFeber, *The New Empire: An Interpretation of American Expansion: 1860–1898* (Ithaca, NY: Cornell University Press, 1963), pp. 316–317.
55. J. A. S. Grenville, *Lord Salisbury and Foreign Policy: The Close of the Nineteenth Century* (London: Athlone Press, 1964), p. 58; and see also Walter LaFeber, *The New Empire*, p. 266.
56. Quoted in Grenville, *Lord Salisbury and Foreign Policy*, p. 63.
57. Ibid., and also see Campbell, *The Transformation of American Foreign Relations*, pp. 214–215.
58. LaFeber, *The New Empire*, p. 315.
59. George B. Young, "Intervention under the Monroe Doctrine: The Olney Corollary," *Political Science Quarterly*, Vol. 57, No. 2 (June 1942), p. 272n; and T. Boyle, "The Venezuela Crisis and the Liberal Opposition, 1895–96," *Journal of Modern History*, Vol. 50, No. 3 (September 1978), p. D1203.
60. LaFeber, *The New Empire*, pp. 315–316.
61. Olney to Chamberlain, 28 September 1896, quoted in W. Allan Wilbur, *The Monroe Doctrine* (Boston: D.C. Heath, 1965), p. 84.
62. Nelson M. Blake, "The Olney–Pauncefote Treaty of 1897," *American Historical Review*, Vol. 50, No. 2 (January 1945), p. 228.
63. Campbell, *The Transformation of American Foreign Relations*, pp. 32–33, 44, and 134–138.
64. Blake, "The Olney–Pauncefote Treaty of 1897," pp. 229–233; and Boyle, "The Venezuela Crisis and the Liberal Opposition," pp. D1191–1192, D1195, D1204, and D1208.
65. Grenville, *Lord Salisbury and Foreign Policy*, pp. 69–73.
66. Bernard Gordon, *The Dimensions of Conflict in Southeast Asia* (New Jersey: Prentice-Hall, 1966), esp. chap. 3.
67. Dewi Anwar Fortuna, *Indonesia in ASEAN* (Singapore: Institute of Southeast Asian Studies, 1994), pp. 24–27.
68. See J. A. C. Mackie, *Konfrontasi: The Indonesia–Malaysia Dispute 1963–1966* (Kuala Lumpur: Oxford University Press, 1974).
69. See Article 2 of the Treaty of Amity and Cooperation in South-East Asia, in ASEAN Documents Series 1967–1988 (Jakarta: ASEAN Secretariat, 1988), pp. 39–41.
70. Yuen Foong Khong, "ASEAN and the Southeast Asian Security Complex," in David Lake and Patrick Morgan, eds., *Regional Orders: Building Security in a New World* (University Park, PA: Pennsylvania State University Press, 1997), pp. 318–339; cf. Amitav Acharya, "Collective Identity and Conflict Management in Southeast Asia," in Emanuel Adler and Michael Barnett, eds., *Security Communities* (Cambridge: Cambridge University Press, 1998), pp. 198–227.
71. See chap. 2 in this volume.

72. US Department of Defense, *A Strategic Framework for the Asian Pacific Rim: Looking towards the 21st Century* (Washington, DC: April 1990).
73. Andrew J. Nathan and Robert S. Ross, *The Great Wall and the Empty Fortress: China's Search for Security* (New York: W. W. Norton, 1997), p. 72.
74. See A. F. K. Organski and Jacek Kugler, *The War Ledger* (Chicago: University of Chicago Press, 1980); Charles Doran and Wes Parsons, "War and the Cycle of Relative Power," *American Political Science Review* (December 1980), pp. 947–965; Edward D. Mansfield and Jack Snyder, "Democratization and the Danger of War," *International Security*, Vol. 20, No. 1 (Summer 1995), pp. 5–38.
75. See David Shambaugh, "Containment or Engagement of China? Calculating Beijing's Responses," *International Security*, Vol. 21, No. 2 (Fall 1996), pp. 180–199.
76. Nathan and Ross, *The Great Wall and the Empty Fortress*, pp. 70–71.
77. This entailed support for congressional tools such as a 1991 Bill requiring China to fulfill the following criteria in order to qualify for renewal of MFN status: the release of all Tiananmen prisoners; the end of long-range missile sales to Syria and Iran; a show of progress in granting free speech and press and religious freedom on China and Tibet; assurances that it would not sell nuclear technology; and an end to the export of prison labor products to the United States.
78. Steven Erlanger and David E. Sanger, "On Global Stage, Clinton Finds Balance as Leader," *New York Times* (29 July 1996).
79. This is how arguments for the renewal of China's MFN status have been framed since 1994; see, for instance, Madeleine K. Albright, "China MFN," Statement before the Senate Finance Committee (Washington: US Department of State, 10 June 1997).
80. Haans W. Maull, "Reconciling China with International Order," *Pacific Review*, Vol. 10, No. 4 (1997).
81. Nathan and Ross, *The Great Wall and the Empty Fortress*, p. 76; Albright, "China MFN," p. 4.
82. Erlanger and Sanger, "On Global Stage."
83. Albright, "China MFN," p. 3.
84. For most of the post-Mao era, the United States was China's largest market, but Asian markets, excluding Japan, now account for 36 percent of China's total exports, compared with 19 percent for the United States and 17 percent for Japan. You Ji, "Economic Interdependence and China's National Security," in Stuart Harris and Andrew Mack, eds., *Asia-Pacific Security: The Economics–Politics Nexus* (New South Wales: Allen & Unwin, 1997), p. 167.
85. Albright, "China MFN," p. 6; Nathan and Ross, *The Great Wall and the Empty Fortress*, p. 77.
86. For a good discussion of interdependence in the context of post–Cold War East Asia, see Harris and Mack, *Asia-Pacific Security*, chap. 1.
87. Tagashi Inoguchi, *Japan's International Relations* (London: Pinter, 1991), pp. 146–148.
88. Robert S. Ross, "Enter the Dragon," *Foreign Policy*, Vol. 104 (September 1996), pp. 18–25.
89. In 1995, China became the world's tenth-largest trader, enjoying favorable trade balances with most of its partners; and it had accumulated the fourth-largest foreign exchange reserves, behind Japan, Taiwan, and the United States. With its internal economies of scale and large pool of cheap labor, China can easily undercut many other economies, inciting protectionism. See Nathan and Ross, *The Great Wall and the Empty Fortress*, chap. 9.
90. Iain Johnston, "Cultural Realism and Strategy in Maoist China," in Peter Katzenstein, ed., *The Culture of National Security* (New York: Columbia University Press, 1996), pp. 251–256.

91. Although China's anger over the bombing of the Chinese embassy in Belgrade was real, the larger worry is the propensity of the United States and NATO to use military force, as in Kosovo, in the name of humanitarian intervention. China would prefer privileging the sovereignty norm.
92. The visions of such a resolution differ: Taiwan sees unification as possible only when China becomes a democracy, whereas Chinese leaders in the 1980s held out various "one country, two systems" assurances to Taiwan at the same time as they did to Hong Kong. Robert A. Scalapino, "Economics, Security and Northeast Asia," in Harris and Mack, *Asia-Pacific Security*, p. 146; Nathan and Ross, *The Great Wall and the Empty Fortress*, p. 209.
93. Nathan and Ross, *The Great Wall and the Empty Fortress*, p. 74.
94. President Jiang Zemin, in an interview with Cable News Network, *A CNN Interview with President Jiang Zemin* (9 May 1997). A full transcript of the interview can be found on the CNN homepage.
95. *Washington Post* (1 July 1998), p. A23.

4
Legitimacy, socialization, and international change

Jean-Marc Coicaud

Introduction

To assume that legitimacy plays a role in peaceful transitions seems reasonable and plausible. The fact that legitimacy contributes to stabilizing and pacifying national politics through its role in the process of social integration and justification, and that the evolution of international affairs shows a tendency over time towards the creation of a global society, only encourages us to think along these lines. There is no reason not to think that the analogy applies. In principle, legitimacy should be able to perform the same function of pacification at the international level as in the national setting.

Questions do arise, however, about this view of legitimacy as an international factor for peace in situations of competition for and transition of power that do not arise when viewed through the national prism. One reason is that different characteristics affect the distribution and exercise of power at the international and national levels. Such differences largely boil down to the fact that the socialization[1] of international politics remains, to this day, much more limited than that of the politics of an integrated nation. Compared with integrated national polities, international relations, even when conceptualized as a social system, still display a profound sense of uncertainty and lack of reciprocity among the various actors. Hence, the lesser role of legitimacy.

Nonetheless, far from ruling out the relevance of legitimacy for peaceful transitions, the problematic nature of the international context enhances its relevance and makes its study even more urgent. In view of the asocial tendency of international politics, overlooking the socializing and pacifying force that legitimacy can offer would certainly be a mistake. This would be a luxury we can ill afford when it comes to the constant process of transition among rising and fading powers, allegedly one of the circumstances most likely to drive international affairs to degenerate into a war, or, more generally, when it comes to a shift of power distribution. The intellectual need to understand how legitimacy can facilitate a peaceful transition among competing powers, and the political need to increase this role so as to reduce the danger that tensions will lead to open war, show us the path to follow.

To give some guidance to our inquiry, we must keep some basic questions in mind. What, for instance, are the attributes and functions of legitimacy that permit it to play a peaceful role in a transition in the distribution and hierarchy of power? How do these attributes and functions play out at the international level? How does legitimacy relate to the two other conditions identified in this book – benignity and order – in situations of transition in the international setting? How can an analysis that includes legitimacy contribute to our understanding of the entire process of change in the current international system?

These questions inform the structure of this chapter, which examines three major sets of issues. The first section focuses on the issue of legitimacy per se, adopting a rather general point of view. In addition, the section touches upon the manner in which legitimacy permits actors to manage and reduce the stress attached to the evolving distribution of power, particularly in the context of democratic legitimacy. It also analyzes international legitimacy and its contribution to the pacification of power rivalries and transition. The second section looks at three historical contexts and levels of regulation to examine the impact of legitimacy upon the peaceful management of power competition at the international level. It draws upon the same cases studies as the book as a whole: the Concert of Europe, the United States–Great Britain rapprochement in the late nineteenth and early twentieth centuries, and the Association of South East Asian Nations (ASEAN). The third section, which also serves as the conclusion, analyzes the implications of the reflections developed in the chapter for the evolution of the current international system. More specifically, the section attempts to decipher what path should be followed by the present international hegemon – the United States – in handling its challengers so that, should a power transition occur in the coming years, it may be conducted in a peaceful manner.

Five main overarching lessons – which constitute a road map for the reading of the chapter – emerge from the issues touched upon and the arguments made throughout the study.

First, the goal of international order is to search for the establishment of socialized instability, and not to create stability at all costs, as is traditionally assumed. Aiming for absolute stability is an illusion, and a dangerous one. It is an illusion because the nature of international relations is to be in a constant state of flux as part of, and as a tool of, history. The state of flux may be more or less settled, but it always has change at its core. Stability as the ultimate goal is also a dangerous illusion in that it tends to artificially freeze the forces of change and to impose upon them a status quo that can become, over time, less and less wanted as it is more and more challenged. As such, imposed stability is likely to generate uncontrolled forms of change. Socialized instability, in contrast, enables change to be controlled because it leaves room for it.

Second, legitimacy is a key element of socialized instability. Just as legitimacy is decisive in ensuring national integration and the acceptance of an asymmetric distribution of power, so legitimacy also contributes to negotiating the acceptance of the unequal distribution of power at the international level. This quality of legitimacy presupposes a number of requirements. One of the most important is that legitimacy has to be based upon values and institutional mechanisms that echo and adequately monitor the strategic aspects of the identity and changes of the social realms to be socialized. If this is not the case, legitimacy is marginalized and, devoid of its integrating capacity, loses its claims to validity – political, social, normative, and emotional. Obviously, so far it has been rather difficult to fulfill these requirements at the international level. The inability of legitimacy to connect with or generate a sense of socialized community beyond borders accounts largely for this state of affairs. This inability is itself explained by the use of international legitimacy for state-oriented goals. In the past, international legitimacy has been envisioned not as an end in itself but as a way to secure the national legitimacy of the states involved in its establishment. Furthermore, even now, the enhancement of a form of democratic international legitimacy within the framework and world-view of the United Nations is part of the double-edged diplomacy of member states. Hence the fact that international legitimacy has been, so far, secondary to national legitimacy, especially vis-à-vis major powers.

Third, the fate of a given international legitimacy tends to be very much attached to the destiny of the main powers. To begin with, the norms and mechanisms of international legitimacy are mainly a projection, at the international level, of key elements of the political culture of the dominant country or countries of the time. This does not come as a surprise because these countries have both the power – material (political, military, financial, etc.) and cognitive (diplomatic, normative, ideological) – and a vested interest in defining the rules of the game at the international level. Having a primary involvement, benefit, and stake in international interactions, they define, monitor, and guarantee the validity of international order. They oversee the establishment of means of international conciliation and socialization. Thus the norms and mechanisms of international legitimacy, and the extent to which they structure the international realm, are likely to echo and be homogeneous with the strategic characteristics of the domestic legitimacy and world-view of dominant powers. Owing to the close bonding between the domestic legitimacy of dominant powers and international legitimacy, the strengths and weaknesses of the domestic legitimacy tend also to be largely the strengths and weaknesses of international legitimacy. In addition, the normative and political viability of international legitimacy rests mainly on the ability of the dominant powers to remain leading actors domestically and internationally. If the domestic legitimacy of the dominant powers erodes, their power to underwrite the international system is hampered. If the international distribution of power that they endorse is decisively undermined, the ability to integrate domestically and generate confidence is likely to be lost at home. This is logical because major powers tend, in one way or another, to make the international dimension part of their national agenda, to establish a strong connection between the two.

Fourth, international democratic legitimacy, as it has been developing in recent decades within the framework of multilateralism, is the way of the future. It is the way of the future when it comes to socializing a plurality of competing interests and national entities at the international level. However, a satisfactory institutionalization of international democratic legitimacy has to meet two main conditions. To begin with, although it is not reasonable to think of getting rid of the national/international divide and of the priorities that it displays in favor of the national,[2] a better balance has to be found between the responsibilities exercised at the national and international levels. As it happens, the burden here is mainly on the major powers. Their unparalleled power of influence simply makes them ethically and politically more accountable. This does not mean, however, that weaker countries should develop a victim and entitlement mentality, expecting major countries to be responsible on all accounts. Weaker countries too have duties. And one of these duties is not to expect everything to come from the outside as regards their national situation. Fulfilling their national responsibilities should be one way of being aware of their international responsibility. In addition, assuming that the establishment of a form of international constitutionalism is the envisioned goal, including mechanisms of checks and balances, international democratic legitimacy cannot be reduced to the universalization of a power hegemony – currently that of the United Sates. The institutionalization of the emerging international democratic legitimacy requires the democratization of hegemony. Democratic hegemony amounts to the organization of the end of unreciprocal hegemony.

Fifth, democratic values are an ideal and extremely effective tool for establishing a contemporary form of international legitimacy. They are highly inspirational, because they are based upon a sense of universality/universalization and of sameness among people; they have the betterment of people's condition as one of their main goals. By aiming to put individuals and countries on an equal footing, they provide the substance and therefore the procedures for imagining and implementing a structured international order in which the various actors can find their place. Nevertheless, these values need to be taken seriously if they are not to become a tool of political expansion, if they are not to trigger violence through people feeling alienated and deceived by them and their undesired effects. This presupposes fulfilling the conditions of inclusiveness, plurality, and mobility at their heart. This requires institutionalizing a web of political power, which has to be strong and open but also identifiable. Indeed, the ability to identify power, its sources, modalities, and effects, is key to its accountability and the evaluation of its legitimacy.

Legitimacy as a socializing force in politics

Legitimacy is a complex enough notion to require some clarification, even in the limited context of this chapter. It will help our purpose to make the generic attributes and functions of legitimacy explicit and to indicate how they contribute to the socialization and pacification of interactions among actors.

On legitimacy and democratic legitimacy

Taken at the most general level, legitimacy is the value that justifies the relationship between the people who are governed and those who govern.[3] It is the process through which both political power and obedience are justified. The recognition of the right to govern is based upon a set of conditions mainly concerning consent, values and identity, and law. It also generates a number of constraints on the exercise and effects of political power involving the notions of responsibility and accountability. If well integrated, these elements allow legitimacy to bring to institutional regulations and arrangements not only a sense of efficiency and order, but also a sense of justice. This is especially the case when it comes to democratic legitimacy, at the national level or at the international level.

At the core of the dynamics of legitimacy is the matrix of rights and duties, of reciprocity and mutual expectations. This forms a system of sociability to which people have to consent. Consent requires a social content to refer to and upon which to agree. Without content, there is nothing to consent to. Such content is provided by the values around which the identity of the collectivity and of its members is built. Values contribute to the establishment of distinctions and hierarchies between principles to abide by, or ideals to aspire to, and courses to eschew. They are part of the process that indicates a consensus on what is commendable and what is condemnable.

Political institutions are expressions and implementation tools of law. They are entities destined and designed to decide, monitor, regulate, guarantee, and enforce policies meant to actualize the level and modalities of reciprocity envisioned by the values that give the identity of society its key features. Their task is to engineer social arrangements to ensure that services are convincingly performed for each member of society and for the group as a whole, allowing reasonably peaceful and integrated interactions to take place among and within the various spheres of society and its members. The role of integration required from political institutions aiming at being legitimate has constraining effects on the exercise of political power. These constraining effects amount to a sense of responsibility vis-à-vis society, which is a key requirement of the legitimate exercise of power.

Because of the centrality of legitimacy in democratic politics, it has sometimes been argued that legitimacy is only a modern and democratic phenomenon. This is not the case, although one has to admit that legitimacy is a key feature of democratic politics. Various elements explain the close bonds, indeed the love affair, between legitimacy and democracy. They boil down to the fact that democratic politics is the enterprise of socialization "par excellence." One of the best illustrations of this situation is found in the ideally tailored properties of democratic values and rights for the exercise of consent and its recognized importance for democratic legitimacy. Values such as freedom and equality in particular and the systems of beliefs and rights they create display the importance of consent and of its required quality, its non-coerced character. They give to people's consent the power and the right – codified and implemented through deliberative and elective mechanisms – to challenge those who govern. The test that this challenge constitutes is a crucial element of the legitimacy of democratic institutions. This means that democracy encourages and integrates as much as possible the evolving distribution of power. In democratic culture, legitimate power is meant to circulate and to be, in principle, accessible to everyone. This largely defines the mission statement of democratic political institutions. They have to do their best to guarantee that power is not permanently held by one segment of society at the expense of others. As such, democracy finds its legitimacy, and therefore its enduring power of socialization, in trying to ensure that a situation of power hegemony existing at a given time is not transformed into a monopoly over power.

International legitimacy as a regulatory force in the distribution of power

In the aftermath of World War II, a comprehensive type of international legitimacy was first established through the United Nations system. Because this is the most global type of international legitimacy ever, we would be ill advised to ignore it in a study on the impact of legitimacy on the peaceful transition of power. This is especially the case since the study is concerned with policy implications for the evolution of the current international system. In this context, the third section of the chapter will show that there are conditions under which the present hegemon, the United States, should handle its future challengers so that their competition does not degenerate into open conflict. These conditions presuppose, among other things, the awareness and integration of stipulations attached to the concept of international legitimacy launched 50 years ago and the framework of political deliberation and action associated with it.

Despite its unparallelled qualities as a system of international legitimacy, the framework of structure and regulation that has emerged since World War II is far from expressing and being able to implement a level of socialization equivalent to that which exists on a national plane, especially in integrated national polities. The shortcomings encountered by the current system of international legitimacy should not come as a surprise since they echo the traditional difficulties of legitimacy in extending its powers of socialization beyond borders. Even when the validity of international legitimacy is recognized, it is never envisioned and entrenched as the only horizon of political actors. As an outgrowth and projection at the international level of domestic legitimacy, international legitimacy continues to be inhabited by state legitimacy and is in competition with it. A telling illustration of this situation is the problematic collection of international principles that gives the present system of international legitimacy its normative foundations and directions and spells out for state actors the main rules of the game of international life.

The interrelationships among the major principles constituting the fundamental standards of today's international law[4] are those of compatibility, competition, and hierarchy. Relationships of compatibility among these principles are required to ensure the relative homogeneity and coherence of international law and of the international system it aims to help structure and regulate. A prime example of this point is the compatibility between the principle of the sovereign equality of states and the principle of non-intervention in the internal affairs of other states. As important as the relationships of compatibility are those of competition among the principles. One of the best illustrations of the relations of competition can be found in the tensions at work between the principle of the sovereign equality of states and that of respect for human rights. Choosing one of these principles over the other is to participate in the establishment of a hierarchy between them. The juxtaposition of these relationships of compatibility, competition, and hierarchy in international law echoes the various demands that the international system is asked to recognize and serve. It expresses the main values that shape the international democratic culture. These relationships are not etched in stone. The products of a historical and political evolution, they continue to evolve. They evolve with the changes affecting the structuring parameters of contemporary culture in its various aspects. They evolve with the changes affecting the identity of national states, the configuration of states' interplay with the international dimension, and, ultimately, the international system and international law themselves.

Assessing the powers of socialization in the current system of international legitimacy leads to the question of the contribution of international legitimacy to the peaceful management of power competition and transition. It certainly tends to curtail power rivalry and facilitate peaceful power transition at the global level, as the handling of the competition between the United States and the Soviet Union showed. As a forum of discussion, the system of multilateral legitimacy established after World War II helped to manage the dangers contained in the East–West confrontation. It also proved to be a useful diplomatic tool at the end of the 1980s and the beginning of the 1990s, when it facilitated the end of the Cold War and a peaceful transition towards a new international power distribution.[5]

International legitimacy and the socializing of power transitions

The magnitude and modes of legitimacy displayed by the three designated case studies of the book – the Concert of Europe, the rapprochement between the United States and Great Britain, and ASEAN – are substantial and diverse. This is why they are a fruitful way to examine the influence of mechanisms of international legitimacy on peaceful power transition. Each provides enough evidence on various aspects of the dynamics of legitimacy to illustrate and test its contribution to the peaceful competition and transition of power in an international setting.

The Concert of Europe: The legitimacy of the past and the attempt to contain the future

Two norms of socialization applied in the Concert of Europe, although at different levels. The first was the balance of power, which functioned as a regulatory norm concerned with the handling of power relations among countries. Second were substantive norms related to the values with which powers identified. Although the Concert of Europe was supposed to call upon these values in a consonant and convergent fashion, their articulation proved to be, in the long run, the reason for its demise. They undermined the Concert because they could not embrace and integrate one of the challenges that it faced all along: nationalism. Indeed, partly designed to restrain France, viewed at the time as an uncontrollable power, the Concert was also meant to contain nationalism, then the emerging new norm of domestic political legitimacy and one that spilled over into the international realm. It was mainly the impotence of the Concert of Europe in coming to terms with nationalism that brought it to an end. How did this happen?[6]

The first norm of socialization was the commitment to the balance of power as a form of power regulation. The architects of the Congress of Vienna recognized that, if Central Europe was to have peace and stability, they would have to undo Richelieu's work of the 1600s. Richelieu had fostered a weak, fragmented Central Europe, providing France with a permanent temptation to encroach and turn it into a virtual playground for its army. To counter this, the statesmen who convened in Vienna set about consolidating, but not unifying, Germany. Austria and Prussia were made the leading German states, after which came a number of medium-sized states that had been enlarged and strengthened. In dealing with the defeated enemy – France – the victors concluded that Europe would be safer if France were relatively satisfied rather than resentful and disaffected. As a result, France was deprived of its conquests but left with its pre-Revolutionary frontiers intact.

After the Congress of Vienna, the commitment to the norm of the balance of power was expressed in two power structures: the Quadruple Alliance, consisting of Great Britain, Prussia, Austria, and Russia; and the Holy Alliance, which was limited to the three so-called Eastern Courts of Prussia, Austria, and Russia. The need for the Quadruple Alliance for the exercise of the balance of power has to be viewed in light of two factors. First, since France in the early nineteenth century was regarded as a chronically aggressive and inherently destabilizing power, a Quadruple Alliance including Great Britain was forged to nip any aggressive French tendencies in the bud through overwhelming force. Second, Great Britain was perceived as a crucial partner because a fixed principle of its foreign policy was to be the protector of the balance of power.

The other segment of the Concert of Europe was the Holy Alliance. The Holy Alliance was altogether different from the Quadruple Alliance. In its own way, it functioned as a substantial norm of socialization, bringing together the Eastern Courts, which were committed to combating revolution and nationalism. It viewed the religious imperative – about which Tzar Alexander I felt very strongly and which he wanted to implement in concert with conservative values to facilitate a complete reform of the international system – as instituting an obligation by the signatories to preserve the domestic status quo in Europe. Metternich considered democratic forces dangerous and unpredictable, and he therefore identified peace and stability with conservative legitimate rule. He expected the crowned heads of ancient dynasties, if not to preserve the peace, at least to preserve the basic structure of international relations. It was in this context that the Eastern powers made conservative legitimacy the cement meant to hold the international order together.

The exclusion of Britain from the Holy Alliance no doubt weakened the Concert more than would have been the case had all its members agreed on common norms. But more important, perhaps, for the limitations of the Concert of Europe was the fact that the Eastern powers themselves possessed goals that could only be in conflict in the long run. Prussia, probably more conservative than Austria but certainly less so than Russia, had expansionist territorial ambitions. Russia was more conservative than Austria and tempted to use the nationalist card in its own interest. Austria was less conservative than Russia, but eager to contain nationalism. The agreement by the three conservative monarchies served as a guidepost for dealing with the numerous crises that arose during the life of the Concert. However, it was not calculated to last forever, for the simple reason that the balance of power was based on the wrong type of substantive legitimacy. In linking the balance of power to an old form of national legitimacy, the Concert disconnected itself from the forces that it should have tried to co-opt: the forces of nationalism.

Such a connection might, in fact, have been impossible, especially for Austria. Austria was a polyglot empire, grouping together the multiple nationalities of the Danube basin in its historic position between Germany and northern Italy. It stood in the direct path of the two storms that would bring about the collapse of the system: liberal nationalism and conservative nationalism. On the liberal nationalism front, the domestic institutions of Austria were less and less compatible with the national and liberal political trends of the century, but were also unable to cope with the demands agitating parts of its empire in northern Italy. On the conservative nationalism front, Prussia loomed over Austria's position in Germany, and Russia over its Slavic populations in the Balkans.

Aware of the increasingly dissonant currents of liberalism and nationalism that threatened its existence, Austria sought to spin a web of moral restraint to forestall tests of strength. Metternich's consummate skill shone brightest in inducing the key countries to submit their disagreements to a sense of shared values. As long as Austria managed to convince its closest allies, Prussia and Russia, each of which represented a geopolitical threat to the Austrian Empire, that the ideological danger posed by revolution outweighed their strategic opportunities, Austria was able to maintain the status quo. Metternich delayed the inevitable by turning Russia – a country he feared – into a partner on the basis of the commonality of conservative values, and at the same time reserving Great Britain – a country he trusted – as a last resort for resisting challenges to the balance of power. However, the more the alliances approached a system of collective security, the more Great Britain felt compelled to dissociate itself. And the more Great Britain dissociated itself, the more dependent Austria became on Russia, hence the more rigidly it defended conservative values. As Austria grew more and more dependent on Russia, the question came to be how long the appeals to the Tzar's conservative principles could restrain Russia from exploiting its opportunities in the Balkans and at the periphery of Europe. The answer turned out to be 30 years, during which Metternich dealt with revolution in Naples, Spain, and Greece while effectively maintaining a European consensus and avoiding Russian intervention in the Balkans.

The Concert of Europe was ultimately shattered by the Eastern Question. This was the result of independence struggles in the Balkans as the various nationalities tried to break loose from Turkish rule. The dilemma this posed for Metternich's system was that it clashed with the commitment to maintain the status quo: the independence movements that today were aimed at Turkey would tomorrow attack Austria. Moreover, the Tzar, who was the most committed to conservative legitimacy, was also the most eager to intervene. But neither Vienna nor London believed that the Tzar would preserve the status quo after his armies had been launched. The war broke out in Crimea in 1854 on the pretext of religious claims – who should be granted the title of Protector of the Christians in the Ottoman Empire, France or Russia? But the real motive was that Tzar Nicholas I was pursuing the ancient Russian dream of gaining Constantinople and the Straits, something that Great Britain could not allow to happen owing to the importance of its interests in the Mediterranean.

Austria at first remained neutral, afraid that siding with Russia would give France a pretext for attacking Austria's Italian territory, and that Russia's advance in the Balkans might increase the restlessness of Austria's Slavic populations. Neutrality was the sensible course. But the threat of France to its Italian positions proved too unsettling, and Austria presented an ultimatum to the Tzar, demanding that Russia retreat from the principalities of Moldavia and Wallachia, which Nicholas had ordered to be occupied. This was the end of a friendship that dated back to the Napoleonic Wars. Once Austria had cut itself loose from the shackles of shared values, this freed Russia to conduct its own policy on the basis of geopolitical considerations. Pursuing such a course, Russia was bound to clash with Austria over the future of the Balkans and, in time, to seek to undermine the Austrian Empire.

The reason the Vienna settlement had worked so long was that the three Eastern powers had seen their unity as the essential barrier to revolutionary chaos and to French domination of Europe. In the Crimean War, however, Austria maneuvered itself into an uneasy alliance with Napoleon III, who was eager to undermine Austria in Italy, and with Great Britain, which was unwilling to engage in European causes. This liberated Russia and Prussia to pursue their own undiluted national interests. Prussia exacted its price by forcing Austria to withdraw from Germany, while Russia's growing hostility in the Balkans turned into one of the triggers for World War I and led to Austria's ultimate collapse.

Faced with the realities of power politics, Austria failed to realize that its salvation had been the commitment to conservative legitimacy. The concept of the unity of conservative interests had transcended national borders and thus tended to mitigate the confrontations of power politics. Nationalism had the opposite effect, exalting the national interest, heightening rivalries, and raising the risks for everyone. Austria had thrown itself into a contest that, given all its vulnerabilities, it could not possibly win. Within five years of the end of the Crimean War, the Italian nationalist leader Camillo Cavour began the process of expelling Austria from Italy by provoking a war with Austria, backed by a French alliance and Russian acquiescence, both of which would once have been inconceivable. Within five years, Bismarck would defeat Austria and secure the dominance of Germany. Once again, Russia would stand aloof and France would do the same, albeit reluctantly. When the period ended, Germany stood as the strongest power on the continent. Conservative legitimacy – the principle of the unity of conservative rulers that had mitigated the harshness of the balance of power system during the Metternich years – had turned into an empty slogan.

Based on a legitimacy that was too narrow and of the wrong kind – being less and less representative – the Concert of Europe was an extremely fragile and unsustainable arrangement in the long run. It resolutely looked to the past and attempted to conserve it. It was formed out of a vision of legitimacy that did not give itself the means to address and integrate the nationalist forces about to reshape the identity of both domestic and international politics and legitimacy.[7] In addition, the fact that the Concert depended upon cabinet politics greatly constrained the decision-making processes and the parameters and goals that they envisioned. It accentuated the politics of narrow consent and hampered the Concert's ability to address and integrate the unfolding changes. The agreement at the top could not bridge the growing gap between the politics of the balance of power and the values of society. In not envisioning mechanisms through which the evolution of this agreement could have been possible, the Concert made itself too much a defense mechanism, a thing of the past, and ultimately relegated itself to that past.

The rapprochement between the United States and Great Britain: Selective value inclusiveness and its unsocializing side-effects

In the late nineteenth century and early twentieth century, the United States rose from its role as a minor actor in international affairs to a position of international influence and became capable of mounting a formidable challenge to British power. The growth of American strength was not confined to the economic sphere. It was also manifested militarily, particularly on the seas. One might have expected Britain to see the United States as the gravest menace to its international position, and the United States to view Britain as the main impediment to its future advancement. Confrontations over the Venezuelan boundary, the isthmian canal, and the Alaskan–Canadian border were all symptomatic of attempts by the United States to advance its strategic and territorial interests and of Britain's attempts to resist. In spite of this, the Anglo-American power rivalry did not end in a hegemonic war. It was resolved through peaceful accommodation. There were good reasons for this outcome.

At the beginning of the twentieth century it had become obvious that Britain's imperial reach was badly overextended.[8] The fiscal pressure, for instance, that the imperial responsibilities were putting on the British Empire showed that some choices had to be made. Where would the necessary trimming and withdrawal of power be the least dangerous and least painful, in real and potential terms? What allies could be found to help ease the pain by occupying the positions from which Britain was retreating without posing a threat to its Empire – indeed becoming, if possible, partners in arms? The answers to these questions were of prime importance, since the British Empire was under attack in a number of its possessions. This was the case in Afghanistan, Persia, Turkey, and India, where British interests were fodder for the Russian territorial appetite. It was the case in North Africa and South Asia, where British interests were clashing with those of France. Even Germany was a concern, since it had embarked upon an ambitious program of naval expansion that threatened to deny to Britain its traditional maritime supremacy. Finally, as the ancient Chinese Empire began to disintegrate and Japan suddenly emerged as a rapidly rising regional power, not to be pushed around easily, the specter of entanglement in a conflict in the Far East arose. None of these threats could be taken lightly, as the war in South Africa and the difficulty Britain encountered in prevailing there revealed. As a result of the rivalries associated with the security threats in these regions, neither Russia, nor Germany, nor France, nor Japan could qualify as a potential partner. The only possibility left was the United States.

Finding an arrangement with the United States made sense for a number of practical reasons.[9] A first reason was the intensity of economic and financial links between the two countries. At the end of the nineteenth century, Anglo-American commerce accounted for more than 40 percent of all US exports and about 18 percent of American imports. For Britain, these figures were 7.5 percent of total exports and 24 percent of total imports. Geopolitical considerations furnished another set of motives. To start with, for Britain to defend its position in the Western hemisphere would have meant launching a war against the United States that it could not have won. With the mounting American naval power, a victory over the United States was clearly out of reach. On the other hand, in accommodating the United States in the Western hemisphere, the British Empire could hope to serve its own interests. Britain would concentrate on the protection of its Empire in other regions of the globe, leaving the United States unchallenged in a zone turned thus into its own backyard. This especially made sense since most of the Latin American countries had by now gained independence and offered only limited opportunities for the Empire. In addition, British statesmen had strong reasons for thinking that America was not the principal threat to their security. Unlike the other continental powers of Europe, the United States was distant from the British Isles and from much of the British Empire. Moreover, in contrast to Britain's other rivals, the United States harbored no real designs on British possessions or spheres of influence. The rapprochement of the United States and Britain in the Western hemisphere was made possible still further by the fact that the United States, too, distrusted Germany for the strengthening of its naval power and its ambitions in the Western hemisphere.

Nonetheless, these views would not have been possible if the Anglo-American friendship had not been perceived as beneficial, even indispensable and natural, owing to the ideological and cultural affinities between the two countries, as a result of the overlap between their core values. The cultural and value affinities that allowed a relationship of trust to develop were initially rooted in an appeal to the common political culture of democracy, liberty, and freedom in the United States and Britain. On the American side, this feeling increased after the reform bills of 1867 and 1884 extending the franchise in England, which largely dissolved the traditional American stereotype of Great Britain as an archaic, hopelessly feudal, and aristocratic country. Similarly, Britain's granting of self-governing Dominion status to Canada helped to erase longstanding American notions of British tyranny. On the British side, although Britain was, as a matter of policy, not concerned with institutions different from its own, it felt warmly about the sense of political commonality with the United States. It felt that the democratic culture of the United States, for all its commitment to equality and meritocracy, was a product of the English world.

The Anglo-Saxon link bringing together Britain and the United States was another factor accounting for a sense of cultural and value affinities between the two countries. This was especially important at a time when the idea of natural selection and of the survival of the fittest was being applied enthusiastically to human relations in the form of social Darwinism. The rival imperialism of Britain, Russia, France, America, and Japan lent considerable credence to the belief that a struggle for world supremacy among the Anglo-Saxon, Slavic, Latin, and Oriental races was indeed under way. In that context, the British and Americans were bound to aid one another if they should clash with those of other racial groups. Furthermore, the white Anglo-Saxon elite and the press in the two countries stressed their unique ability to address the "needs" of non-European peoples and to make the world better through colonization. The various value affinities between the United States and Britain, which played a significant role in the threat assessments of the two countries, therefore led Britain in particular to discount the danger posed by the United States. Although well aware of the United States' rapid growth and its awesome military and industrial potential, Britain simply could not see the United States as a menace to its vital interests. Hence, also, the fact that Britain tended to see American economic success as something to be congratulated and emulated rather than feared. This attitude was even more marked with regard to imperialism. American attempts at expansion were, for the most part, greeted with warm approval, as manifested in the positive British reaction to the Spanish–American War and the seizure of Cuba and the Philippines by the United States. So, instead of meeting in battle, Britain and the United States were reconciled.

Although the tradition has been to wonder at the achievement of the rapprochement, it should not however lead us to be over-impressed, or oblivious to its unsocializing side-effects at the global level. The reasons accounting for the rapprochement, rather than being left uncritiqued, have to be viewed in the light of their negative impact on international order as well. In this context, one has to stress that the affinity of cultures and values, once recognized between the two powers, helped color their relations with other non-Anglo-Saxon countries, which were then portrayed in negative terms, especially if they were at the perimeter of the "civilized" world.[10] This certainly applied to Latin American countries. The attitude of contempt that the Anglo-Saxon world projected toward them provided, among other things, an opportune justification for extending American control over Central and South America. But, more dangerously for the state of peace at the global level, the Anglo-American rapprochement affected the way Britain and the United States saw their immediate challengers, Germany and Japan in particular.

The common value imperatives that bound the two nations provided them with a number of conjoint goals, kept them from warring, made restraint and accommodation easier, and contributed to the development of benign images of one another. But they were also part of a process of selective morality and universality, enhancing the construction of dangerous images of their contenders. As such, they contributed to the failure of the international system at that time to embrace and socialize rising national powers that were craving recognition and inclusion. In disqualifying the claims and ambitions of their challengers as expansionist and dangerous, the rapprochement, clothed in the good conscience and righteousness of Anglo-Saxon liberalism, contributed to the isolation and disenfranchisement of Germany and Japan.[11] Since Britain and the United States were largely at the time in the position of defining the rules of the international game, the joining of forces that the rapprochement constituted ended up being an antagonizing factor vis-à-vis powers that wanted to take part in the international system. The more the major democratic powers of the period – the United States, Britain, and France – were reluctant to make room and share the benefits of international order, the more humiliated and frustrated Germany[12] and Japan[13] would become. Exclusion could only make these two countries, already deeply insecure about themselves and their international standing, more insecure and resentful, and more inclined to resort to the military option.[14] In embracing each other, the United States and Britain helped close the gates of the international system on anxious rising challengers,[15] unintentionally facilitating the eventual possibility of war. This would be a high price to pay for the Anglo-American rapprochement.

84 POWER IN TRANSITION

ASEAN: In search of enhanced internal and regional legitimacy

From the start, the Association of South East Asian Nations (ASEAN) was envisioned as a tool to address and possibly solve two problems of socialization and legitimacy. First, ASEAN was viewed as a way to overcome the weak sense of internal legitimacy that most of the member countries were suffering from. It would do this by strengthening cooperation among nations and enhancing the economic growth, social progress, and cultural development of the region. Second, it was meant to foster a feeling of regional community in order for its member countries to recognize each other as partners and to be perceived as actors to be taken seriously at the international level. Fostering a feeling of regional community was also designed to keep the great powers out of the region and to oppose the spreading of the communist threat.

The extent to which ASEAN has been a solution inside its member countries' borders, the extent to which it has been able to facilitate a transition towards a better power distribution and better social and economic integration, has been limited. The state of the internal legitimacy of a number of nations of South-East Asia has remained shaky and a factor in regional tension owing to the dramatically uneven distribution of social, economic, and political national power. This has been the case in particular with Indonesia, which is especially unfortunate since it is one of the key players in ASEAN. As such, Indonesia is a source of regional instability. Other countries, which have been able to establish well-functioning political institutions – including an efficient state and administration – and a rather strong internal legitimacy, have tended to play an important role in regional negotiation, as the example of Singapore shows. But it is difficult for them to balance out entirely the shortcomings of the pivotal element that Indonesia represents.

The results of ASEAN as a diplomatic device designed to enhance a feeling of regional community are mixed. On the one hand, ASEAN has been relatively successful. To a certain extent, it owes this relative success to the shared experience of colonization and subsequently of decolonization – a major factor in regional identity formation and in the establishment of ASEAN. At the moment of their independence, the common experience of the colonial period – domination and exploitation by colonial powers, treatment as inferior people in their own lands, perceived obstruction by Western powers of their struggle for independence – had created an attachment by the people of nations of South-East Asia to the principles of sovereignty, territorial integrity, and non-interference in domestic affairs. At the same time, the South-East Asian countries viewed themselves as distinct and competitive. The relations among them bore most of the attributes of the European balance of power system of the nineteenth century. Any significant increase in strength by one of them was almost certain to evoke an offsetting maneuver by the others. The combination of these two factors was a decisive motivation for looking for ways to mitigate the Hobbesian dimension of regional politics in South-East Asia and the benefits that outside forces could draw from it. With ASEAN, member states accepted and in large measure abided by key principles in the conduct of their international relations. These principles included mutual respect for political independence, territorial integrity, and national identity; non-interference in one another's internal affairs; peaceful settlement of disputes; renunciation of the threat or use of force; and effective cooperation. Years later, the situation offers no comparison with the early post-independence period. ASEAN member states have now acquired a vested interest in the survival and stability of fellow members. The concerns of other ASEAN states and the consequences for the region have come to figure in the formulation of national interest. In addition, ASEAN countries continue to search for counterweights among one another to balance the influence of China and Japan in the region. Though they will disavow it, they included the feared Vietnam in their group in large part in order to balance China and Japan. And that, too, is why ASEAN is asking the United States to remain engaged in the region while ensuring that it does not become an overpowering factor.

In spite of these achievements, one has to concede that ASEAN is hardly more than an ad hoc regulatory arrangement. It is very far from amounting to a structure of legitimacy able to bring together the countries of the region in a cohesive manner and to reverberate convincingly at the international level. The remaining weak internal legitimacy of some of its members, and especially one of its key members, Indonesia, as noted before, constitutes a major impediment. It is difficult for a group of nations to project strongly outwards if the countries that are part of it are hardly socially integrated. A lack of sound internal legitimacy, of effective political institutions, is all the more problematic considering the cultural and value diversity among and within nations of the region, a diversity that then appears to be another major obstacle to ASEAN ambitions.

Cultural or value affinity is one of the keys to the development of a dynamic of legitimacy and its benefits – because of its influence on identity formation. As a result, one should not overlook the shallow nature of this affinity in the ASEAN region and the negative effect it has. ASEAN countries display to this day a wide spectrum of experiences. ASEAN includes strong and weak states with a variety of political systems and cultural traditions, in different stages of political and economic development. It also displays situations of transition to a market economy, political liberalization and democratization (in some countries), or resistance to political change (in others), or even the two trends at the same time in the same countries. Such differences illustrate the heterogeneity of values characterizing the region. The cultural influences that made their mark throughout its history – South-East Asia is the meeting place of the five great religions (Hinduism, Buddhism, Confucianism, Islam, and Christianity), as well as of many ethnic groups – probably contributed to a certain extent to the development of a sense of regional cultural syncretism. The cohabitation of these influences and ethnic groups did not, however, favor the construction of a real feeling of community, within and among nations of the region. Colonial rule and the struggle against it, while generating a shared experience that had the mobilizing impact mentioned earlier, came also to be a complicating factor in the context of this cultural and value diversity. Far from putting an end to the tense cohabitation of cultures, ethnicities, and values, they often deepened the sense of divide and contributed to the revival of historical animosity. By endorsing certain existing units and arbitrary boundaries, colonial rule contributed to the ethnic and racial diversity, and hence the artificiality, of many states. The inability of the states to function properly as tools of economic, political, and social integration transformed this artificiality of a number of countries of the region into structural weakness. This weakness ultimately translates into the limitations imposed upon the ability of ASEAN to be the important tool of peaceful transition it was initially envisioned to be internally and regionally. The limited extent to which ASEAN has so far brought about a sense of socialization and legitimacy at the regional level echoes the cultural and value diversity keeping apart the nations of the region.

Reflecting upon the case studies: Legitimacy, change, and socialization in an international context

Out of these cases, a number of lessons can, tentatively, be formulated. The first lesson is that change is the ultimate test of international legitimacy.[16] The ability of international legitimacy to integrate change is a moment of truth. It is a moment of truth with regard to how deeply international legitimacy penetrates into the national powers that it is supposed to monitor. It is also a moment of truth with regard to how the values that shape the normative identity of international legitimacy are able to embrace unfolding changes. It appears that not any value will do. Some are fitter than others to welcome and handle change. If the normative content of international legitimacy is too eager to maintain the status quo, this will hamper its integration capacity, especially since conservative-driven values are likely to be echoed by rigid rules and procedures of regulation and negotiation. As such, the system generates a lot of pressure for itself from within, with a tendency to make any challenge into a strategic threat to be viewed through the lens of conflict. Rather than strengthening the system of international legitimacy, it only weakens it, as we have seen with the Concert of Europe.

The second lesson is that the ability to have and maintain a key role in the international system requires a strong home base. A high level of national integration is essential for a country to be a sustainable international power regulator and power broker. If this is lacking, its international capacity can only be fragile and likely to unravel. Conceivably, the whole international system will also go through a profound transformation with the collapse of the key actor. This lesson can be deduced in part from the role played by Austria in the Concert of Europe. Although the internal weaknesses of Austria and its central position in the balance of power accounted largely for the creation of the Concert, they also caused its death. To some extent, this point about the interplay between internal legitimacy and the international system finds an echo in the implosion of the Soviet Union and its loss of influence in the late 1980s and early 1990s. In disintegrating from within, because it had chosen social and political control over social and political socialization, the Soviet Union lost most of its international power. In addition, the international system to whose management it had contributed broke down. This connection between national integration and legitimacy and the ability to be part of the management of the international system should also be a matter of reflection for contemporary China.

The lack of internal integration of a key actor is, however, not an absolute impediment to the international system of regulation if other countries party to the system are able to take over and balance out the weaknesses of the major player. This is the third lesson, drawn from the ASEAN case. It nonetheless presupposes two crucial conditions: the existence of solid alternative partners and a common interest in the continuation of the international arrangement. Clearly, this was not the case in the context of the Concert of Europe, since Austria had more at stake in the Concert than did any of its partners, which ultimately benefited from its collapse. But it is the case with ASEAN. Although Indonesia has been one of its chief actors, the problems that it is now encountering, while weakening it, do not necessarily threaten the existence of the regional arrangement. Besides Indonesia, there are other countries which play an important role in regional regulation and remain committed to the survival and flourishing of ASEAN, and they are able partially to compensate for any present shortcomings of the leading player.

The fourth lesson, deduced from the side-effects of the Anglo-American rapprochement, is that claims expressed by rising contenders should be taken seriously by the international system. It should do its best to integrate them. Their integration is likely to have a double socializing effect. First, integrating the claims does not necessarily mean they must be accepted as they are. The international system could use the eagerness of the claimants to be part of the system as a bargaining chip to get concessions on the nature of the claims and, incidentally, on the nature of the political regimes making them. Second, in making room for the claims, not only could the international system socialize them, but it would probably also increase its own credibility and power of socialization for the future. This presupposes that the values promoted by the international system are rather open, so that they create space for the challengers, and that they are embedded strongly enough to rein in the unreasonable ambitions that such challengers could have and induce them, if necessary, to adapt to the international environment they want to join.

Liberal democratic values are ideally placed to play this role as long as they do not pave the way to non-reciprocal liberalism. This is a fifth and final lesson for us, also drawn from the unsettling side-effects of the rapprochement. Liberal democratic values are likely to play a role of socialization, from normative, institutional, and practical points of view, as long as they organize reciprocity among actors. When this happens, sharing the benefits of the international system also makes it possible and justifiable to share the burden. On the other hand, a unilateral approach to international affairs generates more one-sided attitudes, especially when it originates with the dominant force in the game. In the process, it is not only the liberal structure of the international system that runs the risk of losing its validity; it is also the values and ideas at its foundation – hence, the necessity to ensure that calling upon democratic values in the international setting is not a disguise for universalizing an undemocratic hegemony. This brings us to the third and final section of the chapter.

Socialization of rising security threats and democratic hegemony

It is essential for the hegemonic power being challenged to take into consideration its challengers' claims for recognition. Not doing so runs the risk of putting their interactions on a confrontational path. Although the increasing socialization of the international system, through the formalized system of international democratic legitimacy established after World War II and through the growing links of interdependence, makes war among competing powers an improbable option, we should not be led to rule it out entirely. This is especially the case since American hegemony is likely to be challenged in coming years, and certain conditions will have to be met to ensure that this challenge does not get out of control. The effects of mounting national and regional resentment at a lack of organized reciprocity at the international level must not be underestimated. The potential antisocial consequences should be an invitation to the United States to be wise in the management, defense, and projection of its hegemony.

Legitimacy as the expression and condition of benignity and order

In chapter 2, Charles Kupchan looks for the conditions under which American power could be perceived as benign. In this context, he speaks of the generosity of the hegemonic power. In addition, Yuen Foong Khong argues in his chapter that, when it comes to order, the relevant states must be able to arrive at a mutually acceptable agreement on the central dimensions of order. This entails forging a consensus on hierarchy and on basic rules concerning the use of force, trade, and inter-state relations. It appears that the reflections in the present chapter on legitimacy and democratic legitimacy at both the national and international levels may help to identify some of the conditions under which American power could be benign and order could be achieved. Democratic legitimacy could provide the hegemon and its potential contenders with a framework in which to negotiate their disagreements and embed their agreements. For this to happen, a requirement needs to be fulfilled: American power has to fully integrate the message of democratic legitimacy. Democratic legitimacy states that power competition, at both the national and international levels, is socializable and socialized only as long as the values at the core of democratic culture are implemented continuously and consistently, with all the consequences that this implies for the power holders. Although it is certainly tempting for a hegemonic power to transform its situation into a monopoly, democratic power is conditioned by ethical imperatives. The democratic hegemon must be willing to share and to allow the possibility of the redistribution of power.

The United States as hegemon: Facing hard choices

Democratic legitimacy and its ability to socialize and pacify power competition offer two possible routes to the United States as the only current global superpower. First, it could use its hegemonic position to oppose the continued implementation of democratic legitimacy. This route would be understandable and all too human. Politics is not about sainthood. Being committed to facilitating the success of its competitors is certainly not easy for a hegemonic power, especially when competitors are not equally committed to its success. This, in itself, can be used as a rationalization, if not a justification, for putting self-interest first. However, this route is not necessarily the safest one for American foreign policy, in that it is unlikely to produce conditions for peace, let alone a just peace. It could produce unfortunate consequences in terms of international violence. It could generate envy and resentment, a situation that could fuel the emergence of radical and violent opposition to the hegemonic power. As a matter of fact, this is already happening in various regions of the world, where international terrorism is making the United States its most favorite target. In addition, when there is a perception that a hegemonic power is employing a double standard or inconsistency in its application of democratic values, the values themselves and their power to structure debates and interactions tend to be undermined. This also facilitates the development of unfriendly confrontation.

The second possible path for the United States is the commitment to democratic values at the international level as a way to enhance the socialization of international affairs. There are good reasons to follow this route. To start with, there is the need for the United States to be aware of the normative demands that accompany being the democratic superpower of the time. If it wants to be faithful to its own national mythology and to the democratic creed it professes, it has to give the lead to the expectations of democratic imperatives. This is part of its responsibility, and it is accountable for it. More pragmatically, the enhancement of democratic values at the international level could prove to be, for the United States, a sound strategy for ensuring its own security and the stability of the international system. This is especially the case since there is no shortage of ways to promote this enhancement.

Already largely tested and in the making through the increasingly dense web of multilateral and communal activities initiated after World War II, these methods involve security, economic, commercial, and other negotiations and regulations. As such, they involve trying to secure the establishment of real mechanisms of fairness at the international level, in the political, security, economic, and other such spheres. They imply making as sure as possible that pluralism is expressed, protected, and promoted in strategic areas. Although not yet fully embedded, taking into account these principles, partly in relation to the United Nations system, has certainly already lessened tensions and contributed to the fact that democratic legitimacy tends to be more and more the value of reference, nationally and internationally. For international democratic legitimacy to become more deeply embedded and to contribute more effectively to the pacification of power competition, it is, however, necessary to revisit the notion of hegemony.

Revisiting the nature and role of the hegemon

The understanding of socialization at the international level is an extrapolation of the national dimension, of the process of nation-state formation.[17] This has had two major consequences for the study of international affairs and the envisaged socialization of global politics. First, compared with the internal ordering and integration that national politics has created in modern times, international affairs have appeared unruly and anarchical. Second, borrowing from the concentration of power that construction of the nation-state implied, the idea emerged in the 1980s that hegemony was a prime condition for international socialization. This seemed all the more convenient to American analysts of international affairs in that it appeared fulfilled in the superpower position that the United States acquired after World War II and in its gradually growing influence worldwide, and made it possible to look into the possible theoretical justification for such domination. It is in this context that international relations, as an academic field, mobilized Thomas Hobbes' thoughts on the natural state of anarchy and the need for a Leviathan, as well as Antonio Gramsci's notion of a hegemonic bloc. As a result, hegemony and the concentration, if not monopoly, of power that it implies became one of the core notions of the contemporary American understanding of international politics, one through which order and stability were meant to be achieved and maintained.[18]

This understanding of the role of the hegemon has little to do with democratic legitimacy. Democratic legitimacy, far from being simply the justification for the monopoly of violence elucidated by Weber, who was mainly addressing the issue of legitimacy in a context rather foreign to democratic politics, is in principle the organization of the circulation of power. While it is true that the organizational role of the state involves limiting the access to the means of violence,[19] this should not be permitted to interfere with the very foundation of democratic legitimacy: relatively open access to and participation in power. As a result, if parallels have to be drawn between socialization at the national level and socialization at the international level, they have to be established on clear grounds. In calling upon a somewhat Hobbesian version of the hegemon, theorists of international politics remain dependent upon a pre-democratic vision of national politics that they then superimpose upon the international scene. But, just as contemporary national politics is no longer identifiable with pre-democratic politics, international politics should not be reduced to its pre-democratic features and principles.

It is inaccurate to consider international politics as being in a nascent stage equivalent to that of national politics at the time of the formation of nation-states, and thus requiring an analogous and pre-democratic hegemon. It is especially inaccurate when the current hegemon – the United States – identifies itself with democratic culture. Although it is true that international politics is not fully socialized, especially in democratic terms, it is no longer the raw anarchy that some observers describe. Nor is there anything to indicate that the forms of socialization in international politics are meant strictly to duplicate the way in which the nation-state was historically established and socialized.

The United States' contenders: Seeking hegemony or respect?

Calling for democratization of the United States' hegemonic status does not mean making it a victim of political idealism and romanticism. If democracy tends to structure the overall political culture of our time, it does not imply that democracy is all there is to contemporary political culture. In particular, it does not put an end to power competition and the tensions that competition generates. So, while encouraging the United States to democratize its power, it is important to identify the countries likely to be its challengers and assess how dangerous they could be for a democratized American hegemon.

There are very few possible real contenders at the global level. Among the big powers, Russia and Japan can be eliminated from the start. Russia is no longer in the competition, though one should not underestimate the reactions that could arise from internal resentments attached to its demise.[20] Japan, despite its economic power, has too many problems of self-positioning to be a real threat. Its awkwardness in projecting itself regionally and internationally is a testimony to its limitations and a profound impediment.[21] The two most credible contenders, as more or less homogeneous units, are Europe and China. However, the dangers they represent have to be mitigated. Neither one is likely to challenge the United States for hegemony. They seek respect more than hegemony.

From the beginning, the post–World War II European project was meant to be a key element of the pacification of Western Europe, especially among the European powers that had gone to war in World War I and World War II, such as Germany and France. The outward dimension was no less important. Although not stated in military terms, it was assumed that an integrated and prosperous Europe would be a good protection against the dangers – internally as well as externally from the East – of communism. With the integration of the core of Western Europe largely on its way, the European project is now facing challenges that are results of its success: deciding upon the modalities of further integration, in terms of federation and/or of preserved sovereignty, and upon how far the enlargement should go.

When it comes to the outward projection of Europe, it is interesting to notice that it has evolved over time and that its main target has changed. The Soviet Union is no longer the main outside threat. With the hegemony of the United States, the European construct has for some time now been – and not only under France's auspices – a tool to envision, if not to put into action yet, ways of containing American dominance. This course of action does not mean, however, that Europe aspires to return to world hegemony, or that it is ready to challenge the United States on this ground. Europe is too inhabited by uncertainties and contradictory forces concerning its external future to follow this path. In addition, without even stressing here the importance of the cultural bonds between the United States and Europe, the countries of the European Union are too committed to democratic ideals and mechanisms nationally and internationally to envisage direct confrontation with the United States. The "demilitarized mind"[22] is now a feature too deeply embedded in the West European world-view to make competition for international hegemony likely.[23]

As for China, a number of factors shape it as a self-involved power, not really able to project its ambitions beyond its immediate region. First and foremost, the nature of the values structuring the identity of China does not allow the type of universalization of power that the universal values of the Western democratic message allowed. As a result, even if Asia as a region achieves greater global strategic importance in the future, with China as its leading power, it is still difficult to imagine that without the base of universalizable ideals and values China could project itself globally.

More importantly, perhaps, there is a characteristic that Europe and China share vis-à-vis the United States. This element militates against the likelihood of a confrontation between Europe and the United States, or between China and the United States. It concerns the nature and development of their already noticeable competition. This competition is not and will not be about the replacement of the current beneficiary of world hegemony by a new beneficiary of a hegemonic situation. It is and will be about establishing a more balanced set of relationships among powerful units. Europe and China are, indeed, less concerned with replacing the United States in its hegemonic position than with preventing its hegemony from becoming overwhelming and final. The emerging competition is about the search for reciprocity, mutuality, and respect. It is also about making sure that the international system remains open to change and the possible circulation of power. It is about diversity and reciprocity.

As a matter of fact, it is this search for respect and reciprocity that largely explains the growing regional trading bloc mentality in the European Union, as a way to resist and challenge the globalization of

American order.[24] The search for respect is perhaps even more important for China. Ever since the Opium Wars of the early nineteenth century forcibly opened the country, the West in general, and the United States in particular, have been viewed by the Chinese as the agents of an endless series of humiliations. Equality of status, a fierce insistence on not bowing to foreign prescription, is for Chinese leaders not a tactic but a moral imperative.[25]

Realizing democratic hegemony

The position of domination in which the United States finds itself today is an interesting one. It is tempted to push to the limits what late modernity is normatively and politically allowing in terms of acting as a modern empire.[26] It is tempted to generate a semi-institutionalized imperial regime, a multifaceted imperialism. And, as we know, empires have no interest in operating within an international system. They aspire to domesticate the international realm. They aspire to be the international system. As such, they have no need for a balance of power.[27] The universal character of the democratic values that lie at the core of American culture,[28] and the importance that American foreign policy attaches to their spread, can only facilitate the tactical realization of this temptation, adapted to the *goût du jour*.[29] On the other hand, the democratic culture with which the United States identifies itself places strong constraints on such behavior. One cannot act as a pseudo-empire, as an imperial power, and pretend to be a democratic power – especially when other units of power are growing into challenger status.

If the expression used at one point by Secretary of State Madeleine Albright – that the United States is the indispensable power – has some reason and validity, it cannot possibly mean that other powers are dispensable.[30] This would go against the democratic values that the United States claims it identifies with. It can only mean that the United States' credibility lies in its ability to make the other countries equally indispensable. In considering the spread of democratic representative institutions as a key to peace, the American power should be aware of the consequences that this logically implies: organizing democratic hegemony, rather than using democracy to organize and universalize its own hegemony. To try to have it both ways can only be self-defeating for democracy and its ideals. There is no such thing as a free lunch in the world of democratic legitimacy. Democratic legitimacy is not an *à la carte* menu from which one chooses what is convenient and leaves out what is not. Democratic legitimacy provides benefits – moral and social – only so long as they are accompanied by the possibility that they will be shared. It requires consistency in its deployment to be valid. Democratic hegemony is not the universalization and monopolization of power by the dominating power. It is the organization of the end of unreciprocal hegemony. It is hegemony democratized.[31]

Liberalism, as the ideology of American power within and beyond its borders, does not necessarily help to accomplish this task, since one of its major characteristics is to present itself as an ahistorical and non-ideological world-view, and thus as a "natural" best method for organizing society. Liberalism's philosophy of nature amounts to a depoliticization of the political organization of interactions, at both the national and international levels. It tends to invite the view that the distribution of power it engineers is unavoidable and unchangeable.[32] However, democratic institutions are meant to organize the mobility and circulation of power. Democratic legitimacy is about ensuring relatively open access to and fair competition for power. It is about ensuring power's constant potential redistribution. That is also what the rule of law means, nationally and internationally. That is the price to pay for securing the possibility of peace among competing powers,[33] a peace that is not a *paix armée*, a war in the waiting, but a true celebration of the potentialities of life.[34]

The United States should not forget one of the lessons attached to the end of the Cold War and the collapse of the Soviet Union. The Soviet Union collapsed not primarily because the United States defeated it. It disintegrated because the Soviet Union defeated itself by thinking that it could thrive by feeding on its own society – despite the vital need to organize universality, plurality, and mobility peacefully within itself, despite the demands for socialization and political legitimacy. Because democracy has been rather attentive to the demands for socialization and legitimacy, it remains the only fighter still standing on the field, and on the rise more now than ever. The United States, as part of the democratic culture, benefits from this situation and has greatly contributed to making it possible. As a superpower, however, it should also listen to the lessons this history conveys for the handling of international politics.

The sense of solidarity that American power displayed in the aftermath of World War II in facilitating the reconstruction of the international system and the countries – both victorious and defeated – devastated by war contributed, in the end, to the United States' world hegemony. The United States can once more display its power of solidarity, of interested generosity. Indeed, the United States would benefit – although most likely quite differently from the way it gained from its contribution to the reconstruction of the international system in the aftermath of World War II – by following this path.[35] Acting as a true democratic hegemon, it would finish the job that it began under Woodrow Wilson and continued with the creation of the United Nations. It should do so, but this time by contributing to preparing for its peaceful resignation as the only and overarching superpower, in order to hasten a peaceful return to a pacific, positive and creative multipolarity. As well as political stamina and the proper mechanisms to implement it,[36] this requires moral strength. A sense of urgency should be able to invigorate such a need for moral strength. For, when socializing the rising contenders fails, when the hegemon waits too long to open up, the remaining options tend to be equally unsatisfactory. One is appeasement. It is hardly a good option. By the time it lands on the desk of the decision makers, resentment has usually reached boiling point among contending powers. A confrontational mood has settled in that is difficult to dispel, especially when domestic conditions encourage it. Even accommodation from the still dominant country will be insufficient. Such accommodation is seen as a weakness, and constitutes an invitation to push further and grab more, deepening the atmosphere of conflict. It is then that the chances of open conflict become frighteningly real.

Notes

1. The term "socialization" is used to qualify the process of social integration taking into account the imperative of reciprocity and the dynamics of rights and duties among actors. See also Philip Allott, *Eunomia. New Order for a New World* (Oxford: Oxford University Press, 1990), pp. 152–177.
2. International socialization needs national socialization, at least for the time being.
3. See Jean-Marc Coicaud, *Légitimité et politique. Contribution à l'étude du droit et de la responsabilité politiques* (Paris: PUF, 1997); forthcoming in English, *Legitimacy and Politics. A Contribution to the Study of Political Right and Political Responsibility* (Cambridge: Cambridge University Press, 2002).
4. These are, in particular: the sovereign equality of states, the self-determination of peoples, a prohibition on the threat or use of force, the peaceful settlement of disputes, non-intervention in the internal or external affairs of other states, respect for human rights, international cooperation, and good faith. Each of these principles is essential for the global equilibrium of international law and of the international system that goes with it. See Antonio Cassese, *International Law in a Divided World* (Oxford: Clarendon Press, 1986), pp. 126–165.
5. John Gerard Ruggie, *Constructing the World Polity: Essays in International Institutionalization* (London: Routledge, 1998), pp. 102–103.
6. In this section, I am relying heavily, but not exclusively, on Henry Kissinger, *Diplomacy* (New York: Simon & Schuster, 1994), chaps. 4, 5, and 6, and Karl Polanyi, *The Great Transformation. The Political and Economic Origins of Our Time* (Boston: Beacon Press, 1980), chap. 1.
7. On this issue, see for instance Lucien Febvre, *L'Europe. Genèse d'une civilisation* (Paris: Perrin, 1999), pp. 266–279.
8. See Aaron Friedberg, *The Weary Titan: Britain and the Experience of Relative Decline, 1895–1905* (Princeton, NJ: Princeton University Press, 1988), for instance chap. 3.
9. Stephen Rock, *Why Peace Breaks out: Great Power Rapprochement in Historical Perspective* (Chapel Hill: University of North Carolina Press, 1989), p. 47 for instance.

10. See Michael Mann, *The Sources of Social Power. Volume II. The Rise of Classes and Nation-states, 1760–1914* (Cambridge: Cambridge University Press, 1993), pp. 752–753.
11. Akira Iriye, *China and Japan in the Global Setting* (Cambridge, MA: Harvard University Press, 1992), pp. 15–18.
12. The Germans' frustration and humiliation could only be fueled by a sense of insecurity at the core of the modern German intellectual and political culture. See Louis Dumont, *L'idéologie allemande. France–Allemagne et retour* (Paris: Éditions Gallimard, 1991), chap. 2.
13. See Akira Iriye, *Power and Culture: The Japanese–American War, 1941–1945* (Cambridge, MA: Harvard University Press, 1981), chap. 1.
14. The psychological dimension of international relations should never be overlooked, as it plays a key role in the ways in which countries relate to each other.
15. In this context, it is interesting to look at the reflections of German and Japanese scholars and political analysts upon the international system and international law at the end of the nineteenth and beginning of the twentieth centuries. For Germany, see for instance Michel Koriman, *Quand l'Allemagne pensait le monde. Grandeur et décadence d'une géopolitique* (Paris: Éd. Fayard, 1990), and *Deutschland uber alles. Le pangermanisme 1890–1945* (Paris: Éd. Fayard, 1999). For Japan, see Herbert P. Bix, *Hirohito and the Making of Modern Japan* (New York: HarperCollins Publishers, 2000), pp. 133–135, 146–150.
16. The ability to handle change is also a decisive test of national legitimacy.
17. See Philip Allott, *Eunomia*, pp. 240–250. It should also be noted that Richard Tuck takes another approach to this issue in *The Rights of War and Peace: Political Thought and the International Order from Grotius to Kant* (Oxford: Oxford University Press, 1999), pp. 226–234.
18. The emergence of the notion of hegemony as a structuring paradigm of the academic field of international relations in the United States overshadowed the realist view of achieving international order through the balance of power. The shift corresponds to the rise of the United States as the main superpower and to a change of generation. The supporters of the realist balance of power were often scholars and policy makers originally from Europe (for instance Hans Morgenthau and Henry Kissinger), who contributed to adapting the European notion of *realpolitik* to the American understanding and conduct of power politics throughout the Cold War.
19. In other words, I am advocating here not the end of the state, but the importance and even exclusivity of certain functions to be performed by state institutions, nationally and internationally.
20. Russia suffers domestically from serious and largely self-inflicted problems, among which are a predatory and incompetent state and elite – the worst combination. As a consequence, it appears unlikely that Russia will be able to recover on its own. To a certain extent, its revival depends upon outside forces. However, there are not many international partners. Furthermore, in part rightly so, the help they may offer is rather tentative, if not counterproductive. The Bretton Woods institutions and other private financial actors – which Russia needs because it does not benefit from foreign investments channeled in by an economic diaspora, as is the case for China – are quite hesitant. The United States, which in the end is probably more interested in pushing its advantage over Russia than in bringing it into the international system on the basis of a balanced partnership, is also quite hesitant. The European Union, although cautious as well, is perhaps the best bet for Russia. In the present circumstances, because of Russia's geographical location and its cultural affinity and long shared history with Western Europe, the European Union has the strongest vested interest of all international actors in facilitating Russia's domestic, continental, and international socialization. As a

result, provided that Russian leaders adopt more transparent and efficient modes of governing (which Europe is likely to ask for as a condition of an enhanced partnership, but without the typical ideological righteousness and rigidity of American power), the European Union will probably step in at some point. The question is when the conditions will be met and minds ready on the two sides of the European continent for this to happen.

21. In the 1980s, the technological and economic rise of Japan was viewed as a major threat to the United States. It was mainly in the context of the elevation of this trans-Pacific competition to the global level that the international political economy became a major field of study in international relations. It served as an indication of the changing nature of international power and of the dramatic alterations that the anticipated hegemony of Japan and decline of the United States were envisioned to bring to the global distribution of power. Although based on the impressive economic rise of Japan, the eventuality of such a power transition between these two countries was only a false alarm – largely a self-induced panic attack on the part of the United States. Too many factors pointed toward the extreme improbability of a scenario of Japan's assumption of the mantle of global power. The intensity of the bilateral security relations between the two countries, their mutual need to address and maintain stability in Asia, the almost ontological impossibility of Japan's translation of its economic power into global political power, and the revitalization of the American economy are only some of these factors.

22. The "demilitarized mind" feature in Western Europe – which does not imply total disarmament and a refusal to see the use of military means as a legitimate option in certain circumstances – should not necessarily be perceived as a weakness and a by-product of a lack of agreement on a common defense strategy and policy or of clear strategic thinking on crises arising in Europe (see the European hesitations regarding the intervention in Kosovo). It has also to be understood in the light of a recent historical and cultural European trend – a trend in the context of which the conception and conduct of international relations through the lens of a military world-view appear more and more outdated for a number of situations. This explains why a number of West European countries – not only the internationally friendly countries such as the Nordic countries or the Netherlands, but increasingly even the ones traditionally committed to a certain extent to a global "politique de puissance" (France and the United Kingdom primarily) – are moving away from a foreign policy that is heavily influenced by the military in terms of analysis and means.

23. The demilitarized mind now largely embedded in the West European world-view contrasts with the highly militaristic understanding of foreign policy of the other main world powers: the United States, Russia, and China. This demilitarization of the mind to which the European Union bears testimony could have far-reaching consequences. The Western continent, where the modern nation-state emerged, could now be in the process of organizing its demise or at least of integrating it into a new form of political association: the federation, thus contributing to a new way of doing politics. This type of political legitimacy perhaps in the making is not only regional but also international. First, as it is about to embrace more and more territories, the European Union is tending – rather problematically one has to admit – to extend beyond what some see as the "natural" limits of Europe. Second, this model emulates other regions of the world (for instance the Southern Cone Common Market in South America). Third, it has interesting relationships with two of the models helping to structure international order, apart from the state model: the American model and the United Nations model. There are relationships of complementarity (for example, political and normative complementarity), overlap (normative overlap for instance), division of labor (e.g. UN–NATO and USA–Europe relationships in Kosovo), and competition (USA–UN, USA–European Union).

24. The spread of regional blocs is not necessarily harmless. It might also exacerbate international competition and tensions.
25. Chinese scholars and policy makers in the field of international affairs tend to have a constitutional interpretation of the balance of power. They view it as part of a checks and balances system, of a search for international reciprocity. Their constitutionalist enlightenment is, however, limited. It is typically part of a double standard approach characteristic of power holders more aware and eager to enjoy the privileges of power than to abide by and follow imperatives of justice. Thus it does not prevent most Chinese analysts and policy makers from seeing nothing wrong with China being engaged in macho and ego-inflated politics at the international level, such as being oblivious to the self-determination rights of regions and people located in border areas that China claims are strategic for its own security and interests.
26. The empire – in which institutionalized relationships of hierarchy and vassality exist between the dominating center and the entities of the periphery – is no longer seen as a legitimate form of political regime. The only form of tight supranational association seen as legitimate today is the federation, with relationships of parity and horizontal partnership among countries.
27. Balance of power and hegemony have both positive and negative aspects as ways to ensure international order. Balance of power avoids hierarchy and the alienation of state units but tends to trigger competition and attempts to offset the balance of power and, therefore, stability. Hegemony, by embedding order in overwhelming power, creates a hierarchy that runs the risk of alienating other countries and generating a backlash.
28. Modern France and the United States, each in its own way, put a sense of sameness and equality among individuals and a drive to enhance it as a right at the core of the universal and universalizing dimension of democratic values. This contributed to making their ideological message a very attractive one. It helped create a cultural magnet that progressives from countries at the receiving end have often been eager to emulate at home. At times it was also a convenient mantle to clothe and attempt to legitimate expansion beyond borders. France, when it was at the height of its power, certainly benefited from its version of the universal and universalizing dimension of democratic values. The United States' ability to expand and attract overseas has certainly also gained from the American version of the universal and universalizing dimension of liberal values. In modern times, such a convenient device of international power provided by domestic cultural values is matchless. Take, for instance, the case of Britain. British liberal values, anchored in a rather hierarchical and aristocratic understanding of political republicanism and liberalism, because they are less concerned with social equality than with political liberty, certainly did not lend Britain such ideological attraction at the peak of its international power. Its ability to seduce was targeted more to the elite of the periphery than to the commoners and masses. The cases of pre-World War Germany and Japan are even more striking. Germany was at the time fundamentally insecure about its standing and had no domestic democratic tradition. It viewed its relationships with other nations and cultures essentially in terms of hierarchy and force. Among conservative decision makers, the tendency was to perceive other nations and cultures as different and inferior, to be dominated and subjugated to the greater good of Germany. As for Japan, its insularity and insistence on being different, the combined sense of inferiority/superiority at the core of its self-image, and the ways it related to the outer world, especially vis-à-vis its immediate neighbors in Asia, could only make awkward, unconvincing, and unattractive its attempts to justify its expansion policy in terms of pan-Asian regionalism.
29. See Lea Brilmayer, *American Hegemony: Political Morality in a One-Superpower World* (New Haven, CT: Yale University Press, 1994).

30. Although this probably unfortunately comes close to Albright's interpretation.
31. Spinoza holds that the devolution of all power to one actor is a fatal mistake: "So it is slavery, not peace, that is furthered by the transfer of all power to one man; for peace, as I have said already, is not mere absence of war, but a union or agreement of minds" (*A Treatise on Politics*, chap. VI, paras. 4 and 5, in *The Political Works*, Oxford: Clarendon Press, 1958, p. 317). This certainly also applies at the international level.
32. This conception of liberalism has partly to be understood in connection with the influence of social Darwinism. It is also interesting to note that this view of liberalism cohabits with another core liberal belief, the one emphasizing the individual's power to create artifacts, to manufacture and change reality at will. In the end, liberal forces work hard to ensure that the claims of the superior essence of liberalism prevail historically. They leave nothing to the course of history, which is after all quite unpredictable in its outcomes, even when these are viewed as natural and the best that could happen.
33. One cannot help thinking here about having some equivalent to the US Sherman Antitrust Act, which provides the legal basis for dismantling economic monopoly in the name of open and fair competition and the rights of consumers. It is a piece of social legislation used to limit perceived exploitation and the aggregation of power. Applied to international politics, it would hypothetically put an end to political power monopoly.
34. In *A Treatise on Politics*, Spinoza leads the reader to conclude that democracy is likely to be as close as a political regime can be to reaching a spiritual form of political power where reason, right, freedom, faithfulness to oneself and others, joy, and, ultimately, life with its highest inspirations and aspirations go hand in hand.
35. On this issue, see for instance G. John Ikenberry, *After Victory. Institutions, Strategic Restraint, and the Rebuilding of Order after Major Wars* (Princeton, NJ: Princeton University Press, 2001), pp. 257–273.
36. The proper mechanisms would have to address the domestic level as well as the international plane. Domestically, they imply somehow getting Washington and the US Congress to break away from their parochialism vis-à-vis international affairs. At the international level, they would require the United States to move away from two recurrent shortcomings, which are partly encouraged by the limitations and constant complaints of other international state actors. The first is the politics of paternalism – a politics that tends both to lament other nations' lack of engagement, of taking responsibility in international affairs, and to mock and vilify them when they try to engage and take responsibility. The second is macho politics, which ultimately favors and enjoys unilateral decisions. The effects of these shortcomings (which amount to attempting to have it both ways: calling for burden-sharing while eagerly holding on to the privileges and benefits of power) can be particularly damaging. Because of the dominating position of the United States, any policy that happens to be an outgrowth of them still sets the international agenda.

5
Peaceful power transitions: The historical cases

Jason Davidson and Mira Sucharov

Introduction

In this chapter, we will illuminate the theoretical framework presented in this volume through an examination of three cases of peaceful power management: the United States and Great Britain (1895–1914), the Concert of Europe (1815–1848), and ASEAN (the Association of South East Asian Nations). While the US–UK case is an example of a power transition in the formal sense, the Concert and ASEAN cases exemplify – to greater or lesser degrees – the dynamics of power management and security accommodation integral to our overall topic of interest.

The American–British transition of the turn of the twentieth century is one of the clearest examples of a power transition in modern history. Following Britain's ascent to power in the wake of Dutch decline, the United States gradually drew closer, increasing the likelihood that war might break out between hegemon and challenger. Contrary to what history might have predicted, the transition was completed peacefully. What explains this puzzle? We will argue that the phenomenon of benignity – specifically, the mutual attribution of benign character – was the strongest factor leading to the peacefulness of the transition. We will also illustrate the lesser degree to which agreement on order and legitimacy contributed to the peaceful nature of the transition.

The Concert of Europe also provides fertile ground on which to test the model presented here, as it is a striking example of cooperation in the security realm. We will demonstrate that the exercise of restraint was prevalent throughout the history of the Concert, and that the group's members were willing to forgo their immediate goals in the interests of mutual accommodation. Agreement on order was also highly salient, specifically in the form of agreeing to spheres of influence. Finally, a spirit of shared legitimacy buttressed the Concert, as at least two institutions were imbued with normative significance: the monarchy and Christianity.

Finally, the case of ASEAN, while neither as fully ordered nor as legitimate as a formal security community might be, lends our model a greater degree of geographic and temporal breadth. Now entering its fourth decade, and finally having admitted all the states of South-East Asia, ASEAN stands out as an example of sovereign states agreeing to pursue multilateral aims for the ultimate goal of managing power differentials among members. We will argue that the exercising of strategic restraint facilitated the mutual perception of benignity among the member states, resulting in a more durable dynamic of cooperation within South-East Asia. The institutionalized mechanisms within the organization, agreement on hierarchy within the region, as well as a shared anti-colonialist legacy have helped to further agreement on order and legitimacy.

The remainder of this chapter will explore each of these three cases of power management in turn.

The United States and Great Britain, 1895–1914

The American–British transition of the turn of the twentieth century is the most easily identifiable case of a peaceful power transition in modern history. Nineteenth-century Britain ruled the world's seas with an empire the size of Rome's. By the mid-twentieth century, however, the United States was in a similar position. It dominated international trade and finance, and held a sizable lead over its closest military rival, the Soviet Union. The American–British transition therefore provides an excellent testing ground for the claims made by the model presented in this book. We will argue that, although the evidence for shared legitimacy and agreement on order was sparse (as befits the nascent development of the US–UK relationship), there is much evidence that the two countries exercised restraint and mutual accommodation. We will outline specific acts of accommodation and restraint, and the resulting mutual attribution of benign character. In addition, we will discuss the degree to which order and legitimacy were agreed upon, and will conclude by countering potential critics of our explanation of this case.

Overview

Historical outline

As noted above, British power peaked during the nineteenth century. At the dawn of that century the United States had not yet begun its ascent to great power status and its relations with Britain were anything but peaceful. The War of 1812 was triggered by the rights of neutrals to trade with belligerents and non-belligerents during wartime. The United States, as a non-belligerent in the Napoleonic Wars, sought such trade, whereas the British aimed to keep the Americans from trading with warring parties.[1] The next clash occurred during the American Civil War (1861–1865). Britain ruffled America's feathers by recognizing the South as a belligerent, and later through incidents such as allowing British citizens to fund and man the Southern ship the *Alabama*.[2]

After the Civil War, Britain and America entered an era which historian H. C. Allen refers to as the "Quiet Years," which lasted until our period of interest. The transition period began with the Venezuelan boundary dispute of 1895, which nearly led to war between the two countries. By the Spanish–American War of 1898 Britain was subtly aiding the United States in its bid for power. Two other important conflicts were over the Alaskan boundary and over a Central American isthmian canal that the United States hoped to construct. Internationally, the British were engaged in the Boer War (1899–1902), and then in the contest for an Open Door to China. By the close of this period, the two states had weathered these numerous incidents and had developed a partnership that was to stand the test of time (the crises will be discussed in detail below).[3]

Documenting the transition

We may document the power transition both in terms of capabilities (military and economic) and by noting the issue areas that had the potential to draw the two states into war. The economic aspects of power most clearly demonstrate the transition. In 1860, Britain's relative share of world manufacturing output was 19.9 percent, as compared with the United States' meager 7.2 percent. By 1900, however, it was the young republic that had surged ahead, garnering 23.6 percent to Britain's 18.5 percent.[4] The military dimension, however, presented less of a clear picture. The United States had long downplayed the necessity of a peacetime military force. Consequently, the growth of its navy from roughly 169,000 tons in 1880 to 824,000 in 1910 (compared with Britain's 650,000 to 2,174,000) was noteworthy.[5] Although the United States never challenged Britain's navy, it did become the second-ranked naval power by 1906.[6] The size of the US army was less impressive, even when compared with Britain, which has always had one of the smallest armies in Europe.[7]

However, most observers knew that, like its naval counterpart, the American army was limited only by "the amount of money the American people [chose] to spend on it."[8] In wartime, Americans could draw on their massive population base – second only to Russia's in 1910 – and convert it into one of the greatest armies in the world.[9]

Were there issues that might have led the two powers into conflict? The answer is a resounding yes. The War of 1812 was started by the neutrality/freedom-of-the-seas issue, which remained a constant source of tension between Britain and the United States.[10] However, there are at least three other sets of issues that could have caused war between the two countries. First, there were several outstanding conflicts between the United States and Canada.[11] Because the United States and Canada shared a massive border and the defense of that border was at least in part guaranteed by Britain, war might have resulted.[12] Second, Britain had numerous colonial and commercial interests in the Western hemisphere, where the United States claimed to be the final arbiter of all disputes. Third, and finally, the growth of American naval power could have served as a point of contention between the two.[13] Why, then, despite the evidence of a major transition in power between Britain and the United States, and despite several areas in which the two could have come into conflict escalating into war, did the two resolve their differences peacefully?

Building benignity

We propose that, during this period, the United States and the United Kingdom exercised restraint and practiced accommodation resulting in the mutual attribution of benign character. We will document these moves by discussing four issues. First, we will outline the concessions that each made in their relations with the other. Second, we will document that both the United States and the United Kingdom stopped planning for war with the other. Third, we will note instances where the United States or the United Kingdom actually favored increases in power by the other. Finally, we will cite statements by the United States and the United Kingdom to the effect that the other was seen as benign and therefore could be trusted. Before continuing, however, we should note that the pattern of benign action and attribution of benignity was not symmetrical. Throughout the period Britain both took more benign action and attributed more benign character to the United States than vice-versa.[14]

Restraint and accommodation

The first step in the construction of benignity occurred through concessions made within the US–UK dyad. The first and perhaps most telling incident was the Venezuelan boundary dispute, which was ostensibly between British Guiana and Venezuela.[15] When the British had assumed power from the Dutch in 1814, the border had not been precisely established. As such, British subjects began settling in areas (known as the Schomburgk line) that were contested but formerly held by the Dutch. Furthermore, by the 1890s, both parties began making territorial claims that were beyond any that they had made previously. In this climate, US Secretary of State Richard Olney introduced his "twenty-inch gun" declaration, stating the Monroe Doctrine required that the United States make itself involved (because the dispute was in the Western hemisphere).[16]

In his response several months later, British Prime Minister Salisbury rejected the American claim that it had a role in the conflict.[17] The conflict peaked when President Cleveland declared in a speech to Congress that it was "the duty of the United States to resist by every means in its power" the British action.[18] The crisis was ultimately resolved by concessions on the part of both the United States and the United Kingdom. First, and perhaps most crucially, the British conceded the American right to intervene and to establish an arbitration panel.[19] The United States conceded the specific point that areas settled for more than 50 years would be excluded by the arbitrators.[20] Consequently, the settlement that was eventually achieved largely favored the British at the expense of the Venezuelans.

British concessions were also crucial in resolving the Alaskan boundary dispute and the dispute over an isthmian canal. The former dispute was rooted in an imprecise boundary between Alaska and Canada which the United States had inherited from Russia.[21] Canada accepted the US interpretation of the boundary until gold was discovered in the Klondike in 1896. Despite Canadian claims, a *modus vivendi* was achieved that favored the United States, which Canada accepted under pressure from London. Canada had also pressed the mother country to link American concessions on the Alaskan boundary to British concessions on a proposed isthmian canal (to be discussed shortly). In the event, Britain de-linked the two, angering Canada.[22] In taking this step, the British Ambassador to Washington, Julian Pauncefote, stated, "America seems to be our only friend just now, and it would be unfortunate to quarrel with her."[23] The British conceded in the eventual settlement, angering Canada.[24]

The US–UK dispute over the creation of an isthmian canal began with the Clayton Bulwer Treaty of 1850.[25] This treaty specified that the canal be built by both Britain and the United States, and be strictly regulated in order to keep the canal from biasing one country over others during times of war or peace. When President McKinley reignited the idea of a canal in his address to Congress in 1898, he neglected even to mention the British or the Clayton Bulwer Treaty. More than any of the other disputes between the two parties, the isthmian canal dispute saw the British concede virtually every point demanded by the United States. When the first Hay–Pauncefote treaty (rejected by the US Senate for not being sufficiently favorable to American interests) failed, the British agreed to sign a second treaty, conceding several points that they had initially rejected and gaining virtually nothing from the United States.[26] In making these concessions Britain exercised restraint, contributing to the creation of an image of itself as benign.

In a final dispute the United States conceded in the face of British opposition.[27] In Guatemala, British financiers held most of the country's national debt. When dictator Manuel Cabrera repudiated the claim, the British put pressure on his regime. American Secretary of the Treasury Philander C. Knox strongly suggested that the British give "consideration to the predominant interests of the United States in the Caribbean republics," and allow a takeover of the debts by Americans.[28] Instead, the British stood firm and won. British negotiator Lionel Carden traveled to Guatemala and, backed by a warship, gained restoration of the debt claim.[29]

Benign images

While benignity was encouraged by the concessions that both states made in disputes with the other, perhaps the best *indicator* of mutual attribution of benign character is that each state stopped planning for war with the other. British naval planning had long been based on the "two-power standard," which meant that the island nation's navy must be at least as large as the combined forces of the two next-largest navies.[30] In a memorandum from early 1901, First Lord of the Admiralty Lord Selborne adjusted the standard by explicitly excluding the United States from it.[31] Further evidence of the shifting naval calculation emerges from the negotiations on renewal of the Anglo-Japanese alliance in 1905. Both powers agreed that their combined forces should be capable of matching any two potential rivals, but Britain had difficulty convincing Japan that the "two rivals" should exclude the United States. British Foreign Secretary Landsdowne later reflected on the British policy: "We did not consider it at all likely that we should be at war with the United States."[32]

Similar evidence of the British decision to stop planning for war with the United States occurred when Britain began a full-scale withdrawal of its troops from the Western hemisphere. In 1904, Britain proposed to withdraw infantry at British installations in Halifax, Barbados, Trinidad, Bermuda, and Jamaica.[33] As early as 1906, the last units of British regulars had departed from Canadian soil, leaving it to defend itself against the United States in the unlikely event of war breaking out between the two neighbors.[34]

It is difficult to find evidence to support conclusions about the war plans of the United States, because that country was insular enough not to have been planning as actively for its defense as was Britain. Perhaps the clearest evidence is a statement by President Roosevelt to a junior British diplomat in 1905: "[y]ou need not ever be troubled by the nightmare of a possible contest between the two great English-speaking peoples. In keeping ready for possible war I never even take into account a war with England. *I treat it as out of the question.*"[35]

The next and perhaps most striking example of the mutual attribution of benign character by the United States and Britain is that, at various junctures, both favored increases in the power of the other. The British favored increases in American power in the Spanish–American War, during the American effort to annex the Philippines, and with the American construction of an isthmian canal. In the Spanish–American War, the British could have played a strictly neutral role, and publicly did so. Instead, they supported the American grab for international power in several ways. First, the Royal Navy expedited the sale to the United States of two British-built cruisers which had initially been intended for Brazil.[36] Another biased action occurred when a Spanish squadron that might have challenged the United States in the Far East was prevented from getting there because the British enticed the Egyptians to deny them coal.[37] A final incident occurred when the British allowed American vessels to dock and remain in a Chinese bay that the British were about to occupy (and hence by the laws of neutrality the Americans would have been expelled). The British allowed the Americans to stay by delaying the commencement of British occupation.[38]

The British were more overtly behind American efforts to expand its power by annexing the Philippines. First, the British denied Spanish requests to join with other powers to occupy the island. Second, British officials stated that if the Philippines were to be held by any power other than Spain it should be the United States.[39] The British also actively supported the American effort by lending landing craft to the US navy – a gesture that eased the establishment of American power on Panay Island. In addition, a British gunboat intervened to bring about the surrender of the strategic city of Cebu in the central Philippines to US command.[40] The final and perhaps most dramatic case was that of the American effort to construct an isthmian canal. As noted above, the British had a role in the decision because of a prior treaty between the two countries. Yet, despite numerous memoranda on the deleterious impact the canal would have on the Anglo-American balance of power, the

British conceded the canal to the Americans, with (as noted above) virtually no constraints on American plans.[41]

Similarly, the United States subtly aided British efforts to maintain their power in the Boer War.[42] Theodore Roosevelt, vice-president when the conflict broke out, made the clearest statement of American support, proclaiming "[i]t is in the interest of the English-speaking peoples, and therefore of civilization, that English should be the tongue South of the Zambesi."[43] One major action was that, unlike during the early years of World War I, the United States did not stem the flow of credit to the belligerents. This decision greatly favored the British, as the Boers lacked backing for even the smallest loans, whereas nearly 20 percent of Britain's war costs were covered by US loans.[44] A second step was to continue to export goods that were all but obviously military in nature (despite neutrality laws to the contrary), again favoring the British owing to their vastly greater purchasing power.[45] Finally, although American diplomats handled British interests in enemy countries, they failed to even receive Boer representatives until 1902, and then quickly dismissed complaints of unequal treatment of the two belligerents.[46] In short, unlike relations between most states (even allies), the United States and Great Britain aided each other in the increase or defense of their respective power positions, thus demonstrating the benign view that they held of one another.

General statements made by the United States and Britain also shed light on the mutual attribution of benign character. Some of the most firm statements on the American side are from Theodore Roosevelt. As early as 1901 he stated that the United States had "not the least particle of danger to fear in any way or shape" from the British.[47] By 1905 he made clear that "I regard all danger of any trouble between the United States and Great Britain as over, I think forever," and that "England has a more sincere feeling of friendliness for us than has any other power."[48] British sentiments were similar. In an exchange of letters in 1904, Selborne, First Lord of the Admiralty, stated that "[t]here is no party in the United Kingdom nor even in the British Empire which does not contemplate war with the United States of America as the greatest evil which could befall the British Empire in foreign relations."[49] A. H. Lee, a British civil lord, replied that "I cannot for a moment contemplate the possibility of hostilities really taking place" between the United States and the United Kingdom.[50] On the verge of taking office in 1905, Liberal Prime Minister Sir Edward Grey confirmed that he would stand by the three "cardinal features" of British foreign policy, the first of which was "the growing friendship and good feeling between ourselves and the United States, a matter of common ground and common congratulation to all parties in this country."[51]

Agreeing on order

The degree to which Britain and the United States agreed on order during the period of transition was more embryonic than was the mutual attribution of benignity. On hierarchy, for example, although the British saw the United States as a regional hegemon, time elapsed before they would view it as such in global terms. To the Americans, Britain was already clearly departing from its great power role.[52] The Americans and British did, however, agree upon spheres of influence. The crucial turning point here was the Venezuelan crisis. In that conflict, as noted above, Secretary of State Olney began by demanding an American role because the dispute was within the American sphere of influence.[53] The clash occurred when Lord Salisbury refused to recognize the American prerogative to be involved.[54] However, when the British recognized the Americans as having a role in the conflict despite no direct interest in it, the two states crossed the Rubicon in their relations. The British journal *The Spectator* made this point more clearly than diplomats on either side could, stating:

We want nothing that belongs to America, nor do we claim to interfere with what she considers her special "sphere of influence." Our virtual acceptance of the Monroe doctrine when we agreed to the Venezuelan arbitration has removed the risk of serious quarrel in the future.[55]

Although the United States had long maintained little interest in Europe, Britain's move to bow out of the Americas was crucial to the peacefulness of the power transition.

The US–UK relationship was marked by both agreement and disagreement on the rules governing international economic relations. For instance, the United States and Great Britain disagreed on basic principles of trade during this period. Britain had long been a staunch global advocate of free trade.[56] Conversely, although the United States briefly flirted with free trade in the 1870s and 1880s, by the 1890s it had fully embraced protectionism.[57] On the other hand, the two countries did agree on the rules of the international monetary system. Since the 1870s, the world's leading economies were participants in the British-founded and British-centered "gold standard," wherein national currencies were tied to gold at a legally fixed rate.[58] The United States began to move towards the gold standard by adopting the gold-based dollar as its monetary unit in 1873 (and concurrently demonetizing silver).[59] However, the United States almost shifted away from this policy with William Jennings Bryant's bid for the presidency in 1896. In fact, Bryant based his campaign on the evils of the gold standard.[60] When Bryant was defeated by

McKinley, the new president passed the Gold Standard Act in 1900, consolidating the US commitment to those monetary rules.[61]

In short, the United States and Britain agreed on some parts of order and disagreed on others. Spheres of influence and the gold standard were areas where the two powers found much to agree on. This agreement would obviously reduce the probability of conflict and war between them. On matters related to hierarchy and international trade, however, the two countries disagreed. Perhaps this disagreement did not fuel greater clashes than occurred because of the nascent benign images that the two countries were developing.

Agreeing on legitimacy

Normative agreement between the Americans and British appears to have been manifest in at least three ways. The first was an appeal, made less by statesmen than by public figures and lower-level politicians, to the common political culture of democracy, liberty, and freedom in the United States and Britain. This feeling increased especially after the British Reform Bill of 1832, which expanded the number of voters and increased the power of the House of Commons in Britain.[62] In advocating an alliance between Britain and America, American preacher and editor Lyman Abbott proclaimed, "[w]ho can measure the advantage to liberty, to democracy, to popular rights and popular intelligence, to human progress, to a free and practical Christianity, which such an alliance would bring with it?"[63]

The second pillar of the normative legitimacy the two nations agreed upon was the notion of "the White Man's burden." Repeatedly, elites and the press in the two countries stated that they were bound together by their unique ability to address the "needs" of non-European peoples. Again *The Spectator* provided the clearest statement that "our race is meant to do in the world the work of foreman and ganger" and that at the turn of the century Americans could become "fellow-labourers in the work of the better ordering of the world."[64] In sum, it was argued that the two countries were morally bound to better the world through colonization.

The third and final pillar was Anglo-American racialism. Elites on both sides of the Atlantic viewed the two countries as of the same "race."[65] Moreover, against the background of social Darwinism, many Americans and Britons saw their common race as superior to others.[66] In addition, many understood the core of international relations to consist of conflicts between the races. In that context, the British and the Americans were morally bound to aid one another if they should clash with those of other racial groups.[67] A final point is that Anglo-American racialism meant that a war between the two countries would be akin to fratricide, something that should be avoided at all costs.[68]

These three common moral imperatives bound the two nations, providing them with common goals and keeping them from war. Furthermore, it is likely that the common normative grounds between the two countries made restraint and accommodation easier and contributed to the development of benign images.

Anticipating the critics

Criticisms may be leveled against the arguments we have outlined above. Some have argued that the British faced multiple threats and merely picked the more geographically distant challenger when deciding with whom to ally.[69] This logic might explain a British strategy of distancing itself from the United States or even a traditional alliance to aggregate its capabilities. However, the claim that Britain was merely balancing power cannot explain its efforts to cultivate *better* relations with the United States, even helping it increase its power.[70] According to realist logic, this type of action would be extremely dangerous because today's ally may become tomorrow's enemy. Moreover, this logic fails to explain benign American actions and its increasing view that the British were benign.[71] American behavior is difficult for the critics to explain because the United States neither needed nor sought any formal alliance guarantees from the British. A second more specific critique is that the British conceded in the crises discussed above owing to the balance of power.[72] Yet, the balance of power was never as clearly in favor of the United States as the critics pretend. On the eve of the Venezuelan crisis, for example, the United States had no real navy to speak of (only three first-class battleships) as it faced the greatest navy in the world.[73] Furthermore, in that and other crises the United States had little active support from the other great powers, and might even have faced others as rivals had war broken out between Britain and the United States.[74] In sum, the alternative arguments we have outlined here are inadequate to explain this case.

Summary

The Anglo-American rapprochement can clearly be explained by the model outlined in this volume. First and foremost, the two states exercised restraint and practiced mutual accommodation, which led, in time, to the mutual attribution of benign character. They did so by conceding in dyadic crises, by canceling war plans with each other, and by favoring efforts by the other state to increase or maintain its power. However, the recognition by the United States and Britain of each other's sphere of influence was also important, as was the existence of common norms such as democracy, freedom, and the "White Man's burden."

The Concert of Europe

The Concert of Europe (1815–1848) has long appeared to students of international politics as an anomaly. In contrast to the competitive and violent relations that characterized Europe both before and after, the Concert embodied a peaceful phase in European diplomatic history. For over 30 years between the Congress of Vienna and the revolutions of 1848, the great powers resolved their disputes without resorting to force.

We will first demonstrate that virtually all of the great powers exercised overt restraint at some point during the Concert. Moreover, most states accepted "second-best" solutions to problems when their preferred outcome was rejected. Even when states were fundamentally opposed to a solution reached within the Concert, they voiced opposition but avoided threats of force, in effect abstaining rather than vetoing action. We also argue that the members of the Concert agreed on fundamental aspects of the regional order obtaining in early nineteenth-century Europe. Recognition of spheres of influence was a crucial part of the Concert, and some of its most acute tensions occurred where such agreement was weak. Moreover, the regional hierarchy was largely stable and clear. Finally, we will discuss agreement on legitimate norms. At least three of the great powers – Russia, Austria-Hungary, and Prussia – agreed on the just nature of monarchical political regimes, and all of the great powers professed Christianity. Before turning to these claims, we will begin with an overview of the Concert and its relevant players.

Overview

From 1792 until 1815, Prussia, Austria, Britain, and Russia episodically formed and then dissolved balancing coalitions against France.[75] Britain was the only state that consistently balanced against France, while Austria, Russia, and Prussia entered and exited the various coalitions based on political expediency. However, in 1814 at Chaumont, Britain, Austria, Russia, and Prussia pledged to resist Napoleon until his defeat while refusing to accept a separate peace.[76] By November 1815, the four allies had agreed upon a general European peace settlement – the Treaty of Vienna. A final important development in 1815 was the signing of the Holy Alliance by the monarchs of Russia, Austria, and Prussia, binding them in Christian solidarity.

The Concert faced numerous crises from 1815 to 1848. At Troppau (1820), Laibach (1821), and Verona (1822), the members eventually resolved to send troops to suppress revolutions in Naples and Spain. The great powers also entered into a series of crises over Greek independence between 1821 and 1827. Dynastic questions led to a revolution in Portugal in 1828 and to the Carlist Wars in Spain (1834–1839), which the allies were forced to address. Finally, clashes between Turkey and Egypt between 1831 and 1833 and between 1839 and 1841 occupied great power attention.

When numerous revolutions broke out in 1848, the Concert suffered major blows. In Austria and France new leaders came to power and they were far less enamored with the Concert than their predecessors had been. Britain had long been skeptical of the utility of the Concert and Russia was beginning to bridle at the restraint the Concert placed on its policy in the East. Consequently, it is of little surprise that the Concert failed to prevent the Crimean War (1854–1856) or the Wars of German Unification (1863–1871).

Building benignity

This section will document the actions that members of the Concert took which had the potential to contribute to the construction of benign images. These actions included restraint, wherein a state refrained from pursuing immediate goals in anticipation of a negative action by its peers. Mutual accommodation was also prevalent, as states both accepted options other than their ideal outcome, and did not attempt to veto courses of action to which they were fundamentally opposed. In this period, virtually all of the five great powers both restrained themselves and accommodated others. It is necessary to recognize, however, that, despite these actions, benign character was not mutually attributed in a lasting sense. In part, as will be discussed below, there was a fundamental disagreement on an important portion of the "order" of nineteenth-century Europe, namely the crumbling Ottoman Empire, as well as spheres of influence. However, there were also residues of past behavior that the steps toward benignity could not erase. For example, Russia's aggressive past in Poland and vis-à-vis the Ottoman Empire made its peers skeptical that its actions during the Concert truly signified a change in its character.[77] Our discussion of restraint and accommodation will begin with the Congress itself, and then turn to the Troppau, Laibach, and Verona conferences. That will be followed by a discussion of the Greek independence crisis. Finally, we will explore the Concert's responses to the two Turko-Egyptian crises.[78]

The Concert began with the Congress of Vienna, which witnessed several acts of restraint and mutual accommodation.[79] The first and foremost instance of this was the lenient treatment of France.[80] Britain, Russia, and Austria all had reasons for restraining themselves vis-à-vis prostrate France. The British, led by Viscount Castlereagh, and the Austrians, represented by Metternich, were concerned with preserving a France large enough to counter Russian power on the European continent.[81] Whatever the logic, the three were united in opposition to Prussia, which was totally opposed to the lenient peace.[82] However, the Prussians stood aside in light of the agreement of the other powers and signed on to the peace. A second important example of restraint and accommodation was the German question. The most important issue was the creation of a German confederation and the relative power of Austria and Prussia within it. After much wrangling, a compromise settlement was reached, based on a loose confederation with Austria wielding the presidency, while Prussia exercised de facto hegemony over the states of northern Germany.[83] Equally interesting was the Russian acceptance of Austrian leadership despite an opportunity to disrupt the scheme.[84]

The first test of the Concert came with two revolutions in 1820: one in Spain and one in Naples. In January of that year, the Spanish military rose against their autocratic Bourbon king, Ferdinand VII. They took advantage of the dire straits of the country in the aftermath of the Napoleonic Wars and hoped to institute a constitution that would place the bulk of governing power in an elected parliament.[85] Tzar Alexander of Russia immediately called for intervention to suppress the (as he saw it) illegitimate and contagious revolutionary movement. Castlereagh, the British Foreign Secretary, opposed intervention because the revolution was unlikely to threaten the security of any of the major powers. Metternich was instead concerned that intervention would entail either Russian troops passing through the heart of Europe, or French intervention – with the associated danger that France would attempt to renew the Napoleonic domination of Spain.[86] An important part of the debate over intervention was that, as will be discussed below in the context of order, Spain was not in any single state's recognized sphere of influence. It appeared as if the Concert would be inactive when confronted with its first major crisis.

Fortunately for the Concert, the Spanish revolution was followed by a revolt in Austrian-controlled Naples. There, again, military officers rose against their monarch, Ferdinand I. The response to the Neapolitan revolt was more positive. In large part this was because the great powers recognized Italy and specifically Naples as within Austria's sphere of influence. Therefore, when Metternich declared his aim to intervene on behalf of Ferdinand I, he had the support of the Concert.[87] The Tzar's initial resistance was overcome by Metternich's elucidation of the Europe-wide revolutionary threat that needed to be checked in Naples. Only France continued to oppose intervention, but it, like Prussia with the lenient peace for France, eventually allowed intervention to go forward.[88] At Troppau and Laibach, the Concert powers discussed the revolutions and decided upon an outcome for Naples.[89]

Far more interesting, however, was the return to the question of the Spanish revolt. Because of Naples, Austria could no longer be a strong opponent of intervention. Britain had become even more opposed to intervention in Spain, as the insular George Canning became the new Foreign Secretary.[90] The situation in Spain escalated as well, as Ferdinand VII openly appealed to the Tzar for assistance.[91] In conference at Verona, Austria, Prussia, and Russia agreed that intervention was necessary and sent notes to the revolutionary government in Spain threatening such intervention if the king were not restored.[92] Britain abstained for the aforementioned reasons, while France abstained in protest that it was not formally endorsed as the power to intervene if the rebels did not agree to the appeals of the Concert. In the wake of the notes, France intervened without the consent of the Concert. This action on its face appears to confirm George Canning's reaction at the time that it was "[e]very nation for itself and God for us all."[93] There are two important points to the contrary. First, no state threatened or went to war over French intervention in Spain. Thus, although Britain and Austria in particular opposed French intervention, they abstained rather than actively opposing it. Second, France agreed to several conditions governing its intervention in Spain, most notably that its troops be withdrawn when their objectives were achieved (which they were).[94] In a myriad of ways, then, the revolutions in Spain and Naples demonstrated the restraint and accommodation of the great powers during the Concert.

Whereas the crises surrounding Spain and Naples were based on a desire for regime change, the crises surrounding Greece and Belgium centered on struggles for independence. For the Greeks, the struggle was about their independence from the Ottoman Turks. This was one of the most difficult crises for the great powers, however, because of their drastically conflicting interests and a fundamental disagreement over whose sphere of influence Greece fell into. Russia had the clearest interests, as the power best poised to acquire the spoils of the disintegrating Ottoman Empire as well as being the primary religious patron of the Orthodox Greeks. All the other great powers preferred to preserve Ottoman rule in Greece. Austria-Hungary's interest in the area was based on the fact that Greece was located close to its border with Turkey and to its interests in the Balkans. The French were more concerned with rejuvenating their status (and restraining Russia) than with the specific interests of the

Greek question. Finally, Britain was always interested in the dissolving Ottoman Empire because so many of the issues threatened to impact its interests in wartime and peacetime sea travel.[95] Perhaps most important, however, was not the clash of interests, which was present in all of the crises discussed here, but rather the disagreement on spheres of influence. Russia felt that Greece was within its sphere, but each of the other great powers disputed this claim.[96]

Shortly after the Greek revolt broke out in 1821, Russia sent a unilateral ultimatum to the Turks demanding that they protect Christians, which Turkey summarily rejected.[97] Given the disagreement over spheres, a Russo-Turkish war seemed a certainty. However, Metternich and Castlereagh succeeded in convincing the Tzar to exercise restraint and work towards a Concert-based solution.[98] For the next four years the Russians attempted to find a multilateral solution to the problem, at one point even circulating a *Memoire* which "drew attention to Russia's previous self-denial."[99] By 1825 Russia was frustrated with the lack of recognition of its restraint and a lack of success in resolving the Greek question. The problem was heightened with a renewed Turkish offensive in 1825, which looked to topple Greek resistance, and with the accession of Tzar Nicholas I to the throne in Russia, a ruler more committed to Russian interests than to the Concert.[100] Once again, unilateral intervention by Russia seemed imminent.

Early in 1826, however, British Foreign Minister Canning accommodated the Russians by agreeing to the St. Petersburg Protocol (which France would sign a year later), which entailed a joint offer of mediation between the Greeks and Turks, with Greek independence as its object.[101] After the St. Petersburg Protocol, Russian behavior took a turn that was far less benign. The day following the Protocol, Tzar Nicholas sent a series of demands to Turkey (having nothing to do with Greece) which the Turks, cognizant of the Protocol, quickly accepted in the Convention of Akkerman (1826). Noteworthy is the fact that none of the great powers protested or threatened violence against Russia – not even Austria, which was most threatened by Akkerman.[102] Instead, cooperation proceeded apace. Britain and France sent ships to the Mediterranean to participate in a naval blockade. The three powers eventually destroyed a combined Turko-Egyptian fleet at the battle of Navarino (1827).[103] On the heels of Navarino, the Turks disavowed the Convention of Akkerman and Russia declared war in 1828. Again, although earlier Russian aggrandizement was fundamentally to blame, the other great powers stayed out of the conflict. By 1829 the Russians were victorious over the Ottomans, but they did not press for further gains in the Treaty of Adrianople; instead, it was largely based on the 1826 Convention of Akkerman.[104] Shortly after Adrianople, the Ottoman Empire conceded on the question of Greek independence and the crisis drew to a close.[105] The Greek crisis was colored by Russian impatience and aggrandizement but also by surprising restraint and accommodation by the other great powers, several of which had interests that could have led them to more conflictual, even violent, action.

The crises over Turkey and Egypt began in 1831 with the demand by Muhammad (Mehemet) Ali, Pasha of Egypt, that Turkey cede Syria to it.[106] When Turkey refused, war broke out. While Russia, and to a lesser extent Britain and Austria, sought to preserve the Ottoman Empire against the upstart Ali, the French sought to improve their influence in the region by supporting Egypt.[107] By 1832, Ali's troops were so successful that it appeared as if they might take Constantinople. On the verge of this event, the Turks requested assistance from the Concert powers, and only Russia agreed to intervene. Although the other powers did not protest formally, they were concerned with potential Russian aggrandizement.[108] Instead, Russia convinced Turkey to sign the Convention of Kutahya (1833). While the Russians made no gains, they did sign a defensive alliance with the Turks (Unkiar-Skelessi 1833), signifying that Russia was the Ottoman Empire's protector.[109] Some, notably the British, were concerned about the Russo-Turkish defensive alliance. Instead of expressing concern, Austria chose to combine with Russia (they were later joined by Prussia) in the Treaty of Munchengratz (1833) to guarantee the preservation of Ottoman territories.[110]

Peace reigned between Egypt and Turkey until the Turkish Sultan Mahmud II attempted to regain his losses by attacking Egypt in 1839. Again Turkey suffered massive losses, but this time the Concert powers (excluding France) accommodated each other and agreed on a Collective Note to Mahmud offering to negotiate on his behalf with Egypt.[111] Mahmud agreed and the four developed the 1840 Convention for Peace of the Levant, entailing both general principles on the Ottoman Empire and a specific settlement to the war. France rejected the settlement, and its minister-president Adolphe Thiers made veiled threats of violence to the other four great powers. After Austro-British military efforts against Egypt, the Pasha Ali conceded defeat and accepted the peace settlement.[112] Moreover, Thiers resigned his post as minister-president and France, eager to rejoin the Concert, signed the Straits Convention of 1841.[113] In sum, the Egyptian crises demonstrate a Russian willingness to restrain itself and a general sense of accommodation and cooperative efforts to resolve the crises.

We may glean some general patterns from these complex historical details. First, in almost all of the crises discussed here, most members of the Concert either restrained themselves or accommodated their neighbors. Second, even when they were less willing to do this, they did not threaten violence to achieve their desired settlement. Nevertheless, the record was not all positive, and lasting benign images did not ensue. As noted above, in at least one incident – France and the Turko-Egyptian crisis – violence was threatened. Moreover, Russia, feeling frustrated at the lack of benignity attributed to it, acted without restraint at the Convention of Akkerman (1826). These acts, particularly given residues of past aggrandizement by both these countries, inhibited the development of benign images in Europe during this period.

Agreeing on order

Order was an important part of the success of the Concert, and particularly of the absence of war for nearly half a century. The primary way in which the members of the Concert agreed upon order was through their agreement that particular geographic areas would be the spheres of influence of particular members of the Concert. When agreement on spheres was strong it allowed for a state to deal as it saw fit with crises in its sphere. If, however, two or more states contested a sphere, cooperation was more difficult and conflict more likely. In this section, we will document which powers held what spheres and we will discuss the importance of agreement or lack of agreement on spheres of influence in the different crises discussed above.

Britain was recognized by all of the great powers as having two related spheres of influence. The first was Britain's undisputed mastery of the seas and colonial areas.[114] No crises emerged over colonies or maritime laws, but it is certain that, if they had, Britain would have had virtually a free hand in resolving them. The second British sphere was Portugal. Britain intervened to quash the 1828 revolution in Portugal without support, consent, or formal approval from any of its peers.[115] Similarly, Austria-Hungary was perceived by the Concert to be dominant on the Italian peninsula.[116] As discussed above, Austria's 1823 intervention in Naples was not contested by any of the great powers (even France). Austria also shared a sphere of influence with Prussia over the German Confederation. Consequently, those two states were seen as being responsible for crises in Germany.[117] Because of the aggression of Revolutionary and Napoleonic France, past French spheres of influence, such as Spain and the Netherlands, were contested. This is why French intervention in both crises was tolerated by the Concert only under strict limitations.[118] Finally, Russia's recognized sphere was Poland. Thus, it handled the Polish revolution of 1830 as if it were an internal affair.[119] However, as noted repeatedly above, Russia felt that it had a sphere of influence encompassing the Ottoman Empire, whereas the rest of the

Concert firmly rejected this notion. This disaccord proved problematic in both the Greek and Turko-Egyptian crises.

Another important facet to the agreement of Concert powers on order was a relatively stable hierarchy for the relevant years. Historian Paul Schroeder claims that a "dual hegemony" was shared by Britain and Russia during the Concert.[120] Indeed, after the Napoleonic Wars, Britain was the dominant naval power while Russia maintained the world's largest army.[121] The places of Austria and Prussia were equally clear. Austria, while having turned Napoleon's defeat into a windfall of territorial gains, was evidently in decline.[122] Prussia was on the rise, but still not with the interests or the capabilities to be on par with Austria, not to mention Russia or Britain. It should be clear from the above analysis that Prussia played virtually no part in most of the major crises of the Concert period. Finally, France was the wild card of the Concert period. France certainly had the latent power (even after the Vienna settlement) to challenge Russia and Britain, but lacked both internal cohesion and international status. Consequently, France tried to improve its perceived position in the European pecking order, often, as in the Turko-Egyptian crises, antagonizing its neighbors in the process.

Agreeing on legitimacy

Common normative consensus was a particularly strong element during the Concert, although it was not unanimous. While Russia, Austria, and Prussia shared norms, Britain and at times France usually stood apart. Agreement on legitimacy centered around religious consensus and agreement on domestic political regimes. Concurrent with the Congress of Vienna was the initiation of the Holy Alliance, championed by Tzar Alexander. The Holy Alliance committed Russia, Austria, Prussia, and later France to act, "in their reciprocal relations, upon the sublime truths which the Holy Religion of our Savior teaches."[123] Although there remained significant denominational differences between these four powers, Tzar Alexander appealed to a super-denominational union of Christian monarchs.[124] What the Alliance envisioned was that the monarchs of Europe should act in their relations towards one another with the principles of Christianity foremost in their thoughts. Many at the time, and since, have criticized the Holy Alliance. Castlereagh referred to it as "a piece of sublime mysticism and nonsense," while even Metternich (whose monarch was a member) claimed that it was "high sounding nothing."[125] We should also recognize that Britain remained fully outside both the formal agreement and the sense of normative consensus throughout the Concert period. At minimum, however, the Holy Alliance contributed to the perceived legitimacy of the Concert by the four members. Because Russia, Austria, and Prussia played key roles in constructing the Vienna settlement and sought to preserve it, challenges to the status quo (especially revolutions) would be challenges to the perceived Christian principles as well.[126]

A second and equally important normative element was agreement on the just nature of domestic political regimes. In 1789 the French first raised the question of the "divine right" of kings. By executing Louis XVI in 1793, however, they generated opposition to any form of liberalization that would last over half a century.[127] The three eastern powers – Austria, Prussia, and Russia – were the most convinced of this course. They were so committed to retaining the divine right principle that they suppressed efforts to attain constitutions, even quite conservative ones. For example, Austria backed the Prussian government in resisting efforts by its populace to demand a constitution in 1820.[128] Britain and France were not party to this normative agreement. Yet the agreement on just political regimes by the three conservative monarchies served as a guidepost for dealing with the numerous crises which arose. This logic helped convince Austria of the need for intervention in Spain, and kept Russia from intervening in Greece as long as it did.[129] The exclusion of Britain and France on this issue, and the exclusion of Britain from the Holy Alliance, did not lead to open hostility and tension but no doubt weakened the Concert more than would have been the case had all members agreed on common norms.

Summary

The Concert of Europe was characterized by steps toward mutual attribution of benign character, as well some agreement on order and legitimacy. States repeatedly held back when they could have gained more but knew it would displease their neighbors. They also conceded to their peers if they knew their concession was the only way to reach agreement. Even when states fundamentally disagreed with each other, they would abstain from sanctioning the decision but would not block it. Only once during the duration of the Concert did one state even threaten another with violence (France over the Turko-Egyptian crisis). Agreement on order was similarly robust. States recognized spheres in which others were dominant, and hence could manage crises on their own. Conversely, when conflicts were specifically strong they often had to do with disputes over spheres of influence. Hierarchy was also relatively stable and clear, making for little jostling for rank. Finally, states were bound not merely by their benign acts or by their agreement on rules, but also, for Russia, Austria, and Prussia, by their commitment to common norms. Both

Christianity and the monarchy provided focal points for greater legitimacy and policy coordination.

ASEAN

ASEAN, while not formally a security community, is nevertheless a self-conscious multi-state collective dedicated to preserving economic, sociocultural, and political links within a particular region – and ultimately to preventing war among its member states. In this latter goal they have succeeded, with no inter-member war fought since ASEAN's founding in 1967. Like the Concert of Europe, ASEAN is a good – albeit not flawless – example of an organization aimed at managing the vicissitudes of power among its members, if not power transitions in the traditional sense. In this section, we will present an overview of the organization, documenting its historical evolution, before turning to a discussion of each of the three variables of interest in this study – benignity, order, and legitimacy. We will demonstrate that these phenomena were facilitated by the extension of membership to Indonesia and Vietnam (two of the region's primary belligerents prior to ASEAN's formation), as well as by the shared values of capitalism, self-sufficiency, anti-colonialism, and anti-communism.

Overview

ASEAN was established on 8 August 1967 in Bangkok, with Malaysia, Singapore, Indonesia, the Philippines, and Thailand as founding members. Brunei was the first additional country to be added (in 1984); Vietnam was admitted in 1995, Laos and Myanmar (Burma) joined in 1997, and, most recently, Cambodia joined in April 1999. Bolstering the organizational structure of ASEAN has been the ASEAN Regional Forum (known by its abbreviation ARF), which was formed in 1994. ARF comprises all of the ASEAN members plus the United States, Japan, Canada, the European Union, South Korea, Australia, New Zealand, as well as Russia, China, and India. (Papua New Guinea is an observer.) ARF's mandate is to broaden the discussion of Asian security issues to include the Pacific region, and to contribute to conflict prevention – as distinct from conflict resolution.[130]

Both ASEAN and ARF are the latest in a line of attempts at multilateralism in South-East Asia. The earliest expression of it came in the form of the Bandung Conference of 1955, comprising the newly decolonized states of Africa and Asia. Although the Conference embodied multilateral cooperation, its primary aim was to lobby internationally for the interests of the South-East Asia region. Following that, the collective efforts of the South-East Asian states shifted toward establishing a cooperative environment in which the security aims of each state would be facilitated by the others. In this vein, and more closely approaching what would become ASEAN, the Association of Southeast Asia (ASA) was established on 31 July 1961 by Thailand, Malaya, and the Philippines. The organization was short-lived, however; ASA activities were soon suspended as the Philippines and Malaya suffered tensions over the former's claim to Sabah. (This tension would be a recurring theme in the early years of ASEAN, as will be discussed below.) Moreover, ASA was stymied by its limited membership and by accusations of it being pro-Western.[131] This claim laid the foundation for a more inward-looking organization that would ultimately come in the form of ASEAN.

In the meantime, Maphilindo was formed in 1963, its name invoking the three founding member states: Malaya, the Philippines, and Indonesia. Maphilindo was established in an effort to mitigate tension arising from Malayan border disputes, thus foreshadowing the active attempts at projecting benign images that would become prevalent in the years of ASEAN. With the establishment of Malaysia later that year, the attempt at multilateralism embodied in Maphilindo was ended prematurely.

ASEAN was established in the wake of the ending of the *konfrontasi* (policy of confrontation) between Indonesia and Malaysia (1963–1965). ASEAN exemplified the attempt to deal with regional problems from a regional perspective, and in this goal has been largely successful. In principle, any South-East Asian state was entitled to join, and, with the inclusion of Cambodia, all are now members. The change of regime in Indonesia – from that of communist leader Sukarno to the more conservative General Suharto (in a military coup on 1 October 1965) – enabled the establishment of the organization, whereby the member states could attempt to forge a convergence on ideological and security matters. As the regional hegemon occupying 56 percent of the total land mass of the association's states,[132] Indonesia was "conscious of a regional mistrust" of it and "therefore envisaged better prospects for pursuing regional ambition by attracting the willing cooperation of neighbouring states, including recent adversaries."[133] Therefore, although strategic restraint was certainly a contributing factor to the emergence and maintenance of ASEAN, we should not confuse self-binding with "selfless" behavior.

The aims of the founding members were enshrined in the Bangkok Declaration of 1967, which eclipsed political and security cooperation in favor of economic, cultural, and social linkages. Nevertheless, members pledged to "'ensure their stability and security from external interference' as well as to 'promote peace and stability through abiding respect for peace and the rule of law.'"[134] Given the emphasis on regionalism, members also acknowledged the objective of removing foreign military bases, despite the reluctance by the Philippines, Singapore, and Thailand to forgo the US military presence that they had thus far enjoyed.[135] This sentiment has been termed "collective self-reliance"[136] and emerged out of the anti-colonialist attitude prevalent among the newly decolonized states of the developing world.

Thus, given that security rivalries had historically been the defining aspect of relations among the states of South-East Asia, the ASEAN states attempted to shape their interactions according to the "ASEAN way," guided by a spirit of *mufakat* (consensus) and *musjawara* (consultation) – concepts drawn from Islamic precepts of governance. This does not mean that security rivalries are now absent, only that they are dealt with before full-scale conflict might occur. And, rather than focus upon external military threats, the members of ASEAN have adopted the principle of "regional resilience" to fulfill what they see as the most pressing need: internal security. "Resistance" encapsulates the idea that has become central to much of security thinking in the developing world: the belief that the primary threat to security emanates from domestic dissatisfaction, and that economic prosperity can contribute to domestic stability. As such, one observer has coined the phrase "collective internal security" to describe the organization's aims.[137] Following this, ASEAN has been careful to distance itself from the now-defunct SEATO (Southeast Asia Treaty Organization, 1954–1977), which the region's states now view as a relic of Cold War superpower confrontation. Traditional security co-operation is eschewed in favor of more informal channels for a mutually beneficial regionalism. And, unlike SEATO, which was backed by the United States in an effort to counter Communist China, ASEAN does not bill itself as a collective defense organization, and actively resists external interference in its regional affairs.

We will now turn to a discussion of perhaps the most salient conceptual underpinning of the organization: the projection and mutual attribution of benign images among the ASEAN's members.

Building benignity

Elsewhere, Yuen Foong Khong has written of the gradual sense of "we-ness" that evolved under the terms of ASEAN,[138] and that a sense of "community" was not evident from the organization's beginnings. It is this sense of community that best encapsulates the idea of benignity that is of interest in this chapter. In addition to the Malaysian–Filipino dispute over the Sabah region in Northern Borneo mentioned above, ASEAN carried a legacy of bilateral conflicts into its early years of consensus-building. These tensions meant that the organization has faced more obstacles to reaching the point at which internal power differentials may no longer be seen as threatening. Part of the overall dilemma obstructing harmonious relations between ASEAN's member states has been the issue of different religious and ethnic groups overlapping within state boundaries, many of which were the result of colonial whims. An example of this was Thailand's ongoing fear of Malaysian support for Muslim irredentists within Thailand's southern provinces. Another barrier was the different external threat foci among the organization's founding members: Vietnam for Singapore and Thailand; China for Indonesia and Malaysia.[139] The rest of this section will explore a number of bilateral relationships within ASEAN, illustrating the points at which each member of the dyad attempted strategic restraint, as well as where each was able to form benign images of the other. Following this, we will discuss the operation of benignity at the level of the organization as a whole.

Indonesia–Malaysia

Because ASEAN was established on the heels of Indonesia's *konfrontasi* policy toward Malaysia, the Indonesian–Malaysian dyad is perhaps the most pertinent relationship to examine in order to determine the degree to which benignity, order, and legitimacy have facilitated peaceful relations. The change from the Sukarno to Suharto regimes has already been discussed, as has the role of that event in facilitating the establishment of ASEAN itself. Not only did Indonesia attempt to portray itself as a less malevolent power in the region, but it actively sought to signal to its neighbors that it had benign intentions. Thus, it began its association with ASEAN by cooperating with Malaysia against communist insurgents in Northern Borneo[140] – a clear acknowledgment of the communist legacy it was attempting to bury.

Later years saw continued Indonesian attempts at self-restraint. Whereas *konfrontasi* had been sparked initially in September 1963 by Indonesia's attempt to prevent the union of Malaya with Singapore, Sabah, and Sarawak, by 1966 Indonesia explicitly agreed to support the sovereign wishes of the Sabah and Sarawak residents, thus in effect legitimating Malaysia's control over these areas.[141] And the following year, the two countries exchanged diplomatic recognition – on 31 August 1967, less than a month after the establishment of ASEAN. During the next two decades, Indonesia and Malaysia entered into agreements to curtail the entry of illegal workers (in 1984)[142] and undertook joint border patrol efforts.

However, as Michael Antolik notes, both Indonesia and Malaysia had strategic reasons for exhibiting mutually reassuring behavior. First, Indonesia had suffered significant economic costs arising from its previously belligerent policies in the region, including inflation, loss of exports, and the accrual of a significant debt. For this reason too, "good behavior" would help to entice creditors to reschedule its debts. Finally, as the new regime was in the midst of trying officials associated with *konfrontasi*, Suharto was going to do everything in his power to distance himself from his predecessor's era of more belligerent relations.[143]

On the Malaysian side, that country was in the midst of experiencing internal dissent in the form of its Islamic movement, and therefore needed to focus its energies domestically. Compounding this internal problem was the influx of refugees that Malaysia had absorbed from southern Indonesia from 1978 onward. Finally, the largest threat as perceived by Malaysia came in the form of China, thus underscoring the need to focus its energies away from Indonesia.[144]

Malaysia–Philippines

As was mentioned above, ASEAN was established in the wake of the Sabah dispute between Malaysia and the Philippines. However, the two countries signed an anti-smuggling agreement in September 1967, thus paving the way for improved relations. Nevertheless, less than a year later, in March 1968, what has come to be called the Corregidor Affair erupted at the military camp of the same name in the Philippines. A group of Filipino Muslims who were being trained to infiltrate into Sabah were killed by their officers. Rather than use ASEAN to mediate between the two countries, Malaysia turned to the United Nations and cut off bilateral talks. In response, the Philippines withdrew its ambassador from Malaysia, and soon after introduced an act in Congress stating that the Philippines would unilaterally extend sovereignty over Sabah. Malaysia responded by abrogating the anti-smuggling agreement as well as recalling its ambassador. Soon after, Malaysia commissioned British jet fighters to fly over Sabah's capital. Ultimately, at the ASEAN Ministerial Meeting in December 1969, the two countries agreed to restore relations. It is unclear, however, whether this was due to the good offices of the organization, or out of fear of the Nixon Doctrine.[145] The latter stated that the United States would no longer support conventional defense (by American forces) against communist challenges in the region,[146] though it would back local forces attempting the same. Relations finally improved further with the election of Corazon Aquino as president of the Philippines, followed by a new constitution (in February 1987) that in effect acknowledged Malaysia's hold over Sabah. Thus, although ASEAN did play a role in smoothing relations between the two members, the organization must be seen against a broader backdrop of geopolitical imperatives.

Malaysia–Singapore

Relations between Malaysia and Singapore have been necessarily tentative, owing especially to the fact that Singapore was created out of Malaysia in the form of the August 1965 separation. Unlike Eve from Adam's rib, however, Singapore was less than amorous towards its larger neighbor. Nor did it place much trust in ASEAN in the association's early years. Indeed, the city-state feared that ASEAN would simply serve as a "launching pad" to further Indonesian and Malaysian designs upon the region.[147] Thus, Singapore embarked on what has come to be called a "poison shrimp" policy: a deliberate course of deterrence intended to make any potential attack upon it unduly costly. It was not until it aligned with the United States (primarily to expand its market access) that it managed to improve relations with its neighbors,[148] thus underscoring another channel for projecting benignity: alliance choices. Once Singapore's neighbors witnessed it allying with a power they too considered friendly, they were assured of Singapore's benign intentions. This dynamic illustrates a point of convergence between what we are arguing here and classic geopolitical assumptions. Thus, although Singapore had economic reasons for allying with the United States, this decision nevertheless served as a way of transmitting benign intentions towards its neighbors.

Another catalyst for improved relations was the identification of other, more salient, adversaries – China in the case of Malaysia, and Indonesia in the case of Singapore. Finally, the efforts by Singapore actively to nurture a national identity among its citizenry alleviated Malaysia's fears about Singapore supporting insurgents within Malaysia, specifically its own ethnic Chinese minority.[149] Nevertheless, tensions arose with the visit to Singapore by Israeli President Chaim Herzog in November 1986. This was coupled with Singapore's declaration of itself being a "little Israel," which invoked images of a "defensive" country existing in a sea of hostile Muslim enemies.[150] However, despite this diplomatic *faux pas*, this sort of statement could nevertheless be interpreted as at least a projection by Singapore of defensive aims, however inaccurate (and inflammatory) the analogy might have been in reality. Ultimately, though, and despite several uncertain periods, fairly good relations have prevailed. This has been partly due to Singapore fearing a Malaysian dictatorship or an ethnic Chinese communist regime, while Malaysia has wanted to prevent a pro-Chinese regime from taking power in Singapore.[151] Thus, both countries took active measures to support the status quo. Here, too,

ASEAN can be viewed as facilitating – but not determining – peaceful relations between its members.

Indonesia–Singapore

Indonesia and Singapore have also not escaped tense periods in their varied history, but theirs is one that has ultimately achieved a high degree of normalcy. One event in particular serves to underscore the difficulties the two countries experienced in the early years of ASEAN. In October 1968, two Indonesian marines-turned-saboteurs were executed in Singapore, despite Suharto's attempts to obtain clemency for them. The result was domestic disorder in Indonesia, while Suharto "concealed a deeply felt sense of personal slight."[152] Indeed, the only real action taken by Suharto was a move toward suspending trade relations with Singapore, and this not much more than in name only. Five years later, Singapore's President Lee visited Indonesia and went so far as to place flowers on the tombs of the soldiers that his own government had executed.[153]

While exemplifying the difficulties the two countries faced in the early years, this example also demonstrates the effect of self-binding behavior on paving the way to better relations in the future, as well as Suharto's ability to resist domestic pressure in favor of preserving peace within the region. Indeed, the current state of affairs between the two countries is characterized by a healthy degree of economic interdependence, as Singapore has shifted from labor-intensive industries toward the service sector – a shift that Indonesia has appreciated for its mitigating economic competition between the two states.[154] Finally, Singapore also deferred to Indonesia when it waited to open diplomatic relations with China until Indonesia did so; this move served to mitigate Indonesia's perception of Singapore as being too "Chinese" in character.[155]

Multilateral benignity

The acts of self-restraint evident in the bilateral relationships among ASEAN's members are underscored by ASEAN's "code of conduct," which explicitly mandates "self-inhibiting behavior."[156] This code is embodied in the principles of non-interference in domestic affairs, non-use of force, peaceful dispute resolution, and the eschewing of external intervention in favor of regional solutions.[157] Antolik offers a more instrumental account of what led the ASEAN states to practice self-restraint. That is, given the illegitimacy of many of the states' boundaries, the larger states fear the potential for smaller states to support secessionist or terrorist movements should relations turn sour, and small states of course are fearful of their larger counterparts out of the basic idea that anarchy breeds uncertainty.[158] Nevertheless, the notion of ASEAN contributing toward policies of self-restraint was well understood by the region's smaller members. Indeed, it has been argued that Brunei chose to join ASEAN in 1984 for the reason that the "five founding states would be obliged to be restrained ... towards it."[159]

With the idea of benignity established in the ASEAN case, we will now turn to the phenomenon of order, illustrating the degree to which it has been agreed upon at the multilateral level.

Agreeing on order

Through the "ASEAN way," the members of ASEAN have managed to build at least a rough agreement on the status quo, despite the numerous bilateral tensions plaguing the region. An underlying, though tentative, sense of order has been achieved through a combination of norms and strategic policies, including anti-communism as well as a general commitment to capitalist economic development.[160] In terms of agreeing on hierarchy, Indonesia was originally the central target of most states' concerns. As Michael Leifer writes, ASEAN's extension of membership to Indonesia "was contemplated as both a way of catering for [sic] the natural political ambition of the most powerful regional state and of trying to contain its objectionable interventionist disposition. [That] Indonesia was the object of this kind of calculation ... was well understood in Jakarta in August 1967."[161] This was despite the "sense of entitlement"[162] that Indonesia nevertheless experienced, owing in part to its highly populated, resource-filled land mass, but also because it was the only state of the five founding members that had to fight actively for its independence. (Thailand was never colonized, and the others were granted sovereignty peacefully by their respective colonial powers.)

Moreover, agreement on order has not been easy to achieve, because each member of ASEAN arguably has one or more border disputes with the others. Indeed, there were 17 points of inter-state dispute within the ASEAN-7 alone.[163] Although this state of affairs has encouraged military modernization, weapons are more likely to be trained inwards rather than upon each other in order to prevent domestic insurgency.[164] National "resilience" is the credo by which ASEAN members focus their security concerns. Another way in which these tensions are kept in check is through the sharp distinction made between bilateral issues and multilateral ones within the organization's forums.[165]

Attaining a regional order mostly acceptable to the member states has been facilitated by a number of institutionalized arrangements for dialogue. Emphasizing diplomatic rather than military security or economics, the annual meeting of ASEAN states is attended by their respective foreign ministers (in the form of the Annual Ministerial Meeting, or

AMM). Each capital city hosts a "national secretariat" to complement an overarching ASEAN secretariat, which has been based in Jakarta since 1982. In addition to these permanent features, there are various standing ad hoc committees, and heads-of-state summits are held occasionally; the first was held in 1976 in Bali. There, the Treaty of Amity and Cooperation (TAC) was introduced as a mechanism for dispute resolution, and the ASEAN Concord was declared, which legally bound members to the established rules of conduct. Through the Concord, members pledged "'mutual respect for the independence, sovereignty ... territorial integrity of all nations'; 'non-interference in the internal affairs of one another'; 'settlement of differences or disputes by peaceful means'; and 'renunciation of the threat or use of force.'"[166] Implicit in ASEAN's formation was the isolation of Vietnam. However, Indonesia and Malaysia objected to this goal, preferring a strong Vietnam in order to counter China, which was deemed the larger threat. Ultimately, Indonesia and Malaysia relented, thus supporting the idea that the organization's collective interest took precedence over individual member states' claims.[167] This is all the more significant in that Indonesia and Malaysia are the most powerful among the founding members, thus underscoring the fact that, as in the case of the Concert of Europe, the member states have forgone their immediate preferences in order to safeguard the collective interest – a strategy that, in any event, ultimately buttresses the goals of the member states themselves.

Agreeing on legitimacy

Despite detailed, institutionalized procedures for multilateral cooperation within ASEAN, a deep sense of legitimacy has not been easy to obtain. It is true that the self-conscious principles of "consultation" and "consensus" embodied in the celebrated phrase "the ASEAN way" have gone part of the way towards establishing a framework for norm-based cooperation tinged with proud self-sufficiency accompanied by regional efforts. Nevertheless, consensus among the member states has not been automatic. Different ethnicities and religious groups existing in a region characterized by arbitrary post-colonial borders mean that any normative sense of legitimacy that is reached must be deliberately built on through institutional mechanisms. This means that some norms will exist on paper long before they are internalized by the member states. Ultimately, though, a consultative approach to regionalism has largely prevailed in practice, embodied in the November 1971 declaration drafted at an ad hoc meeting of foreign ministers in Kuala Lumpur. There, the members agreed "to continue to consult each other with a view to fostering an integrated approach on all matters and developments which affect the

Southeast Asian region."[168] Thus, an anti-colonial legacy coupled with a strident attempt at regional self-sufficiency has imbued ASEAN with at least a modicum of agreement on the normative framework within which the member states interact.

Summary

The case of ASEAN illustrates the importance of benignity, order, and legitimacy in managing power relations among members of a security community. Although it is far from a formal and entrenched security community within which war is unthinkable, the ASEAN states have at least succeeded in managing their power relations to the extent that war has not occurred among the members. This section has shown that the major states exercised self-restraint in their relations toward one another, even in the midst of acute diplomatic crises. Admitting Indonesia into ASEAN meant that Sukarno's belligerent legacy could be ushered out along with Suharto being ushered in. Agreement on order was facilitated by a collective anti-communist sentiment coupled with a drive toward capitalist economic development. The latter also facilitated self-restraint among the region's members, as policies were shaped in part to facilitate economic linkages. Finally, the legacy of anti-colonialism and the drive toward self-sufficiency imbued the organization's explicitly normative principles with at least some degree of legitimacy.

Conclusion

In this chapter, we have applied the theoretical framework of this volume to three cases of power management. The US–UK case is one of history's clearest examples of a peaceful power transition, while ASEAN and the Concert of Europe are cases of multi-state collectives – one contemporary (and less formal); the other historical (and properly a security community). It is evident from the discussion presented here that benignity is perhaps the most powerful of the three variables, but the addition of legitimacy and order makes the framework not only a necessary cause of peaceful power management, but a sufficient one as well.

Benignity results from the exercise of self-restraint and mutual accommodation. The various dyads examined here all exhibited such self-binding behavior, imbuing what might have been adversarial relations with an element of trust. Order is facilitated by agreement on hierarchy and spheres of influence. While hierarchy is crucial to all three cases examined here, the importance of spheres of influence has faded in recent years (thus, spheres play little role in ASEAN). Agreement on legitimacy centers around common normative ideas. In the cases examined here, these ideas focused on religion (Christianity in the case of the Concert); regime type (the Concert powers' proclivity for monarchy; the ASEAN members' distaste for communism); economic policy (capitalism in the case of ASEAN); and historical exigencies (ASEAN's spirit of anticolonialism).

The empirical cases examined in this chapter point to the geographical and temporal breadth suggested by the framework presented in this volume. As benignity, order, and legitimacy have supported peaceful power management across two centuries and three regions, and among states on either side of the colonial divide, it appears that this formula will serve us well for the power transition that may arise as American preponderance wanes.

Notes

1. On British–American relations during this period, see H. C. Allen, *Great Britain and the United States: A History of Anglo-American Relations, 1783–1945* (New York: St. Martin's Press, 1955), pp. 300–356.
2. Ibid., pp. 452–517.
3. This period will be discussed in detail below. The best overview is Bradford Perkins, *The Great Rapprochement: England and the United States, 1895–1914* (New York: Atheneum, 1968).
4. Figures as cited in Paul Kennedy, *The Rise and Fall of the Great Powers* (New York: Vintage, 1987), p. 149. For even more extreme estimates see Aaron Friedberg, *The Weary Titan: Britain and the Experience of Relative Decline, 1895–1905* (Princeton, NJ: Princeton University Press, 1988), p. 26.
5. Kennedy, *The Rise and Fall of the Great Powers*, p. 203.
6. Ranking by *Jane's Fighting Ships*, cited in Allen, *Great Britain and the United States*, p. 561.
7. Figures as cited in Perkins, *The Great Rapprochement*, p. 48.
8. Lord Selborne, First Lord of the British Admiralty, cited in Friedberg, *The Weary Titan*, p. 135.
9. Kennedy, *The Rise and Fall of the Great Powers*, p. 199. For instance, the United States multiplied its standing force of 1890 nearly ten-fold for the brief Spanish–American War. See Kenneth Bourne, *The Balance of Power in North America, 1815–1908* (Berkeley: University of California Press, 1967), p. 338.
10. Allen, *Great Britain and the United States*, pp. 276–281.
11. These include fisheries disputes, naval armaments on the Great Lakes, and a dispute over Behring seals.
12. Formal British responsibility for the defense of Canada was less than clear. After 1867 Canada was formally responsible for its day-to-day defense. However, Canada expected British support if it were attacked and most Canadian diplomacy was channeled through Britain until 1927. On the ambiguous nature of the commitment, see Sean M. Shore, "No Fences Make Good Neighbors: The Development of the Canadian–US Security Community, 1871–1940," in Emanuel Adler and Michael Barnett, eds., *Security Communities* (Cambridge: Cambridge University Press, 1998), pp. 335–336, 342.

13. Many observers have claimed that the rise of Germany's navy can serve as at least part of an explanation for the outbreak of World War I. For a discussion, see Paul M. Kennedy, *The Rise of the Anglo-German Antagonism, 1860–1914* (London: Ashfield Press, 1980), pp. 410–432.
14. The widely accepted historical consensus is that Britain always conceded more and cared more about the relationship than did the United States. Perkins is explicit on this point. See *The Great Rapprochement*, pp. 4, 7.
15. An excellent introduction is J. A. S. Grenville, *Lord Salisbury and Foreign Policy: The Close of the Nineteenth Century* (London: Athlone Press, 1964), pp. 54–73.
16. Ibid., p. 57.
17. For the full text of Lord Salisbury's response, see *Foreign Relations of the United States, 1895* (Washington DC: US Government Printing Office), Vol. 1, pp. 563–567.
18. Ibid., pp. 542–545.
19. Perkins, *The Great Rapprochement*, p. 18.
20. Ibid., p. 19.
21. For an overview see ibid., pp. 162–171.
22. Ibid., p. 165.
23. Cited in ibid.
24. Ibid., p. 171. See also A. E. Campbell, *Great Britain and the United States, 1895–1903* (London: Longman, 1960), p. 124. Consequently, the costs to Britain were less the concessions on the boundary than the anger that they incurred from Canada.
25. See Campbell, *Great Britain and the United States*, pp. 48–88.
26. Ibid., see especially p. 72; and Perkins, *The Great Rapprochement*, p. 183.
27. See Perkins, *The Great Rapprochement*, p. 196.
28. Cited in ibid.
29. Ibid.
30. For an excellent discussion see Friedberg, *The Weary Titan*, pp. 135–207.
31. Ibid., pp. 172–173.
32. Quoted in Perkins, *The Great Rapprochement*, p. 230. For another instance of the decision to remove the United States from British calculations, see Bourne, *The Balance of Power in North America*, p. 369; see also p. 361.
33. Friedberg, *The Weary Titan*, pp. 195–197.
34. Bourne, *The Balance of Power in North America*, p. 389.
35. Quoted in Perkins, *The Great Rapprochement*, pp. 106–107 (emphasis added).
36. Ibid., p. 33.
37. Ibid., pp. 44–45.
38. Ibid., p. 45.
39. Grenville, *Lord Salisbury and Foreign Policy*, p. 216.
40. Perkins, *The Great Rapprochement*, p. 50. There is debate on the extent of British support. See Grenville, *Lord Salisbury and Foreign Policy*, p. 216.
41. See, for example, the memorandum by Major Gen. Ardagh, Director of Military Intelligence, in *British Documents on Foreign Affairs: Reports and Papers from the Foreign Office Confidential Print, Part I, Series C North America, Vol. 10, Expansion and Rapprochement, 1889–1898* (Washington, DC: University Publications of America, 1993), pp. 468–470; see also *Vol. 11, 1899–1905*, pp. 3, 127–128.
42. Another instance of American support for British efforts to maintain its power was American pleasure upon the commencement of the Anglo-Japanese alliance. See the discussion in Raymond E. Esthus, *Theodore Roosevelt and the International Rivalries* (Waltham: Ginn-Blaidsell, 1970), p. 64.
43. Quoted in Perkins, *The Great Rapprochement*, p. 93. For another statement on the heels of the 1902 election see pp. 97–98.
44. Ibid., p. 95.

45. Ibid. American exports to Britain rose by over US$100 million during the war.
46. Ibid., pp. 95–97.
47. Quoted in Esthus, *Theodore Roosevelt*, p. 38.
48. Quoted in Perkins, *The Great Rapprochement*, p. 172, and Esthus, *Theodore Roosevelt*, p. 63, respectively.
49. Quoted in Bourne, *The Balance of Power in North America*, p. 381.
50. Ibid.
51. Quoted in Perkins, *The Great Rapprochement*, p. 275.
52. See Friedberg, *The Weary Titan*, p. 164, and Perkins, *The Great Rapprochement*, p. 53.
53. See n. 16 above.
54. See n. 17.
55. Quoted in Campbell, *Great Britain and the United States*, p. 79.
56. For an excellent discussion of the trade policies of the two countries during this period, see Peter Gourevitch, *Politics in Hard Times: Comparative Responses to International Economic Crises* (Ithaca, NY: Cornell University Press, 1986), pp. 71–123.
57. See Walter LaFeber, *The American Search for Opportunity, 1865–1913* (Cambridge: Cambridge University Press, 1993), pp. 77, 78, and 133. Note that, although the McKinley tariff had a reciprocity provision that might have led to freer trade, it was highly restrictive and largely unused.
58. See Benjamin Cohen, "A Brief History of International Monetary Relations," in Jeffrey A. Frieden and David A. Lake, eds., *International Political Economy: Perspectives on Global Power and Wealth* (New York: St. Martin's Press, 1995), pp. 209–214.
59. See ibid., p. 210. Opponents of this decision labeled it the "Crime of '73."
60. See Perkins, *The Great Rapprochement*, pp. 21–25. Perkins also discusses the British reaction to Bryant's campaign.
61. LaFeber, *The American Search for Opportunity*, pp. 133–134.
62. John Owen sees this as a major fulcrum preventing war between the two countries. See John M. Owen, "How Liberalism Produces the Democratic Peace," *International Security*, Vol. 19, No. 2 (Fall 1994), pp. 108–119.
63. Quoted in Perkins, *The Great Rapprochement*, p. 55.
64. Quoted in ibid., p. 84. Note also that the Rudyard Kipling poem "White Man's Burden" was published in the American magazine *McClure's*. See ibid., pp. 84–85; see also pp. 43, 52, 57, 64.
65. For elite statements to this effect, see Stephen R. Rock, *Why Peace Breaks out: Great Power Rapprochement in Historical Perspective* (Chapel Hill: University of North Carolina Press, 1989), pp. 50–52.
66. Stuart Anderson, *Race and Rapprochement: Anglo-Saxonism and Anglo-American Relations, 1895–1904* (Rutherford: Farleigh Dickenson, 1981), p. 11.
67. Ibid.
68. See specifically Anderson's discussion of the Venezuelan boundary dispute of 1895; ibid., pp. 95–111.
69. Those who make this or a similar case include Aaron Friedberg, *The Weary Titan*, p. 168; R. G. Neale, *Great Britain and United States Expansion: 1898–1900* (East Lansing, MI: Michigan State University Press, 1966); and, more specifically with reference to the Venezuelan crisis, Christopher Layne, "Kant or Cant: The Myth of the Democratic Peace," *International Security*, Vol. 19, No. 2 (Fall 1994).
70. Stephen Rock notes that a large part of this decision was not just geostrategic but also based on a British understanding of American intentions. *Why Peace Breaks out*, pp. 36–37.
71. Rock documents that British elites did not expect the United States to be as supportive of Britain as it was; ibid., p. 35.
72. See Layne, "Kant or Cant," p. 25.

73. Campbell, *Great Britain and the United States*, p. 29.
74. Germany, for instance, had constant designs on Latin America; see ibid., pp. 31–33.
75. For this period see Steven T. Ross, *European Diplomatic History, 1789–1815: France against Europe* (Malabar: Krieger, 1969).
76. This outline draws upon Paul W. Schroeder, *The Transformation of European Politics, 1763–1848* (Oxford: Oxford University Press, 1994). See also Norman Rich, *Great Power Diplomacy, 1814–1914* (New York: McGraw-Hill, 1992).
77. On the impact of Russian behavior in Poland, see Rene Albrecht-Carrie, *The Concert of Europe, 1815–1914* (New York: Harper, 1968), p. 31.
78. Owing to space constraints, we are not able to discuss the Concert's reactions to the Portuguese revolution of 1828, the Carlist Wars in Spain, or the Belgian Revolt of 1830. A failure to discuss those cases should not be problematic, however, because they are largely in keeping with our argument. We focus on tougher cases such as the Greek independence and Turko-Egyptian crises. See Rich, *Great Power Diplomacy*, pp. 58–68.
79. On the Congress, see Harold Nicolson, *The Congress of Vienna, A Study in Allied Unity: 1812–1822* (San Diego: Harcourt, Brace, Jovanovich, 1946).
80. The details are most clearly stated in Rich, *Great Power Diplomacy*, p. 25. See also Schroeder, *The Transformation of European Politics*, p. 556.
81. For clear statements of this view see Rich, *Great Power Diplomacy*, p. 25; and Alan Palmer, *Metternich* (New York: Harper & Row, 1970), p. 124.
82. In the words of Harold Nicolson, the Prussians were out for "revenge and loot." See *Congress of Vienna*, pp. 232–233.
83. Schroeder, *Transformation*, p. 547. See also Rich, *Great Power Diplomacy*, pp. 20–21.
84. Schroeder, *Transformation*, p. 548.
85. Ibid., pp. 607–608.
86. These logics are outlined in Rich, *Great Power Diplomacy*, p. 36.
87. Schroeder, *Transformation*, p. 608. See also Rich, *Great Power Diplomacy*, p. 37.
88. Schroeder, *Transformation*, pp. 609–610. The British did not formally endorse the intervention for domestic political reasons. However, Metternich said of Castlereagh's opinion on the issue that he "was like a music-lover in church; he wished to applaud but dared not."
89. Rich, *Great Power Diplomacy*, pp. 37–38.
90. Canning replaced the pro-Concert Castlereagh when the latter committed suicide.
91. Schroeder, *Transformation*, pp. 622–624.
92. Ibid., pp. 624–626; Rich, *Great Power Diplomacy*, pp. 40–41.
93. Quoted in ibid., p. 40. On French intervention see Schroeder, *Transformation*, p. 626.
94. Strangely, Schroeder, who takes a highly pessimistic view of French intervention, does not cite the conditions. See Schroeder, *Transformation*, p. 627. For a discussion of the conditions, see Rich, *Great Power Diplomacy*, p. 41.
95. For a discussion of these interests, see Loyal Cowles, "The Failure to Restrain Russia: Canning, Nesselrode, and the Greek Question, 1825–1827," *International History Review*, Vol. 7, No. 4 (November 1990), p. 692.
96. Schroeder, *Transformation*, pp. 637–638.
97. The clearest chronology is in Rich, *Great Power Diplomacy*, pp. 49–57.
98. Schroeder, *Transformation*, p. 621. See also Rich, *Great Power Diplomacy*, p. 51. Korina Kagan argues that Russia restrained itself in 1822 because of fear of revolution. See Kagan, "The Myth of the European Concert: The Realist-Institutionalist Debate and Great Power Behavior in the Eastern Question, 1821–41," *Security Studies*, Vol. 7, No. 2 (Winter 1997/98), p. 27. It is irrelevant to our argument *why* Russia restrained itself; we are only concerned that it did.

99. Cowles, "The Failure to Restrain Russia," p. 693. On the general Russian frustration with the Concert, see Kagan, "The Myth of the European Concert," p. 29.
100. Rich, *Great Power Diplomacy*, pp. 51–52.
101. Ibid., pp. 52–53. Note, again, that there is some controversy as to why the British sought accommodation. Loyal Cowles argues that Canning feared Russian strength in the Balkans. However, if this were the case, one would expect him simply to abstain and allow Russia to act as it would, rather than cooperating with it. See Cowles, "The Failure to Restrain Russia," pp. 691–697.
102. The primary gains of Akkerman were a grant of Russian protectorate over Serbia, Moldavia, and Wallachia, all bordering on the Austro-Hungarian Empire. See Rich, *Great Power Diplomacy*, pp. 53–54, and the map on p. 48. On Austrian policy, see also Schroeder, *Transformation*, pp. 649–650.
103. Rich, *Great Power Diplomacy*, p. 54.
104. Schroeder, *Transformation*, pp. 658–659; and Rich, *Great Power Diplomacy*, p. 55. Again, Kagan raises the question of why Russia restrained itself, which we are less concerned with. See "The Myth of the European Concert," pp. 33–34.
105. Owing to bickering within the Concert over who the monarch would be, Greek independence was not actually declared until 1832. See Rich, *Great Power Diplomacy*, p. 56.
106. Ibid., pp. 69–74. Ali had already demanded and received gains in the Sudan and Arabia from the Sultan.
107. Ibid., pp. 69–70; Schroeder, *Transformation*, p. 728.
108. Schroeder, *Transformation*, pp. 728–729.
109. Ibid., pp. 729–730; Kagan, "The Myth of the European Concert," p. 40.
110. Schroeder, *Transformation*, p. 731; Rich, *Great Power Diplomacy*, p. 71. A secret provision also stipulated that, if the Ottoman Empire dissolved, the members of the treaty would work to preserve the balance of power.
111. Schroeder, *Transformation*, p. 743; Rich, *Great Power Diplomacy*, p. 72. See also Kagan, "The Myth of the European Concert," p. 43.
112. On the Austro-British military cooperation, see Rich, *Great Power Diplomacy*, p. 74.
113. Whereas Rich implies that Thiers was forced to resign because of the threat to the European powers, Schroeder argues that his resignation was also bound up with an armaments campaign. See Rich, *Great Power Diplomacy*, p. 73; Schroeder, *Transformation*, p. 747.
114. Rich, *Great Power Diplomacy*, pp. 4, 22. On the colonial concessions see Nicolson, *The Congress of Vienna*, pp. 72, 99.
115. Ibid., pp. 63–64.
116. France later contested Austrian dominance of Italy, primarily through its support of Italian Unification. See ibid., pp. 123–146.
117. Schroeder, *Transformation*, p. 547. See also the discussion on the German question at the Congress of Vienna above.
118. Rich, *Great Power Diplomacy*, pp. 40–41, 61.
119. Schroeder, *Transformation*, p. 707.
120. Ibid., pp. 580, 657.
121. Paul Kennedy, *Rise and Fall of the Great Powers: Economic Change and Military Conflict from 1500 to 2000* (New York: Vintage Books, 1989), p. 99.
122. See Alan Sked, *The Decline and Fall of the Hapsburg Empire, 1815–1918* (London: Longman, 1989).
123. Full text cited in Albrecht-Carrie, *Concert of Europe*, pp. 33–34.
124. Hans Georg Schenk details the philosophical underpinnings of the Tzar's stance in *The Aftermath of the Napoleonic Wars: The Concert of Europe, an Experiment* (London: Oxford University Press, 1947), pp. 1–23.

125. Ibid., p. 40.
126. Henry Kissinger's claim that "legitimacy" held the Concert together is not so far from this mark. See Kissinger, *A World Restored: Metternich, Castlereagh and the Problems of Peace, 1812–22* (Boston: Houghton Mifflin, 1957).
127. For a discussion that clearly draws the links between the revolutionary threat and the reactionary nature of the European elites, see Mack Walker, "Introductory Essay," in Walker, ed., *Metternich's Europe* (New York: Walker, 1968), pp. 1–22.
128. Schroeder, *Transformation*, pp. 602–603.
129. See Rich, *Great Power Diplomacy*, pp. 36, 51. See also discussion and citations above. To garner the Tzar's support on intervention in Naples, Metternich penned an 8,000-word document he called "a profession of political faith." See Palmer, *Metternich*, p. 196.
130. Sheldon Simon, "Security Prospects in Southeast Asia: Collaborative Efforts and the ASEAN Regional Forum," *Pacific Review*, Vol. 11, No. 2 (1998), p. 210.
131. Roger Irvine, "The Formative Years of ASEAN: 1967–1975," in Alison Broinowski, ed., *Understanding ASEAN* (New York: St. Martin's Press, 1992), p. 9.
132. Donald K. Emmerson, "Indonesia, Malaysia, Singapore: A Regional Security Core?" in Richard J. Ellings and Sheldon W. Simon, eds., *Southeast Asian Security in the New Millennium* (London: M.E. Sharpe, 1996), p. 46.
133. Michael Leifer, *ASEAN and the Security of South-East Asia* (London: Routledge, 1989), p. 20.
134. Quoted in Yuen Foong Khong, "ASEAN and the Southeast Asian Security Complex," in David A. Lake and Patrick M. Morgan, eds., *Regional Orders: Building Security in a New World* (University Park, PA: Pennsylvania State University Press, 1997), p. 326.
135. See Kusuma Snitwongse, "Thirty Years of ASEAN: Achievements through Political Cooperation," *Pacific Review*, Vol. 11, No. 2 (1998).
136. Roger Irvine, "The Formative Years of ASEAN," p. 17.
137. Leifer, *ASEAN and the Security of South-East Asia*, p. 3.
138. Khong, "ASEAN and the Southeast Asian Security Complex."
139. Amitav Acharya, "Collective Identity and Conflict Management in Southeast Asia," in Emanuel Adler and Michael Barnett, eds., *Security Communities* (Cambridge: Cambridge University Press, 1998), p. 203.
140. Leifer, *ASEAN and the Security of South-East Asia*, p. 22.
141. Michael Antolik, *ASEAN and the Diplomacy of Accommodation* (Armonk, NY: M.E. Sharpe, 1990), p. 21.
142. Ibid., p. 23.
143. Ibid., p. 24.
144. Ibid., pp. 28–33.
145. Leifer, *ASEAN and the Security of South-East Asia*, p. 35.
146. Ibid., p. 35.
147. Ibid., pp. 18–19.
148. Antolik, *ASEAN and the Diplomacy of Accommodation*, p. 23.
149. Ibid., p. 41.
150. Ibid., pp. 35–36.
151. Ibid., p. 44.
152. Leifer, *ASEAN and the Security of South-East Asia*, p. 32.
153. Antolik, *ASEAN and the Diplomacy of Accommodation*, p. 47.
154. Ibid., p. 49.
155. Ibid., p. 47.
156. Simon, "Security Prospects in Southeast Asia," p. 197.
157. Ibid.

158. Antolik, *ASEAN and the Diplomacy of Accommodation*, p. 8.
159. Leifer, *ASEAN and the Security of South-East Asia*, p. 47.
160. Acharya, "Collective Identity and Conflict Management in Southeast Asia," p. 207.
161. Leifer, *ASEAN and the Security of South-East Asia*, p. 23.
162. Antolik, *ASEAN and the Diplomacy of Accommodation*, p. 21.
163. Jörn Dosch and Manfred Mols, "Thirty Years of ASEAN: Achievements and Challenges," *Pacific Review*, Vol. 11, No. 2 (1998), p. 170.
164. Simon, "Security Prospects in Southeast Asia," p. 200.
165. Snitwongse, "Thirty Years of ASEAN," p. 185.
166. Quoted in Khong, "ASEAN and the Southeast Asian Security Complex," p. 333.
167. Ibid., p. 334.
168. Quoted in ibid., p. 58.

6

The change of change: Peaceful transitions of power in the multilateral age

Emanuel Adler

This chapter breaks with the pack; it neither focuses on one or more of the book's organizing concepts, nor uses historical cases to illustrate their importance. Rather, the chapter aims to apply the security community concept to the subject of major power transitions, reflecting on how the security community concept may help us better understand peaceful transitions of major powers and how the emergence of security communities may ease or complicate the onset of peaceful transitions. More generally, the chapter deals with changes in the institutional context within which the next power transition may take place. It argues that, in the future, we are likely to witness the change of change itself, i.e. the transformation of the mechanism or mechanisms that regulate power transitions. Although multilateral diplomacy and social learning may at least partly replace war as mechanisms of major power transitions, especially within security communities, unfortunately this change does not necessarily presage a less violent world outside security communities, and between members of security communities and other states. Owing to changes in historical and institutional contexts, however, power will probably be more horizontally and vertically diffused, thus we may fail to recognize a major power transition when we see one.

The multilateral age

> *Nature and Nature's laws lay hid in night:*
> *God said let Newton be, and all was light ...*

> *But alas:*
> *It did not last: the Devil howling 'Ho!*
> *Let Einstein be!' restored the status quo.*
>   (Arthur Koestler)[1]

Not too long ago, international relations were, or seemed to be, in a Newtonian-like stage. States were sovereign and thus independent to act at will;[2] when state interests clashed with other states' interests, the contest was resolved (how else?) by the use of force. In the "Newtonian" age of world politics, states were measured by their mass, i.e. material assets such as territory, population, natural resources, industry, and military gear. At the same time, change meant the replacement of one "top dog" by another, usually after a bloody encounter, in which the stronger side did what destiny called for, and the weaker side did what it must – it became a regular country haunted by memories of a long gone empire. In this Newtonian world of international relations, both balance of power theory and its rival, power transition theory, made sense. Unlike balance of power theory, which asserted that balance had a beneficial effect in preventing war, power transition theory asserted that balance was an omen of war.[3] In a more or less balanced yet changing situation the likely result from a process of power transition was *war* – either because a rising power would use violence to achieve the world status that befitted its material resources, or because the declining power would attempt to prevent the inevitable before it was too late. A recent study that assessed the results of empirical tests to which the theory was subjected concluded that, "[f]or the most part, stated results have substantiated the theory."[4]

"But alas, it did not last." What seemed so neatly explained by mass, equilibrium, and static change may, at least in parts of the world, be a thing of the past. At the same time that the indicators of transition theory are being scrutinized, and that the statistical methods that are used to analyze it are being appraised, there is a feeling of obsolescence about the entire theory. This is not because nation-states have come to an end – far from it – or because organized violence between them is a thing of the past – unfortunately this has not occurred. Rather, the sense of obsolescence comes from the notion that we have left behind "the imperialist age," that we no longer live in the "balance of power age" or the "Cold War age," and that, instead, we are entering a new stage in history, which, for lack of a better word, I call *the multilateral age*. One of the first symptoms of this new age was the end of the Cold War and of the Soviet Empire.

What appears so new in this coming multilateral age (although it has not fully arrived yet) is how international conflicts between major powers will be handled. In other words, what seems to be changing is the mechanism of change itself. If, in the past, conflict arising from power transitions was settled by force, in the foreseeable future, similar conflicts hold the potential (although not the certainty) of being resolved "benignly," by peaceful change. To begin with, the use of force among major powers has become too expensive, and the material incentives of cooperation are too rewarding,[5] for total war to be justifiable as a rational enterprise.[6] Moreover, since the end of World War II, the United States has been using its economic, political, and military power to constitute an international order that transcends rather than perpetuates anarchy. Most important, however, is the fact that in the multilateral age, at least in some parts of the world, geopolitical and geostrategic considerations – thus also intrinsic notions of security – seem not to arise either exclusively or even primarily from the balance of material resources in a power politics game. Rather, they also seem increasingly to arise from the values and norms people live by, from the compatibility of norms and values across national borders, and from collective social identities. These days, therefore, security seems to be increasingly related, not only to how many tanks and missiles a state has in relation to other states, but also to whether or not they all inhabit a common space characterized by common values and norms. Consequently international politics seem to be veering from balance of power and alliance mechanisms to multilateral diplomacy and *social learning* mechanisms, which, primarily aimed at creating a common normative milieu, promote trust-building practices and thus encourage peaceful change.

Thus when the balance of power or violent transitions of power were collectively perceived as the only game in town, stratification of material power – the number of "poles" in a given international system – was the game's middle name. When, however, collective perception seems to be moving from material capabilities to the rules that bestow meaning upon them (material resources have meaning only within the context of identities), the stratification of power becomes only one of the structural factors that matter at the systemic level. Other factors are (a) the "stratification" of the actors' identities, institutional arrangements, and rules, (b) the evolution of new legitimate practices, and (c) whether and how people spatially construe new political spaces to which they attach a sense of belonging, and the structural differentiation between these spaces.[7]

More formally, we may characterize the multilateral age according to what seem to be its most distinctive characteristics:

1. Thick webs of international institutions are beginning to reduce anarchy, at least in some parts of the world. International structure in the multilateral age, thus, is better portrayed as *punctuated anarchy*, i.e. anarchy that is punctuated by areas where anarchy is tempered by shared values and norms and is managed by international institutions, and where, generally, people do not expect violent conflict to arise across national borders.

2. Increasingly, international problems are being handled by multilateral diplomacy. This is true with regard not only to "low-level politics" but, primarily, to international security. Thus, for example, a shift is occurring from classic "coercive diplomacy"[8] – according to which a state, usually a major power, threatens to use force or uses force against other states in order to compel them to bend to its will – to *multilateral coercive diplomacy* – according to which the threat and/or use of force is undertaken, usually in defense of international community principles, by multilateral institutions such as the North Atlantic Treaty Organisation (NATO). It is a sign of the times that the European Union (EU) is now moving to turn the Western European Union into the EU's operational option of multilateral coercive diplomacy.
3. The multilateral age is also characterized by the growing globalization of the economy and culture around the world. Increasing globalization of trade, finance, investment, and labor markets leaves no options for states other than going to multilateral forums, such as the World Trade Organization (WTO), to jointly manage these markets. Economic globalization, however, has helped to bring to the fore the existence of two global cultures. The first global culture is the "Davos culture" of the transnational economically liberal corporate world, which, to a large extent, is responsible for the trillions of dollars' worth of goods, services, and investment that now move around the world. The second global culture, as the 1999 WTO meeting in Seattle, Washington, showed, is a global "counterculture." Facilitated by the Internet, this global counterculture has helped a transnational coalition of individuals to organize around symbols, such as the WTO, in order to exert "global pressure" against what they take to be globalization's downside, i.e. growing unemployment, poverty, and environmental degradation.
4. The multilateral age also seems to be characterized by a small, albeit perceptible, movement from state sovereignty to what UN Secretary-General Kofi Annan has characterized as "individual sovereignty."[9] Not only are people more sensitive to what occurs to other people in other parts of the world, but, for humanitarian reasons, they are also willing to pressure their governments into intervening to stop gross human rights violations. Sometimes people also organize in a private fashion to provide humanitarian help and to mobilize public opinion against injustice. In the multilateral age, thus, we find a proliferation with "transnational advocacy groups,"[10] which, working side by side of states, promote the solution of humanitarian problems. And dictators, such as Chilean General Augusto Pinochet, who were engaged in gross human rights violations, are not safe any more to roam around the world without fear of being prosecuted for their crimes. Moreover, increasingly, at least in some parts of the world, a norm of account-

ability is taking hold, where states are accountable to other states for what they do to their own people. For example, the 55 members of the Organization for Security and Co-operation in Europe (OSCE) have agreed on injunctions based on this norm.[11] In part, this norm also helps explain why Western countries forced the Serbs to be accountable for their gross human rights violations in Kosovo, and why they are now trying to induce Russia to be accountable for violations of human rights in Chechnya. For their part, Russians seem to apply the same measure when they complain that the West too ought to be accountable for the human suffering that NATO forces inflicted on the Serbian people.

5. In recent years, it has become increasingly clear that the international system is not composed entirely of "like-units," as was generally thought, and, that, therefore, some units are more like-units than others. One political formation that escapes description in classical terms is the EU: it is more than a mere intergovernmental cooperative venture between 15 states, and less than a unified or unitary state.[12] In the future, the multilateral age may thus be characterized by the coexistence of classic nation-states with EU-like formations. Some of these formations may develop along lines of civilization, for example in the Far East, although they may also develop across civilizations, reified cultures, and religions, such as along the shores of the Mediterranean Sea. These formations, however, are likely to take many decades to develop. The above means that, in the multilateral age, identities may fluctuate, first from nation to region, second from state to individuals, and third from nation and individuals to attributes connected with planet earth.

6. In contrast to eras when the balance of power seemed to be paramount, including the Cold War, the upcoming era seems to rely increasingly on rules for the management of change. Since primeval times, social relations have been constituted and regulated by sets of rules that give meaning to social action, help constitute identities, and, thus, are the sources of people's wants and needs. Here, however, I am referring to explicit rules that the international (and transnational) community is developing, not just to know how to proceed, but to manage the complex problems raised by technological change, interdependence, and globalization. Whether in the fields of international trade and finance, the global environment, human rights, or humanitarian multilateral intervention, the international (and transnational) community seems more self-conscious about explicit rules of the road than at any previous time in history, and indeed it is eager to use the rules when problems arise.

7. Finally, although the multilateral age seems to be characterized by an

increase in the use of low-level violence, violent ethnic conflict, ethnic cleansing, and terror, this holds only for regions whose people have yet to achieve a high level of pluralistic integration. On the other hand, people who have achieved a high level of pluralistic integration can be described as belonging to *security communities*, characterized by dependable expectations of peaceful change. Owing to the importance of this subject, I will deal with it separately. In the context of this chapter, I am particularly interested to explore to what extent security community-like processes may be affecting the likelihood that the next power transition will be peaceful.

To end this section, I raise two caveats and one epistemological and methodological point. Starting with the caveats, first, my argument that we may be entering a new international relations era and that this era may best be characterized by multilateral practices, globalization, a variety of political actors or forms, and, most important, a learning mechanism does not necessarily mean that we are entering a "brave new world," or that we may have reached "the end of ideology"[13] or "the end of history."[14] Nothing could be further from the truth. By watering down the practices of state sovereignty, traditional diplomacy, and, to some extent, balance of power (on which the Westphalian inter-state order has been based for the past three hundred years), the multilateral age may be opening the way to numerous new conflicts between people within and across state borders. Moreover, it is increasingly becoming apparent that globalization's integration potential has a dark side, i.e. the widening of the welfare gap between various groups within nations and between rich and poor nations themselves, and the propensity for every local or regional "flu" to become a global "epidemic." The dark side of globalization, thus, may open the gates of collective frustration, alienation, and, ultimately, violence. When taken together, these threats may amount to an insurmountable barrier to the work of international organizations and to the fixation and stableness of common norms and values. In other words, these threats may impede the development of new security communities, and may compromise the stability of enduring security communities. Finally, some of the technologies that, like the Internet, are facilitating entry into the multilateral age are also means by which people can achieve new levels of evil, suffering, and destruction. All of the above means that, although the multilateral age creates the potential for learning and, thus, for peaceful change in some regions of the world, and for peaceful transitions between major powers, this potential first needs to be actualized by political agents. Of course, from a theoretical perspective, it is therefore crucial to understand, not only the structural situations that political actors find themselves in, but also what political actors do, sometimes in spite of the structures that constrain and empower them.

In other words, when trying to explain peaceful change among major powers, processes are as important as structures.

My second caveat is that it would not be implausible to argue that the attributes of what I call the coming multilateral age are but expressions or representations of American hegemonic, mainly material, power. I read Charles Kupchan's chapters in this volume as saying that, if and when American hegemony wanes, the conditions that allow for benevolence in the present international order and, thus, for peaceful transitions between major powers are also likely to disappear. Obviously, in order to test the validity of this argument empirically, we must wait for America's hegemony to decline. When taking everything into consideration – including (a) the notion that an increase in the material power of the EU and China may not necessarily lead to a parallel diminution of America's power, and (b) what Joseph Nye has called America's "soft power," i.e. America's ability through culture and economic welfare to attract rather than repel people of other nations[15] – it is possible that Kupchan and I may not be able to settle our differences on empirical terms in the foreseeable future. This is why, in the meantime, we need to address this debate in logical and theoretical terms.

In short, my arguments have to do with understanding change in international relations. First, it is undoubtedly true that hegemonic powers may have a paramount influence over the international orders that they help constitute. And it is also true that material power plays an important role in this constitution, as both carrot and stick. On the other hand, it is also true that, owing to the nature of long-term learning processes, international practices that reflect deeply institutionalized normative and cultural changes are likely to continue to exist, even after the material power that played a role in their institutionalization wanes or disappears. Otherwise, international practices such as diplomacy, sovereignty, and self-determination would have vanished together with the hegemonic powers in whose time they were developed. In other words, international governance and international practices are based neither exclusively on material power, nor solely on the function they perform. Rather, they are also based on the attachment of meaning to material reality. Once meaning becomes institutionalized and embedded in routines, it helps to define the identities and interests of the communities in which it becomes rooted, and thus acquires a life of its own.[16]

Second, power transitions are not predetermined and, thus, whether they are benign or not will depend less on the intrinsic or primordial characteristics of the actors involved than on their interaction and, therefore, also on benignness actually becoming a practice. To put it another way, *power transitions are socially constructed.*[17] More specifically, whether a power transition is benign or violent depends not only on the powers' material capabilities, their quantity and quality, and their intrinsic attributes, but also on interactive processes through which the identities and interests of the rising and declining powers become established, and on the context (time, space, culture, technology, etc.) of their interaction. In other words, it is the major powers' collective understandings and actions, their reciprocal interaction, and the material, cultural, and historical contexts of actions that determine whether the powers will end up framing their joint situation as a "power transition" (thus expecting the worst and fulfilling these expectations with every reciprocal action) or, for example, as an evolving "Concert of Power" (thus expecting cooperation). This, of course, means that power transitions are one big self-fulfilling prophecy. Either, by means of reciprocal threats, major powers are led to articulate antagonistic interests that did not exist prior to interaction, or, by means of dialogue, they may discover shared interests, whose potential already existed, but which they were unable or unwilling to articulate. The socially constructed nature of power transitions also highlights the crucial importance of domestic politics in whether the transition will be peaceful or violent. Thus, evoking a constructivist "two-level game,"[18] state–society relations are crucial for the development of affinity at the level of identity, which, as Yuen Foong Khong argues in this volume, is a precondition for the development of shared notions of international order at the inter-state level and, thus, for peaceful transitions. To a large extent, therefore, peaceful transitions will depend on the ability and willingness of leaders, in both the rising and the declining powers, jointly to discredit, delegitimate, and disempower domestic societal actors who play a role in constructing reciprocally conflicting images, identities, and interests.

Third, all of the above does not mean, however, that the attributes of the coming multilateral era and peaceful power transitions will be grounded only in culture. Rather, they will be and already are related to technological and economic developments, such as globalization, that probably are more "powerful" and lasting than any hegemonic state. True, a cataclysmic event, such as a major nuclear war, might return the world to pre-globalization times. In the absence of catastrophic events, however, it would be as hard to believe that globalization could be undone by decree by the next hegemonic power, as that the Internet's long-term consequences could be stopped by religious decree. Does my approach mean that change is linear, progressive, and irreversible? Again, nothing could be further from the truth. For example, the EU-type political form is a priori neither progressive nor regressive. It remains to be seen, and for us to determine, whether the EU is helping more or less permanently to decrease violence, human misery, and injustice across national borders (or whatever is left of them), and, thus, whether it is progressive.[19] Moreover the EU political form is evolving dialectically and non-linearly, as a result of historical processes characterized by self-reflection and the clash between localizing and globalization forces. And, of course, regardless of the final political and institutional form that the EU ends up taking, like all other historical political forms that now exist only in history museums and historical memory, the EU also will one day evolve into something else and disappear.

Finally, to the epistemological and methodological point. The multilateral age requires changing the way we explain international relations. In other words, if social learning and multilateralism are substituting for violent conflict as a mechanism of power transitions, we ought to pay attention not only to material power but also to the collective knowledge and meaning that are attached by political actors to material reality. Moreover, the onset of the multilateral age forces us to inquire how collective identities across national borders become stable and, thus, whether new political communities may be in the process of formation. In addition, it obliges analysts to recast social explanation, paying more attention than in the past to changes in social mechanisms and their nature. From the nature of social mechanisms and from an empirical assessment of whether or not they are changing, we may then be able cautiously to predict the types of practices in which states and non-state actors will probably engage, and, thus, also their propensity to be used habitually.[20]

Security communities

The multilateral age is characterized by both "thin" and "thick" interaction forces. The thin forces of multilateralism refer to the proliferation of multilateral organizations and practices, for example in international trade, finance, and international security. Thin multilateral organizations and practices respond to the instrumental logic of self-interested states, which coordinate their policies – and thus construct a thin vision of international society – on the basis of consensual principles of conduct.[21] Thick multilateralism refers to people's self-conscious efforts to construct regional identities by the use of multilateral diplomacy and organizations. In other words, whereas thin multilateralism aims at better policy coordination between states, thick multilateralism aims at constructing security communities. Michael Barnett and I recently defined security communities as "transnational regions comprised of sovereign states whose people maintain dependable expectations of peaceful change."[22] The concept, however, goes back to Karl Deutsch and his associates, who defined security community as "a group of people which has become integrated." By this, they meant "the attainment within a [transnational] territory, of a sense of community and of institutions and practices strong enough and widespread enough to assure for a 'long' time, dependable expectations of peaceful change."[23]

According to Deutsch, security communities may be either "amalgamated" or "pluralistic." In an amalgamated community, two or more (sovereign) states formally merge into an expanded state. A pluralistic security community, on the other hand, retains the legal independence of separate states but integrates them to the point that the units entertain "dependable expectations of peaceful change." A pluralistic security community develops when its members possess a compatibility of core values derived from common institutions and mutual responsiveness – a matter of mutual identity and loyalty, a sense of "we-ness," or a "we-feeling" among states.

The concept of security community and the concept of peace are closely related, which means, of course, that security community-building processes may be strongly related to peaceful power transitions. In fact, the condition or state of peace between states is actually a practice constituted through collective understandings – primarily collective identities – which is best identified with the concept of security community. Peace thus refers to a condition in which states constituting pluralistic security communities find themselves.[24] This is true of "loosely coupled" pluralistic security communities, which possess few or no institutional and political arrangements between the member sovereign states. It is even truer of "tightly coupled" pluralistic security communities, which, like the EU, possess a political regime that lies somewhere between the sovereign state and centralized regional government. The latter kind of community is something of a post-sovereign system, comprising supranational, transnational, and national institutions and some form of collective security system.[25] Thus, from the perspective of both loosely and tightly coupled pluralistic security communities, real positive peace does not require the transcendence of the nation-state or the elimination of existing cultural and ethnic loyalties and identities or full integration into a single state. It merely requires sovereign states to adopt a novel form of regional governance that, relying on collective identity and mutual trust for coordination and compliance with norms, sustains dependable expectations of peaceful change.[26]

Security communities are structured around a core of strength, which is endowed with superior material and human resources. Because "cores of strength" produce expectations of security and economic welfare, powerful states need not force themselves into other weaker states by violent means or by the threat of the use of violence. Rather, regions may form around them, and common norms and identities may then grow within them.[27] Thus, in special circumstances and within the cognitive boundaries of these regions – for example, the Euro-Atlantic security community (roughly including states associated with the EU and NATO); the North American Free Trade Association (NAFTA) countries (the United States, Canada, and Mexico); the Southern Cone of Latin America (mainly Argentina, Brazil, Chile, Paraguay, and Uruguay); and the still-evolving community around the Association of South East Asian Nations (ASEAN) – people may acquire mutual responsiveness, that is, they may gain the ability to more or less predict one another's behavior and come to know each other as trustworthy. Within some regions, then, people, although organized into states, may nevertheless be able to exploit this mutual trust to develop pluralistic systems of intraregional governance that minimize or even eliminate the threat of war in that community region.

In sum, thick multilateralism refers to the development of security communities, or security community-building processes, around powerful states, by means of social communication and collective identity-building practices, on the basis of normative knowledge forged through new and/or pre-existing institutions.

The changing mechanism of change

The mechanism of change that is associated with the development of security communities, and which may be replacing violent confrontation in power transitions, is something very much like social learning. This is not a new argument. Over 10 years ago, George Modelski argued that evolutionary learning may be replacing major power war as the mechanism that accounts for the replacement of one long cycle (roughly one hundred years) of international relations by another long cycle. According to Modelski, however, it is not agents, whether individuals or political communities, who learn but the long-cycle systems themselves. Following structural functionalism, Modelski thus suggests that it may have become functional for systems to transform themselves through learning rather than through war.[28]

I understand learning differently. First, I define social learning as "an active process of redefinition or reinterpretation of reality – what people consider real, possible and desirable – on the basis of new causal and normative knowledge."[29] Second, learning thus has to do with agents, whether individual or political communities or groups. Third, agents do not just adapt to a changing environment or emulate behavior that has proven successful in other places and times. Rather, social learning "represents the capacity and motivation of social actors to manage and even transform social reality by changing their beliefs of the material and social world and their identities."[30] Fourth, social learning does not represent only a change of individual beliefs, which can be transient. Rather, the transformation of what individuals know and believe amounts to a mechanism of change, because as a result they constitute the social structures that give meaning to their social life in different ways than in the past, and thus they perpetuate, in fact they institutionalize, that which was learned. It is thus the change not only of individual minds but also of social structure that leads to the enlargement of the group of people who practice a certain practice, such as peaceful change.

Power transitions, which are managed by a learning process, rely on agents actively involved in "thick" social interaction and communication processes, the aim of which is not just to persuade each other but, primarily, to institutionalize the practice of peaceful change. Thus, because of changes in the material world, and of transformed knowledge that is attached to material objects, through interaction and social communication, agents are susceptible to changing their collective understandings of their condition, interests, and aspirations; indeed, they may adopt social identities that are consistent with peaceful change. In so doing, not only may they recursively institutionalize the new practices, but, most important, they may also transform "their very concept of problem solving."[31] Thus, if and when a learning mechanism replaces war as the mechanism of change, what once seemed natural, almost desirable, now becomes non-natural, undesirable, and wrong. In other words, regardless of the fact that, in the foreseeable future, inter-state wars may still be distinctively possible, indeed that they are likely to occur (although probably by different means than in the past), managing power transitions through social learning means that *even victorious wars among major powers become undesirable and close to unthinkable.* It also means that, taking everything into consideration, major powers will tend to choose peaceful rather than violent means of achieving their goals. Moreover, in these circumstances, they will tend to be more cautious than in the past and will self-bind to domestic and/or international arrangements to prevent a war that can only mean mutual annihilation.

It follows from the above that it is not just the deterrent potential of weapons of mass destruction in the possession of major powers that may lead to a peaceful transition;[32] wars due to crisis escalation and miscalculation may still occur. And it is not only the calculus associated with expectations of economic progress that may explain the increase in the disparity between the expected utilities of peace and war. Rather, what more than anything else may explain the onset of peaceful transitions in the future is the increasing collective acceptance of practices that, because war has become normatively unacceptable, rely on mutually reciprocal expectations of peaceful change.

It also follows from the above, however, that, lacking a learning mechanism, liberal democratic values – indeed, the "democratic peace" interpretation, according to which liberal democratic states do not make war with each other – are insufficient in and by themselves to explain peaceful power transitions.[33] Rather, only a learning mechanism can explain why a democratic space or shared identity and joint practice become established in a particular space or region and, in our case, among rising and declining powers. Thus, I fully agree with Jean-Marc Coicaud in this volume when he argues that democracy becomes important for the legitimacy of a given international order only insofar as, through socialization, power hegemony "is not transformed into a monopoly over power."[34]

Social learning is the mechanism of change within security communities. But can learning also become the mechanism of change between security communities and outsiders? May we see the development of security community-making processes between security communities and outsiders, even if the former never manage to integrate the latter within their circle of nation-states that entertain dependable expectations of peaceful change? I now turn to these questions.

Power transitions within and across security communities

Charles Kupchan's necessary conditions of peaceful transitions – (a) reciprocal benign images; (b) agreed principles of hierarchy and international order; and (c) international order's legitimization[35] – can thus be said to work differently, depending on whether transitions occur within or across security communities. In the former case, it is also important to consider the scope and depth of collective social identities within security communities. Thus, within security communities, power transitions are likely to be inherently peaceful. This is particularly true for "tightly coupled" security communities, such as the EU, which are characterized by strong shared social identities. On the other hand, power transitions between security communities and outsiders – or between major powers from different security communities – will be peaceful only to the extent that the actors have adopted the mechanism of social learning, use multilateral diplomacy to manage the transition, and actively cooperate in reducing domestic political pressures against managed and peaceful transitions.

One reason power transitions are likely to be peaceful within security communities is the notion that, in these communities, increases in the power of states are either inconsequential or welcome. For, in security communities, power becomes "a magnet."

In a community formed around a group of strong powers, weaker members will expect to share the security and (potentially) other benefits associated with stronger ones. Thus those states that belong to the core of strength do not create security, *per se*; rather because of their positive image, security communities develop around them. This is clearly the case of Europe, where the former Communist states, rather than being invited to form part of the security community, issued their own invitations.[36]

Moreover, particularly in "tightly coupled" security communities, the capabilities of their most powerful agents increasingly serve a common purpose. In these communities, states still act on the basis of their own preferences, as long as these preferences are cognitively framed by the shared understandings of the community. Thus, it would be safe to argue that, for the foreseeable future, no power struggle will occur between EU states, even in the absence of the US security guarantee. Furthermore, in "loosely coupled" security communities too, such as the Euro-Atlantic security community, the likelihood of a violent power transition is small. Thus, it would also be safe to argue that, for the reasons discussed above, a power transition between the United States and the EU is likely to be peaceful. As Barnett and I have shown, what holds a "loosely coupled" security community together are collective identities and mutual trust: "Trust and identity are reciprocal and reinforcing: the development of trust can strengthen mutual identification, and there is a general tendency to trust on the basis of mutual identification."[37] What keeps a collective identity and mutual trust stable, however, are (a) the *institutionalization* of shared practices, (b) *expectations* that arise from a shared social structure, and (c) *power*, understood as the capacity to attach meaning to material reality such that these meanings become naturalized or taken for granted. These conditions are even truer for tightly coupled security communities, in which common political institutions and the distribution of political authority among supranational, national, and subnational institutions make any attempt at "deconstructing" the community very hard to achieve.

Between security communities and outside powers, however, the ability to agree on hierarchy and the basic elements of global legitimate order, and to construct reciprocal benign images, will depend on the evolution of a social learning mechanism among them. To assess this prospect in practical terms, we need to ask where competition against the Euro-Atlantic security community might come from. Russia may one day recover from its current weakness and present a challenge to the community. This seems unlikely, however. First, Russia's weakness vis-à-vis the Euro-Atlantic security community is not a transient matter. It will take major structural economic, technological, military, social, and political changes to bring Russia on a par with NATO countries. Second, NATO countries are making a major effort to transform Russia in their own image and to help incrementally integrate it as part of the West. The jury is still out, however, on whether they will succeed. Third, "security communities are neither security alliances nor collective security systems; nor are they state-like units, only larger. Rather, they are transnational non-territorial 'cognitive regions' where peaceful change is practiced."[38] Thus, in itself, a security community cannot pose a threat, any more than peaceful inter-state relations can be mutually threatening. However, outsiders may feel threatened by a security community that is also organized as a defense alliance. Indeed, many Russians still fear NATO, in spite of repeated attempts by Western powers to persuade them that, rather than threatening Russia, the new NATO offers Russia the opportunity to become integrated with the West, if and when domestic conditions in Russia allow it. But, then, it is not only military capabilities that lie at the source of these fears, and that will determine whether Russia will one day choose to balance against the Euro-Atlantic security community, but also Russians' understanding (or misunderstanding) of the rules of the game in the multilateral age. In other words, it matters whether Russians perceive NATO as a defense alliance poised to profit from Russia's weakness, or as a security community (with a defensive alliance in its midst) that seeks European security through integration rather than through balancing practices.

Balancing against security communities, however, may also arise from dividing lines between civilizations and the social construction of enmity across them. One can think about – although barely imagine – the prospect that Muslim fundamentalism will succeed in creating a solid front of Muslim states against the West and, as argued by leading Islamists, that it will strive to replace the Western order with a Muslim fundamentalist order.[39] But, then again, Islam should not be interpreted merely as a fundamentalist threat, as some people in the West do. Thus, whether or not a future challenge to the Euro-Atlantic security community arising from civilization dividing lines results in power-balancing practices between the parties will to a large extent depend on whether actors across civilizations end up negotiating rules of the road that, because they take into account the cultural sensibilities of both sides, have the potential to result in peaceful change.

Moreover, a peaceful transition between a security community and outsiders will depend on the ability of both the security community and the outsiders to control domestic forces that fuel the practice of power balancing. In addition, exclusion from the benefits of a security community may fuel resentment and ultimately bring about the return of traditional power balancing. Thus, the real concern is not power balancing per se, but exclusion leading to cultural balancing and then to power balancing. Failure to develop a mechanism of social learning between security communities and outsiders will thus rest not only with outsiders who still do not practice peaceful change, but also with actors within security communities who are politically unable or unwilling to engage in a cultural debate with outsiders and to share with them some of the economic and security benefits that their security communities have been able to secure for themselves. Thus, as both Coicaud and Khong argue in this volume, a peaceful transition between the United States and China may depend not only on Chinese leaders adopting peaceful practices but also on North American and European leaders treating Chinese culture and people with the respect they deserve.

This raises another issue, however. Should an existing security community attempt to enlarge itself in order to bring within its embrace large powers that lie outside its "borders"? Or should security community actors content themselves with socializing these powers into accepting security community notions of hierarchy, order, and legitimacy? Alternatively, should security community actors encourage outside powers to establish their own security communities? To begin with, where possible – i.e. where geographical, cultural, socioeconomic, and political conditions exist – it is in the interests of peace for an existing security community to try to incorporate major powers on its periphery. Indeed, this was the approach taken by the OSCE (which until 1994 was called the Conference on Security and Co-operation in Europe) after the break-up of the Soviet Empire. The OSCE adopted the view that it must first let the largest possible number of states believe that they are part of the same cultural region. Only then, when member states have formally and instrumentally accepted the shared institutional normative structures and practices, does the OSCE socialize state elites by means of continuous diplomatic interaction and a wide range of community-building practices. Thus, it was crucial for the OSCE to make Russia feel that it is inside the "Common European House"; otherwise Russians might turn into "the other," and thus against "us."

NATO, however, was in no position to bring Russia in. This is not only because of Article 5 of NATO's Charter, according to which NATO countries commit themselves to come to the defense of their fellow members, if attacked, but also because Russia's political and economic institutions have not been reformed enough for it to be considered as part of the West. But NATO could not leave Russia out either. Thus, since 1991, NATO has been wavering between the two poles, unable to accept Russia until it substantially changes its political and economic institutions, and yet engaging Russia enough (for example through the Partnership for Peace) to give it a sense that, in the future, it could join the community. Since 1991, it has been NATO, and not the OSCE, that has been the main player on the European security scene. NATO, however, still has a great deal to learn from OSCE practices in dealing with "outsiders," and should keep Russia engaged, culturally and politically. The reason is that the Euro-Atlantic security community and Russia must agree on the rules of the road and develop shared understandings on hierarchy, order, and legitimacy. More generally, they all need self-consciously to adopt a shared learning mechanism and to act in concert to help remove domestic opposition to practices of peaceful change.

Should the Euro-Atlantic security community also attempt to bring states of other regions, such as Latin America or East Asia, within its ranks? Or should it encourage these regions to create their own security communities? Because, as argued above, security communities are not alliances or state-like units (only larger) but are regions where peaceful change is practiced, security communities may easily overlap, as do, for example, the Euro-Atlantic region, the EU, and Scandinavia. This means that, were a security community to develop in the Western hemisphere, it would partially overlap with NAFTA and the Euro-Atlantic security community. A Western hemisphere security community not only would not pose a threat to other security communities, but also would help establish social learning as a mechanism of change in the entire Western hemisphere, and would help institutionalize common rules and shared beliefs about order, hierarchy, legitimacy, and peaceful change. Thus both the United States and the EU should encourage the development of a security community in the Western hemisphere. Although Euro-Atlantic security community states are culturally closer to the Western hemisphere than to East Asia, and although in East Asia China may be willing and able to challenge Western attempts to set regional rules of the road, the Euro-Atlantic security community should nonetheless encourage East Asia to become a security community. At the same time, Euro-Atlantic security community states should be sensitive about not imposing their views of hierarchy, order, and legitimacy on East Asians and should leave East Asians to take the lead in the development of security community-like processes, as ASEAN has done for the past 30 years. Otherwise, attempts to construct joint mechanisms of social learning may backfire and tensions across cultural divides may promote rather than constrain mutual suspicions and fears. On the other hand, in order to build consensus on a mechanism of peaceful change, the Euro-Atlantic security community should promote, and participate in, institutionalized dialogues with East Asia, as it has started to do in the past decade (e.g. Asia Pacific Economic Cooperation).

Still another question is whether or not an attempt should be made to homogenize culture around the world. One could persuasively argue that, regardless of people's motivations, cultural globalization is already taking place. On the other hand, it is one thing to argue about the increasing development of global "cultures," such the "Davos culture," as I did above, and quite another to argue on behalf of achieving global cultural homogeneity. The latter goal is a chimera and should be discouraged. The world is *not* converging toward a common set of guiding principles and it would be senseless to work for such a goal. Even with respect to the United States and Europe, there are differing views of ordering principles.

In this context, we must take into account that there are powers, such as the United States, that, owing to the nature of their culture, frequently attempt to shape other states' principles and norms in their own image, regardless of these states' geographic and cultural location. On the other hand, there are the eastern powers, such as China and Japan, that, because their culture is inward looking, see the regional level as their natural area for hegemonic control. This asymmetry between global-oriented powers and regional-oriented powers could lead to misunderstandings and thus enhance mutual fears across civilization lines. This might lead to difficulties over mutual agreement on rules and, thus, over the peaceful management of a power transition. To deal with these dangers, the Euro-Atlantic security community should start by engaging China and Japan in a dialogue about the conceptual and practical differences between regional hegemony and security community. Thus, the name of the game with regard to a peaceful transition between the United States and China or Japan is not just economic and political engagement. Rather, a peaceful transition depends also on US willingness to adapt international rules and multilateral institutions so that they reflect other powers' cultural values and norms. By means of dialogue, then, without compromising their own culture and beliefs, Americans should be ready and willing to negotiate *new* multicultural rules and institutions that express a compromise between cultures and signal an inclination jointly to learn.

As an example of what may turn out in the future to be a collective learning process, I can point to the Mediterranean area. Since 1995, the EU has been involved in a tenuous and obviously self-interested project – better known as the "Euro-Mediterranean Partnership" or "Barcelona Process" – aimed at constructing a Mediterranean region. The prospects are dim of finding common interests between the West and Islam and between the rich North and the poor South, let alone shared cultural and political attributes, that would promote the development of a Mediterranean identity. And yet, in order to avert a "Clash of Civilizations"[40] in the Mediterranean area, it is imperative to jumpstart pluralistic integration processes as soon as possible, even if these processes may bear fruit only in the very long term. Techniques of security community-building and the adoption of social learning as a mechanism of change thus represent the quintessential anti-"clash of civilizations" project.

To end this chapter, it would be useful to speculate whether or not there is a distinct possibility that, in the future, not only will the nature and mechanisms of power transitions change, but, rather, power transitions as we know them may come to an end. The reason for this speculation is the idea that technological and economic changes, as well as changes in what Ruggie called "epistemes" (what people collectively know about themselves and others, or intersubjective images of reality),[41] may be leading to a profound transformation in the nature of actors in the international system. This transformation may then trigger a horizontal diffusion of power – from major powers to a large number of state and non-state actors – and/or a vertical stratification of power, i.e. the spread of rule and authority across supranational, national, and subnational institutions. In such a world, the concept of power transition might still be relevant but it would mean something very different. Future research projects on power transition should therefore explore what would happen to hierarchy, order, and legitimacy and, in general, to power transitions in a world in which power is widely *and deeply* dispersed.

Notes

1. Arthur Koestler, *The Act of Creation* (London: Picador, 1975), pp. 229–230.
2. For a dissenting view see Stephen Krasner, *Sovereignty: Organized Hypocrisy* (Princeton, NJ: Princeton University Press, 1999).
3. A. F. K. Organski, *World Politics* (New York: Knopf, 1958); A. F. K. Organski and Jacek Kugler, *The War Ledger* (Chicago: Chicago University Press, 1980).
4. Jonathan M. DiCicco, "Power Transitions, Parity, and War Onset," paper prepared for the 39th Annual Meeting of the International Studies Association, Minneapolis, Minnesota, 17–21 March 1998. For a dissenting view see Jack Levy, "The Causes of War: A Review of Theories and Evidence," in Philip E. Tetlock et al., eds., *Behavior, Society, and Nuclear War, Volume I* (New York: Oxford University Press, 1989).
5. Stephen G. Brooks, "The Globalization of Production and the Changing Benefits of Conquest," *Journal of Conflict Resolution*, Vol. 43, No. 5 (October 1999), pp. 646–670.
6. Donald Kagan, Eliot A. Cohen, Charles F. Doran, and Michael Mandelbaum, "Is Major War Obsolete? An Exchange," *Survival*, Vol. 41, No. 2 (Summer 1999), pp. 139–152.
7. See, for example, John Agnew, "Mapping Political Power beyond State Boundaries: Territory, Identity, and Movement in World Politics," *Millennium*, Vol. 28, No. 3 (1999), pp. 499–521.
8. Alexander George and Richard Smoke, *Deterrence in American Foreign Policy: Theory and Practice* (New York: Columbia University Press, 1974).
9. Kofi Annan, "Two Concepts of Sovereignty," *The Economist*, 18 September 1999.
10. Margaret Keck and Kathryn Sikkink, *Transnational Advocacy Networks* (Ithaca, NY: Cornell University Press, 1998).

11. See Emanuel Adler, "Imagined (Security) Communities," *Millennium*, Vol. 26 (1997), pp. 249–277.
12. See Jakob Oehrgaard, "Less Than Supranational, More Than Intergovernmental: European Political Cooperation and the Dynamics of Intergovernmental Integration," *Millennium*, Vol. 26 (1997), pp. 1–29.
13. Daniel Bell, *The End of Ideology* (Cambridge, MA: Harvard University Press, 1998).
14. Francis Fukuyama, *The End of History and the Last Man* (New York: Free Press, 1992).
15. Joseph Nye, Jr., "Soft Power," *Foreign Policy*, Vol. 80 (Fall 1990), pp. 153–171.
16. Emanuel Adler, "Seizing the Middle Ground: Constructivism in World Politics," *European Journal of International Relations*, Vol. 3 (September 1997), pp. 319–364.
17. See, for example, Adler, "Seizing the Middle Ground"; Friedrich Kratochwil, *Rules, Norms, and Decisions: On the Conditions of Practical and Legal Reasoning in International Relations and Domestic Affairs* (New York: Cambridge University Press, 1989); Nicholas Onuf, *World of Our Making: Rules and Rule in Social Theory and International Relations* (Columbia: University of South Carolina Press, 1989); John G. Ruggie, *Constructing the World Polity: Essays on International Institutionalization* (London and New York: Routledge, 1998); Alexander Wendt, *Social Theory of International Politics* (New York: Cambridge University Press, 1999).
18. Robert D. Putnam, "Diplomacy and Domestic Politics: The Logic of Two-Level Games," *International Organization*, Vol. 42, No. 3 (Summer 1998), pp. 427–460.
19. Emanuel Adler and Beverly Crawford, eds., *Progress in Postwar International Relations* (New York: Columbia University Press, 1991).
20. Adler, "Seizing the Middle Ground."
21. John G. Ruggie, *Multilateralism Matters* (New York: Columbia University Press, 1993).
22. Emanuel Adler and Michael Barnett, *Security Communities* (Cambridge: Cambridge University Press, 1998), p. 30.
23. Karl Deutsch et al., *Political Community and the North Atlantic Area* (Princeton, NJ: Princeton University Press, 1957), pp. 5–6.
24. Emanuel Adler, "Condition(s) of Peace," *Review of International Studies* (December 1998), pp. 165–191.
25. Adler and Barnett, *Security Communities*, p. 30.
26. Adler, "Condition(s) of Peace," p. 177.
27. Deutsch et al., *Political Community*, and Adler and Barnett, *Security Communities*.
28. George Modelski, "Is World Politics Evolutionary Learning?" *International Organization*, Vol. 44, No. 1 (Winter 1990), pp. 1–24.
29. Adler and Barnett, *Security Communities*, p. 43.
30. Ibid., p. 44.
31. Ruggie, *Constructing the World Polity*, p. 20.
32. If power transition theory is right to believe that war results from a calculation by either the rising power or the declining power, nuclear weapons would tend to affect these calculations in the direction of caution and a peaceful management of the transition. Not only would a nuclear war between the rising and the declining power help to produce "parity" at the lowest denominator level, but it would also benefit third parties, which would then rise to a hegemonic position. Thus, for example, were the United States and China to choose to go to war as a result of a hypothetical transition conflict between them, both countries would experience losses and destruction that would put them out of the race, and therefore would allow other powers, such as Europe, to achieve preeminence.
33. On the "democratic peace" theory, see Michael W. Doyle, "Kant, Liberal Legacies, and Foreign Affairs, Part I," *Philosophy and Public Affairs*, Vol. 12 (Summer 1983), pp. 205–233, and Bruce M. Russett, *Grasping the Democratic Peace: Principles for a Post–Cold War World* (Princeton, NJ: Princeton University Press, 1993).

34. Chapter 4 in this volume.
35. Chapter 1 in this volume.
36. Emanuel Adler and Michael Barnett, "Governing Anarchy: A Research Agenda for the Study of Security Communities," *Ethics and International Affairs*, Vol. 10 (1996), p. 83.
37. Adler and Barnett, *Security Communities*, p. 45.
38. Adler, "Condition(s) of Peace," p. 180.
39. See, for example, Abdulrahman A. Kurdi, *The Islamic State: A Study Based on the Islamic Holy Constitution* (London: Mansell, 1988). For a view of Islam that is not inconsistent with Western liberal ideas, see Bassam Tibi, *The Challenge of Fundamentalism: Political Islam and the New World Disorder* (Berkeley: University of California Press, 1998).
40. Samuel Huntington, *The Clash of Civilizations and the Remaking of World Order* (New York: Simon & Schuster, 1996).
41. John G. Ruggie, "Territoriality and Beyond: Problematizing Modernity in International Relations," *International Organization*, Vol. 47, No. 1 (Winter 1993), pp. 139–174.

7
Conclusion: The shifting nature of power and peaceful systemic change

Charles A. Kupchan

The opening chapter of this book contends that global politics are on the verge of entering a period of systemic change. As this new century progresses, the unipolar system that emerged after the end of the Cold War will give way to a landscape in which power and responsibility are more equally shared. The bloody record of past power transitions serves as a point of departure for this volume and underscores the importance of new efforts to think through how to manage systemic change peacefully.

The claim that a systemic change is looming on the horizon is admittedly contestable. The United States enjoys a stark material preponderance that shows few signs of dissipating in the years ahead. America's economic output far surpasses that of any other country. The United States spends more on defense than the next five major powers combined and more on research and development in the defense sector than the rest of the world combined.[1] Its qualitative edge in technology suggests that its economic and military supremacy is likely to be sustained for some time to come. Furthermore, America's material preponderance is backed up by a quite impressive portfolio of "soft power" stemming from the breadth and depth of its cultural reach.

The stark power asymmetries between the United States and potential challengers should not, however, breed complacency that systemic change is necessarily far off. To focus only on material indicators of power is to assume that power transitions of the future will look like those of the past, in which a rising state pursues and eventually overtakes the reigning hegemon. But, for three critical reasons, the next systemic change may bear little resemblance to past transitions.

First, the most likely near-term challenger to the United States is not a unitary state, but a Europe in the midst of integration. For the foreseeable future, the European Union is likely to fall well short of becoming an amalgamated polity. At the same time, a single market and single currency give Europe a distinctively collective character; at least in the economic realm, the EU is already a counterweight to the United States. Whether or not the EU develops a military capability commensurate with its economic resources and whether or not authority continues to be concentrated at the supranational level, a more balanced Atlantic relationship is likely to evolve as the twenty-first century progresses – with as yet undetermined consequences for global polarity.

Second, even if the United States maintains its economic and military supremacy, effective unipolarity also depends upon America's willingness to continue expending its resources and serving as the global protector and guarantor of last resort. In this respect, initial signs indicate a distinct possibility of a shrinking American internationalism. The United States did lead NATO into battle over Kosovo, but with a distinct lack of enthusiasm.[2] Centrist politicians from both of America's main parties argued passionately that the interests at stake in Kosovo did not warrant US military intervention. In the aftermath of the air campaign, the Senate unanimously approved a resolution that bemoaned the "significant shortcomings" in European defense capabilities and urged the EU to rectify the "overall imbalance" within the alliance. The Senate's rejection of the Comprehensive Test Ban Treaty and the momentum building behind the deployment of missile defense further indicate a United States that may seek to reduce its external commitments and cordon itself off from potential external threats. In this sense, systemic change may be precipitated by the retrenchment and turning inward of the reigning hegemon more than by the rise of new challengers.

Third, changes in the nature of power and in the nature of the polities that wield power mean that a coming shift in the structure of the system may take place in a new international environment. The advent of nuclear weapons, globalization, the spread of democracy, changes in the sources of wealth – these are all developments that could profoundly alter the process and the consequences of systemic change. What constitutes a pole could be undergoing change as well as the forces that will shape relations between poles.

The purpose of this closing chapter is to reflect on the nature of contemporary systemic change and to evaluate the extent to which the lessons of the past speak to the challenges of the future. I begin by looking at how changes in material factors are likely to affect systemic change.

I then examine how the relatively benign character of the reigning hegemon is likely to affect relations with rising challengers. In the nature of its polity and in the practice of its policies, the United States represents a departure from the past. Finally, I discuss the implications of the emergence of security communities for systemic change. North America and Europe have carved out a zone of stable peace and virtually eliminated security competition between themselves. How can this existing security community be protected against unraveling? Should this security community be enlarged? Should similar zones of peace be replicated in other regions? The answers to these questions will shed light on the nature of contemporary systemic change and help guide policy makers seeking peacefully to manage coming shifts in the international distribution of power.

Changes in material conditions

There are sound reasons for believing that changes in military technology and the sources of wealth may dampen security competition and make systemic change easier to manage peacefully than in the past. Nuclear weapons breed caution and may succeed in limiting the intensity of strategic rivalry between competing poles of power. Predatory conquest and control over land and labor no longer represent the best pathway to economic and military supremacy; today's great powers may be able to attain the wealth and influence they desire without aggression. Furthermore, contemporary globalization, more far-reaching in both quantity and quality than ever before, may help encourage multiple power centers to pursue joint gains rather than seek individual advantage. I consider each of these claims in turn.

Nuclear weapons

Nuclear weapons do decrease the chances that systemic change will be accompanied by major war. The prospect of nuclear devastation may well be sufficient to prevent reigning hegemon and rising challenger from engaging in the great contests for primacy that usually accompany the decline of one great power and the rise of another. At the same time, the nuclear revolution may make systemic change more precarious for three distinct reasons.

First, if nuclear weapons do not succeed in deterring conflict among contenders for primacy, the resultant conflict among nuclear-armed power centers would be catastrophic. History makes clear that systemic change brings with it powerful war-causing forces. That these forces will be unleashed during the nuclear age warrants considerable thought about how best to dampen the possibility of hegemonic war. Furthermore, nuclear weapons in the hands of third parties increase the chances that systemic instability, even if not accompanied in the first instance by conflict among power centers, could have very dangerous consequences.

Second, nuclear weapons may embolden contenders for primacy and make them less willing to compromise to find a mutually acceptable order and new hierarchy.[3] Even if nuclear weapons do restrain parties from going to war, they may also make them less pliant partners because of the bargaining strength associated with nuclear capability. A declining hegemon may hold its ground because of its ability to threaten nuclear retaliation; despite the loss of its material superiority, it may seek to cling to its position in the global hierarchy. A rising challenger may be equally obstinate because of its nuclear capability.

Third, even if nuclear weapons prevent contenders for primacy from engaging in outright war, they may do little to facilitate rapprochement among leading power centers – and indeed may stand in the way of such rapprochement for the reasons just cited. A multipolar world in which stability is maintained by mutual nuclear deterrence is far preferable to war, but far less preferable than a multipolar world in which stability is maintained through cooperation. In this sense, scholars and analysts alike need to address how to bring about a systemic transition that leads to a warm, rather than a cold, peace.

State power

Changes in the sources of state power may act to moderate the war-causing potential of systemic transition. Territorial conquest pays less than it used to; economic primacy is now rooted in technological innovation and communication, not land and labor. The proliferation of weaponry to many parts of the world also increases the costs of conquest to the aggressor.

Although it is plausible, if not likely, that major powers will, for utilitarian reasons, engage in less predatory behavior than their imperial predecessors, a world in which power centers regularly engage in strategic restraint is not necessarily a stable world. Strategic restraint, while reducing direct rivalry between contenders for primacy, could result in the underprovision of security in third areas. Rather than compete for market access and strategic influence in developing areas, major powers may seek to cordon themselves off. The result could be an incremental return to disorder in the periphery, which ultimately would have the potential to undermine order in core areas. Imagine what might have happened in the Balkans had both the European Union and the United

States refrained from military engagement throughout the 1990s. Conflict might well have spread throughout the Balkan peninsula, ultimately threatening the broader European and Atlantic security order. The ongoing proliferation of weapons of mass destruction also raises the stakes of instability in third areas.

It is also possible that contenders for primacy, even if they do not initially clash over territory, will engage in status competition.[4] Systemic change, after all, upsets the existing hierarchy, creating demands by rising powers for more voice and influence. A direct conflict of interest may therefore not be necessary for rivalry to begin and escalate. The sources of World War I, for example, lay not in disputes over borders or territory but in Germany's desire for a level of influence in Europe commensurate with its economic capability. Status competition thus has the potential to escalate into geopolitical competition.

Globalization

Globalization, according to its many proponents, contributes to stability through several different pathways. High levels of international trade and investment and the globalization of production increase the costs of geopolitical rivalry. As Thomas Friedman has persuasively argued, the global marketplace is also imposing a "golden straightjacket" on states that enter it, leading to a convergence of domestic structures and ideology.[5] If states want to have access to international capital and the global market for goods and services, Friedman argues, they have to adhere to a relatively constraining set of political dictums and business practices. This domestic convergence may in turn reduce the likelihood of conflicts of interest.

Parsing out the consequences of globalization for systemic change is complicated by the fact that globalization is itself an ambiguous and elusive term. If taken to be the global diffusion of trade, investment, production, and communication, then the phenomenon has both positive and negative effects on the prospects for peaceful systemic change. To be sure, high levels of cross-border trade and investment are encouraging leading states to pursue mutual advantage. The global diffusion of production sites is of particular importance because they constitute a more durable – and less easily moved – asset than equity investment. In addition, most of the world's wealthier states and those aspiring to such wealth are converging around a core set of capitalist values and practices, decreasing the likelihood of diverging interests. All of these features of a globalized economy may promote stability amidst structural change.

But globalization also brings with it forces that could magnify the destabilizing effects of transition. Should sectoral or regional economic shocks take place, a fast, interdependent market will transmit such shocks globally. The 1930s made clear the extent to which spreading economic crisis can lead to geopolitical instability. Globalization may well widen the bandwidth within which market disturbances can occur without destabilizing the broader system. But, once a certain threshold has been crossed, disturbances may spread with a vengeance.

The domestic convergence engendered by globalization also has negative as well as positive consequences for systemic stability. Developing states are converging around a common set of values and practices in order to encourage foreign investment and participate fully in the global economy. But strict adherence to economic principles imposed from outside can also have powerful backlashes if such adherence does not pay off. States buffeted by the international economy at times fight back, fostering the authoritarian tendencies that can in turn trigger external ambition and geopolitical rivalries. In *The Great Transformation*, Karl Polanyi linked twentieth-century fascism to excessive adherence to market principles and the gold standard.[6] His analysis has cautionary implications for today's global economy and the discipline of Friedman's golden straightjacket.

In sum, material conditions provide cause for both optimism and pessimism about the prospects for managing systemic change peacefully. At a minimum, the above analysis suggests that there is little room for complacency in confronting the geopolitical consequences of a return to multipolarity.

Changes in polity and practice

One of the most puzzling aspects of the current strategic landscape is the absence of balancing against the United States. France, Russia, and China may cavil at what they see as America's overbearing, imperial behavior. But, behind the scenes, they quietly welcome the presence of US troops in Europe and Asia and the stability they engender. Far from balancing against the United States, most countries of the world behave as if they cannot get enough of American power and purpose.

This unusual absence of balancing against the hegemon is the product of three factors. First, America's location, with large expanses of water to its east and west, limits the threat it poses to major powers in Europe and Asia. Were a country of the size and power of the United States to be located on the Eurasian land mass, it would be far more likely to trigger balancing. America's direct neighbors, Canada and Mexico, simply do not have the option of balancing because of stark power asymmetries.

Second, the scope of the power gap between America and potential rivals calls into question the feasibility and desirability of attempting to balance against the United States. With US military spending roughly equal to that of the next five powers combined, no single state could realistically seek to act as a counterweight to US power. Furthermore, with the United States underwriting and in effect fashioning the key multilateral institutions and practices in both the security and economic realms, challenging American dominance would bring with it considerable costs. To be sure, were coalitions of major states to form against the United States, those coalitions would have the wherewithal to act as counterweights to US power. However, such coalitions simply are not taking shape. Europe is gradually emerging as a collective entity equal to the United States in economic terms. But the European project is being fueled primarily by efforts to escape national rivalry within Europe, not a wish to balance against the United States.

That coalitions are not forming against the United States brings us to the third reason that balancing is not taking place: the character of American power. Were the United States engaging in predatory behavior – regularly invading other states and pursuing exploitative policies – balancing coalitions would no doubt form. Instead, the United States engages in policies that succeed, for the most part, in reassuring other states about its intentions. Put differently, because of the nature of its polity and its practice, other states attribute to the United States a benign character.[7]

Democratic government partially explains this perception of the United States. The American polity is transparent and porous. The vagaries of partisan politics are in plain view, as are the self-checking mechanisms associated with three competing branches of government. That the United States regularly engages in both self-binding (unilateral restraint) and co-binding (multilateral restraint) further reassures others about US intentions. And as more countries become democratic and share a sense of affinity and commonality, they are likely to join the grouping of states within which security competition has been muted, if not eliminated.

A key question for the future is whether or not the absence of balancing against the United States will continue even as global power becomes more equally distributed. Will American policy change and become more aggressive when the United States is confronted with more capable rivals? Will the Atlantic security community be threatened by a more self-possessed Europe? How should the Atlantic community manage its relationship with other regions? To address these questions, I turn to the role that security communities are likely to play in preserving order and facilitating peaceful change. If systemic change is on the horizon, a key determinant of its geopolitical consequences will be whether or not the security community formed across the Atlantic will withstand a new balance of power. It is equally important to speculate about how existing security communities can be enlarged or new ones created in order to incorporate rising powers such as China and Russia.

Peaceful change and security communities: The West against the rest?

As I argued at the close of chapter 2, the Atlantic democracies are unlikely to become security competitors even as a more equal balance of power emerges between North America and Europe. As the war over Kosovo and its aftermath have made clear, the United States is tiring of its role as Europe's protector of last resort, meaning that Europe will have to rise to the occasion and develop the political will and the military capability to assume more responsibility for its own security. But a more autonomous Europe is a logical consequence of the end of the Cold War and the decreasing need for a dominant American role, not a sign that Europe and the United States are growing apart. Firmly embedded in a shared history, common values and political culture, and a thick network of institutions, the existing security community of the Atlantic democracies is likely to weather coming changes in the distribution of power.

The formation of a security community among the Atlantic democracies took decades. The threat posed by the Soviet Union provided critical impetus. The prospects of mutual economic gain helped bind states together and institutionalize cooperative behavior. And the cultural and historical affinity that exists between North America and Western Europe was an important facilitating condition. The durability of the political space occupied by the Atlantic democracies has been manifested not just in its continued existence, but also in its efforts to expand. Both NATO and the EU have embarked on ambitious plans of enlargement, seeking to integrate the new democracies of Central Europe into the Atlantic community.

A key unknown of this process of enlargement is its consequences for Russia and for East Asia. Russia could balance against Europe, especially if NATO and the EU exclude Russia in their plans for enlargement. At the same time, depending on politics in Moscow and in Western capitals, Russia could ultimately be included in a broader Europe. Should Russia end up being excluded from the European space, the potential is high for a return of competitive geopolitics to Eurasia. For reasons of both security and status, Russia would likely seek to reconstitute itself as an independent power center, increasing the chances that Moscow try to reassert control over its immediate neighbors. Exclusion from Europe would also affect Russian identity, encouraging Russians to see Europe as the other, not the self. As Russia comes back on line as a major player, it is therefore important to ensure that its power, influence, and identity are arrayed with, rather than against, a power center in Western Europe. NATO and the EU should therefore make the drawing westward of Russia and its embrace in the Atlantic security community a top priority.[8]

Mapping out a geopolitical trajectory for East Asia is far more complicated. East Asia is unlikely to become part of an Atlantic security community. None of the conditions that brought together the United States and Europe pertain. The Atlantic community and East Asian states do not face a common threat. They do not share a cultural affinity. And they are at different stages of economic and political development. Furthermore, deep political cleavages still exist in East Asia, meaning that the states of the region will for the foreseeable future be preoccupied with each other, rather than with their collective relations with Europe or North America. The risk in the near term is the return of intraregional balancing and rivalry, especially if American internationalism wanes and the United States seeks to reduce the scope of its commitments in East Asia. From this perspective, facilitating cooperation and rapprochement among proximate poles of power *within* East Asia is a far more immediate and important challenge than fashioning East Asia's relations with other regions. Forming a security community within East Asia is thus a necessary condition for drawing the region into a broader zone of peace.

Regional reconciliation and rapprochement depend first and foremost on improving relations between China and Japan. Efforts to build a stable regional order will falter if East Asia's two major states remain estranged. Just as reconciliation between France and Germany was the critical ingredient in building a stable zone of peace in Europe, so too is Sino-Japanese rapprochement the *sine qua non* of a stable peace in East Asia.

Primary responsibility for improving Sino-Japanese ties lies with Japan. With an economy and political system much more developed than China's, Japan has far more latitude in exploring openings in the relationship. Japan could also make a major step forward by finally acknowledging and formally apologizing for its behavior during World War II. The United States could further this process by welcoming and helping to facilitate overtures between Tokyo and Beijing. Washington should also help dislodge the inertia that pervades politics in Tokyo by making clear to the Japanese that they cannot indefinitely rely on American guarantees to ensure their security. Japan therefore needs to take advantage of America's protective umbrella while it lasts, pursuing the policies of reconciliation and integration essential to constructing a regional security order resting on cooperation rather than deterrence.

If overtures from Tokyo succeed in reducing tensions between China and Japan, the United States would be able to play a less prominent role in the region, making possible an improvement in its own relations with China. As it buys time for Sino-Japanese rapprochement to get off the ground, the United States should avoid rhetoric and policies that might induce China to intensify its efforts to balance against Japan and the United States. Talk of an impending Chinese military threat is both counterproductive and misguided; the Chinese military is nowhere near world class.[9] The United States should also avoid provocative moves, such as deploying anti-missile defenses in the theater or supporting a Taiwanese policy of moving toward formal independence. China could do its part to strengthen its relationship with the United States by containing saber-rattling over Taiwan, halting the export of weapons to rogue states, and avoiding actions and rhetoric that could inflame territorial disputes in the region.

The road ahead

The central message of the above analysis is that, despite reasons to be optimistic that contemporary power transitions should be easier to manage peacefully than those of the past, any complacency about the challenges ahead would be unwarranted. Post-war periods are usually followed by a period of relief and optimism and a sense of safety and final escape from geopolitical competition and war. But time and again such optimism has proved illusory; peace turned out to be only a hiatus from war, not a lasting condition.

Changes in material conditions do suggest that conquest pays less than it used to; major powers may well be more restrained with each other and with third parties than in the past. At the same time, contests over critical resources (water, oil, lines of communication) may still occur. And even if material interests do not clash, competition over status and hierarchy has the potential to spill over into the security realm. Perhaps most importantly, the causes of today's relatively peaceful international setting are overdetermined. It may be unipolarity, not nuclear weapons, the declining returns to conquest, or democracy that is preserving stability. If so, the return of a multipolar world may well overwhelm these other peace-causing variables. This uncertainty points to the importance and urgency of beginning to plan for systemic transition. It is better to map out a strategy for the future while unipolarity still holds than to wait until multipolarity has already begun to make the international landscape more intractable.

A second admonition stems from the observation that globalization, although under certain conditions it can promote stability and integration, can also have exactly the opposite effect. Protecting against the downsides of globalization involves several steps. First, mechanisms to limit the global transmission of economic shocks should be built into the international financial architecture. Just as the New York Stock Exchange automatically suspends trading when volatility reaches extreme levels, so should international capital markets introduce "circuit-breakers" to prevent the contagion-effect of unforeseen shocks. Second, major states should protect against the possibility of a political backlash against globalization should there be a world-wide economic downturn. If the United States, Germany, and Japan, rather than Malaysia and Thailand, are eventually the victims of a globalized economy, the consequences could be severe. The states that underwrite the system would then be compelled to withdraw from that system, risking the breakdown of the international economy and the adoption of more mercantilist policies by the leading states. Having policies on the shelf to prepare for such contingencies can help prevent the unraveling of a liberal trading order. It is better to recognize the potential need for such cushions and have them ready to deploy than to be left in the lurch.

A third admonition concerns US policy and the need to find the right balance between self-binding and engagement. The stability of the current system depends in large part on American restraint and Washington's willingness to underwrite an international order that contains a healthy dose of consensual governance. But America's ability to find the correct mix of leadership and accommodation will be more difficult as power asymmetries diminish and Washington's influence is reduced. As already demonstrated by the US Senate's rejection of the Comprehensive Test Ban Treaty, America's pursuit of national missile defense, and Congress's lack of enthusiasm for US intervention in the Balkans, US policy is likely increasingly to oscillate between unilateralism and isolationism. While the former would likely induce allies and adversaries alike to distance themselves from US leadership, the latter would likely produce unwanted security vacuums, especially in East Asia and third areas. Accordingly, fashioning a new American internationalism – one that remains multilateralist at its core and that can be sustained politically over the long term – is an essential ingredient of efforts to manage systemic change.

The creation of a security community in the West that seems ready to outlast the distribution of power that led to its formation similarly provides good reason for guarded optimism. The vitality and strength of the Atlantic community demonstrate that stable zones of peace are in fact possible and that they can exist even in the absence of the conditions that made them possible. Nonetheless, elites and publics in both the United States and Europe cannot afford to take the Atlantic link for granted; they must appreciate the revolutionary nature of this stable zone of peace and take whatever steps are necessary to preserve it. Furthermore, it will be no easy task to promote security communities in other parts of the world or to ensure peaceful relations between the Atlantic community and other regions. Especially as Russia, China, and other emerging powers take the stage, shifts in regional and global balances of power will again try the skills of statesmen in facilitating peaceful systemic change.

In closing, I return to the three concepts that form the conceptual core of this study: benign character, order, and legitimacy. We have argued that peaceful transition is a product of these three variables working in sequential fashion. The mutual attribution of benign character is the starting point: it enables contenders for primacy to pursue rapprochement and to replace mutual threat with mutual trust. Agreement on order is the next step: it produces a new hierarchy and a new set of rules of the road. Legitimacy is the capstone of the process: it helps create a new political space that transcends the boundaries of the original parties and locks in a stable zone of peace.

The important role that the mutual attribution of benign character plays in facilitating peaceful change leads to two questions. First, what policies are needed to ensure that parties that already see one another as benign continue to do so? Second, what can be done to promote a mutual sense of benign character among parties that are current or potential antagonists?

As to the first question, the first post–Cold War decade provides cause for optimism. The Atlantic democracies continue to prosper as a security community despite the lack of a pressing external threat. No signs of security rivalry between North America and Europe have yet emerged. At the same time, Europe is still finding its way as a collective actor and remains under US tutelage, especially on matters of security. As the balance of power and influence becomes more equal, both parties should be sure to continue engaging in acts of self-binding and co-binding. Passing up on opportunities for individual advantage, relying on consensual, multilateral governance, and engaging in collective ventures will help ensure that benign images do not gradually give way to malign ones. Public education, increasing cultural and educational exchanges, and deeper institutional linkages will also help.

Promoting benign images where they do not already exist will be a far more formidable task. Two sobering conclusions emerge from the above analysis. First, strategic necessity plays an important role in triggering the reconstruction of social identities and efforts to turn enemies into partners. Second, a preexisting cultural or linguistic affinity appears to be a necessary condition for the mutual attribution of benign character. These two observations do not augur well for rapprochement between the United States and China. Neither faces a pressing need to reduce external commitments. And the cultural divide between the two countries is wide. Nonetheless, both Americans and Chinese should take into consideration how important are the broader images that the two polities hold of one another. Politicians on both sides should therefore exercise great caution and avoid using diatribes against the other for domestic political purposes. The top priority for the future is not getting the balance of power right and making sure that both sides deploy defensive rather than offensive weapons systems. Instead, the goal is to embark on a long-term process of rapprochement that will eventually succeed in fostering the mutual attribution of benign character. On the Chinese side, domestic political liberalization would be an important step in the right direction. On the American side, more deference to Chinese concerns and according China a greater voice in regional and global affairs would similarly move the relationship down the right path.

As Yuen Foong Khong makes clear in his chapter, even if the United States and China succeed in sending each other signals of benign intent, reaching agreement on order in East Asia will be no easy task. The two powers remain relatively far apart on several important dimensions, including human rights and political reform, bilateral trade, the norm of multilateralism, arms proliferation, and resolution of territorial disputes (Taiwan in particular). Khong notes that differences on these issues stem at least in part from China's perception that the United States does not accord it sufficient status and weight in the international arena. Washington's willingness to deal with Beijing on a more equal basis could help resolve substantive disagreement on ordering norms. Renegotiating order in the Asian region is complicated by the role of Japan. Japan continues to follow America's lead in the region. But its views on and place in a new regional order will be integral to managing systemic change in the region peacefully. In light of continuing tensions between China and Japan, the United States certainly faces a considerable challenge in crafting a regional order that will simultaneously satisfy Beijing, Tokyo, and Washington.

In developing the notion of democratic hegemony, Jean-Marc Coicaud places the challenges ahead in a broader political and normative context. As Coicaud elucidates, scholars and practitioners alike should cease equating hegemony with order and the end of hegemony with disorder. Instead, the current hegemon as well as rising challengers should seek to build a legitimate international order – one that rests on acceptance of change, reciprocity, respect, and democratic norms. The alternative,

Coicaud argues, is the gradual erosion of the current order – owing less to changes in the distribution of power than to the delegitimation of an undemocratic and unreciprocal hegemony. The United States should therefore use its primacy while it lasts to socialize rising powers, encourage a more balanced set of relationships among powerful units, and seek to bring about an international system that remains open to change and the circulation of power. The result would be an international system ready for and able to withstand change – a hallmark of democracy within states – rather than yet another static hegemonic system that seeks to perpetuate itself in the name of order.

Emanuel Adler's focus on social learning provides hope that Coicaud's vision could ultimately become a reality. If Adler is right that what is changing is not just the material distribution of power but the mechanism of change itself, then the coming power transition – as long as it occurs among states that have internalized the same basic norms – should occur peacefully. It is here that Coicaud's and Adler's perspectives intersect. For democratic and reciprocal hegemony is essentially about mutual socialization and reciprocal social learning. A benign United States imparts to the international system its rules of the game and notion of order, but also makes room for and adjusts its own grand strategy to the rules of the game and notions of order of other major states. The result is perhaps a messy amalgam, but at least one that would enjoy democratic legitimacy and accord rising units the status they seek. Perhaps such "socialized instability," to use Coicaud's turn of phrase, is the best one can hope for. Indeed, in light of the alternative – great power war in the nuclear age – striving for socialized instability and seeking the democratization of hegemony may well offer the best prospects for managing international change peacefully.

Notes

1. William Wohlforth, "The Stability of a Unipolar World," *International Security*, Vol. 24, No. 1 (Summer 1999), pp. 5–41.
2. See Charles Kupchan, "In Defense of European Defense: An American Perspective," *Survival*, Vol. 42, No. 2 (Summer 2000), pp. 16–32.
3. See Robert Gilpin, *War and Change in World Politics* (Cambridge: Cambridge University Press, 1981).
4. Randall Schweller, "Realism and the Present Great Power System: Growth and Positional Conflict over Scarce Resources," in Michael Mastanduno and Ethan Kapstein, eds., *Unipolar Politics* (New York: Columbia University Press, 1999), pp. 28–68.
5. Thomas Friedman, *The Lexus and the Olive Tree* (New York: Farrar, Straus, Giroux, 1999).
6. See Karl Polanyi, *The Great Transformation* (New York: Octagon Books, 1975).

7. The proposition that the peoples of most countries attribute to the United States a benign character is admittedly controversial. Especially in countries whose populations have suffered because of direct or indirect military intervention by the United States, anti-American sentiment runs strong. At the same time, I would contend that the United States is far less predatory and exploitative than most other great powers in history. The best testimony to such qualities is the absence of balancing against the United States despite its stark material preponderance.
8. See Charles Kupchan, "Rethinking Europe," *The National Interest*, No. 56 (Summer 1999), pp. 73–79.
9. See Bates Gill and Michael O'Hanlon, "China's Hollow Military," *The National Interest*, No. 56 (Summer 1999), pp. 55–62.

Contributors

Charles A. Kupchan is Associate Professor of International Affairs in the School of Foreign Service and Department of Government at Georgetown University and Senior Fellow at the Council on Foreign Relations.

Emanuel Adler is Associate Professor, Department of International Relations, The Hebrew University of Jerusalem.

Jean-Marc Coicaud is a Senior Fellow at the United States Institute of Peace (Washington, DC), while on leave from the Peace and Governance Programme of the United Nations University (Tokyo), where he serves as a Senior Academic Officer.

Yuen Foong Khong is a Fellow of Nuffield College, Oxford University. From 1998 to 2000, he was Acting Director and Professor, Institute of Defence & Strategic Studies, Nanyang Technological University, Singapore.

Jason Davidson is Visiting Instructor of Political Science and International Affairs at Mary Washington College.

Mira Sucharov is Assistant Professor of Political Science at Carleton University (Ottawa).

Index

Abbott, Lyman 110
accommodating change 13
accountability 11, 71, 141–2
Acharya, Amitav 27
advocacy groups, transnational 141
affinity, emotive
  benign character 11, 31, 171
    Anglo-American rapprochement 23–4
    ASEAN 28
    attribution 20
  legitimacy
    Anglo-American rapprochement 82, 83
    ASEAN 85–6
  order 49
    Anglo-American rapprochement 45, 46
    Japan's rise 43–4
aggressor states 9–10, 19
Akkerman, Convention of (1826) 116, 118
Alaska 103, 105
Albright, Madeleine 94
Alexander I, Tzar
  benign character 114–15, 116
  legitimacy 77, 78, 119
Ali, Muhammad (Mehemet) 117

Allen, H. C. 103
amalgamated security communities 147
anarchy 140
Anglo-American rapprochement 14, 15, 101, 102–4, 111–12
  benign character 21–4, 104–8
  legitimacy 80–3, 87, 110–11
  order 35–6, 37, 44–9, 109–10
Annan, Kofi 141
Antolik, Michael 124, 127
Aquino, Corazon 125
arbitration 48–9
ASEAN *see* Association of Southeast Asian Nations
ASEAN Regional Forum (ARF) 121
Asia Pacific Economic Cooperation 154
Association of Southeast Asia (ASA) 122
Association of Southeast Asian Nations (ASEAN) 14–15, 102, 121–3, 130
  benign character 26–8, 123–8
  Concord 129
  legitimacy 84–6, 87, 129–30
  order 52–4, 128–9
  security communities 148, 154
  Treaty of Amity and Cooperation (TAC) 52, 53, 129
Australia 28, 31

Austria, and Concert of Europe 112, 113
  benign character 25–6, 114–15, 116, 117
  legitimacy 76–8, 79, 87, 119, 120
  order 118, 119

balance of power theory 139
Balfour, Arthur 47
Bandung Conference (1955) 121–2
Bangkok Declaration (1967) 122
Barcelona Process 155–6
Bayard, Thomas 47
Belgium 115
benign character 9–11, 18–20, 170–1
  attribution 20–1
  contemporary power transition 29–31
  historical cases
    Anglo-American rapprochement 21–4, 104–8
    ASEAN 26–8, 123–8
    Concert of Europe 24–6, 113–18
  legitimacy 89
  USA 10, 165
Bismarck, Otto von 79
Boer War 44, 45, 81, 103, 108
Borneo *see* Sabah; Sarawak
Bosnia 5
  see also Yugoslavia, former
British Guiana *see* Venezuelan border crisis
Brunei 121, 128
Bryant, William Jennings 109–10
Bull, Hedley 37
Burma 121
Bush, George (Sr) 5, 56, 60
Bush, George W. (Jr) 61

Cabrera, Manuel 106
Cambodia 121, 122
Canada
  Anglo-American rapprochement 104
  benign character 22, 105, 107
  legitimacy 82
  and USA, power asymmetries between 164
Canning, George 115, 116
Carden, Lionel 106
Castlereagh, Viscount 114, 116, 119
Cavour, Camillo 79
Chamberlain, Joseph 47, 48
change of change 138, 148–50
  multilateral age 138–46
  security communities 146–8

power transitions within and across 150–6
Chechnya 142
Chile 141
China
  Anglo-American rapprochement 46–7, 103
  ASEAN
    benign character 27, 28, 124–7
    legitimacy 85
    order 129
  historical parallels 15
  legitimacy 87, 92, 93–4
  order 36, 37
    Anglo-American rapprochement 46–7
    Japan's rise 39, 40–1, 42
    rise 54–61
  security communities 153, 154, 155, 167–8, 170
  sources of structural change 4
  systemic change, future 171
  US hegemony 1, 4
classical realism 9–10
classic overtake cases 14
Clayton Bulwer Treaty (1850) 105–6
Cleveland administration 44, 105
Clinton, Bill 5
  China 56, 57, 60, 61
cold peace 7
Cold War
  cold peace 7
  internationalism 1, 6
  legitimacy 75
  order 54–5
colonialism *see* imperialism
compatibility relationships, international law 74–5
competition relationships, international law 74, 75
Comprehensive Test Ban Treaty 160, 169
concert diplomacy 39
Concert of Europe 14–15, 101–2, 112–13, 120–1
  benign character 24–6, 113–18
  legitimacy 76–80, 87, 119–20
  order 118–19
consent and legitimacy 73
constructivism 7
continuity 13
Corregidor Affair 125

INDEX 177

counterculture, global 141
Crimean War 78–9
Cuba 47–8, 82

Davos culture 141, 155
defense
  EU 4, 10
  US policy 3, 5
democracy 7–8
  changing mechanism of change 150
  legitimacy 71–4, 88–96
  order 39, 45
  USA 165
Deutsch, Karl 146–7
diplomacy 39, 141
dispute resolution
  arbitration 48–9
  ASEAN 28
  China's rise 59

Eastern Question, Concert of Europe 78–9
economic interaction
  benign character 20–1
  legitimacy 81
  order 35, 36
    Anglo-American rapprochement 44–5, 46–7, 109
    China's rise 56–9
    Japan's rise 40, 42
Egypt 117, 118, 119, 120
emotive affinity *see* affinity, emotive
Euro-Mediterranean Partnership 155–6
European Union (EU)
  benign character 10, 29–31
  diplomacy 141
  legitimacy 13, 92–4, 97–8n.20
  multilateral age 142, 145–6
  security communities 147, 148, 150–1, 154, 155
    systemic change 166–7
  sources of structural change 4, 6
  systemic change 160
    future 170
    polity and practice, changes in 166–7
    security communities 166, 170
  US hegemony 1
external threats 11
extraterritoriality 42

Ferdinand I 114
Ferdinand VII 114, 115

force, rules of 35, 43, 59–61
France
  Concert of Europe 112, 113
    benign character 24, 25–6, 114, 115–16, 117, 118
    legitimacy 76–7, 78–9, 119
    order 118, 119, 120
  Japan's rise 36, 41, 42
  legitimacy 92, 93, 99n.28
    Anglo-American rapprochement 81, 83
    Concert of Europe 76–7, 78–9, 119
  US hegemony 4
free trade 5
Friedman, Thomas 163
future 168–72

G-8 55
Gelber, Lionel 23
General Agreement on Tariffs and Trade 35
Germany
  benign character
    Anglo-American rapprochement 22, 23, 24
    Concert of Europe 114
    self-binding 19
  globalization 169
  legitimacy 92, 99n.28
    Anglo-American rapprochement 81, 83
    Concert of Europe 76, 78, 79
  order
    Anglo-American rapprochement 45
    Concert of Europe 118
    Japan's rise 36, 41, 42, 43
    US hegemony 1
    World War I 163
Gilpin, Robert 35, 38
globalization
  cultural 154–5
  multilateral age 141, 143, 145
  systemic change 163–4, 169
gold standard 109–10
Gramsci, Antonio 91
Great Britain
  Concert of Europe 112, 113
    benign character 25–6, 114, 115, 116, 117
    legitimacy 76–7, 78, 79, 119, 120
    order 118, 119

Great Britain (cont.)
  legitimacy 99n.28
    Anglo-American rapprochement
      80–3, 87, 110–11
    Concert of Europe 76–7, 78, 79, 119,
      120
  order
    Anglo-American rapprochement
      35–6, 37, 44–9, 109–10
    Concert of Europe 118, 119
    Indonesia's bid for regional hegemony
      50, 51, 52, 53
    Japan's rise 36, 40, 42, 43
  and the US, rapprochement between
    14, 15, 101, 102–4, 111–12
    benign character 21–4, 104–8
    legitimacy 80–3, 87, 110–11
    order 35–6, 37, 44–9, 109–10
    see Anglo-American rapprochement
Greece 115–17, 119
Grey, Sir Edward 108
Guatemala 106

Harcourt, Sir William 47
Hay–Pauncefote treaty 106
hegemonic instability theory 38
Herzog, Chaim 126
hierarchical relationships, international
  law 74, 75
Hobbes, Thomas 91
Holy Alliance 112
  benign character 26
  legitimacy 76, 77, 119–20
Hong Kong 60
human rights issues 141–2
  China 56, 57, 60

ideational contestation 8–9
  order 34, 37
    ASEAN 52, 53
    conceptualizing 37
identity 8
  benign character 11, 20, 29
    Anglo-American rapprochement 23,
      24
    ASEAN 27, 28
    attribution 21
    Concert of Europe 25, 26
    legitimacy 13
    multilateral age 142
    order 12, 36

Anglo-American rapprochement 46
  Japan's rise 43
  peaceful power transition 39
  security communities 151
imperialism
  legitimacy 94
    Anglo-American rapprochement
      80–1, 82, 110
    ASEAN 84, 86
  order
    Anglo-American rapprochement 48
    Indonesia's bid for regional hegemony
      50, 51
    Japan's rise 43
India 48
Indonesia
  ASEAN 121, 122, 130
    benign character 26–8, 124–5, 126,
      127
    legitimacy 84, 85, 87
    order 52–4, 128, 129
  Maphilindo 122
  order 36, 37
    ASEAN 52–4, 128, 129
    bid for regional hegemony 49–54
Industrial Revolution 46
influence, spheres of
  Concert of Europe 112, 116, 120
  order 35
    Anglo-American rapprochement 110,
      112
    China's rise 59–61
    Concert of Europe 118–19
    Indonesia's bid for regional hegemony
      50, 51
    Japan's rise 43
institutions 8
  benign character 9–10
  legitimacy 71–2, 73
  multilateral age 140
  order 37
  security communities 146
intellectual property rights 57
interaction
  economic *see* economic interaction
  social 20–1
interdependence theorists 38–9
Internet 141, 143
Islam 152
Israel 28, 126
isthmian canal 103, 105–6, 107–8

Italy 78, 79
Iwakura Mission (1871–1873) 40

Jameson raid 45
Japan
  benign character
    Anglo-American rapprochement 106
    ASEAN 27
    self-binding 19
  globalization 169
  legitimacy 92, 99n.28
    Anglo-American rapprochement 81, 83
    ASEAN 85
  order 36, 37
    China's rise 58
    Japan's rise 39–44, 49
  security communities 155, 167–8
  systemic change, future 171
  US hegemony 1
Jiang Xemin 60

Kennedy, Paul 45, 46
Kissinger, Henry 97n.18
Knox, Philander C. 106
konfrontasi 122, 124, 125
  order 51, 53
Korea 40, 41, 42
Kosovo 5, 142, 160, 166
  see also Yugoslavia, former
Kruger, Paul 45
Kurils 43
Kutahya, Convention of (1833) 117

Landsdowne, British Foreign Secretary 106
Laos 121
law, international 74–5
learning *see* social learning
Lee, A. H. 108
Lee Teng-hui 60, 127
legitimacy 9, 12–14, 68–72, 170
  case studies 75–6, 86–8
    Anglo-American rapprochement 80–3, 110–11
    ASEAN 84–6, 129–30
    Concert of Europe 76–80, 119–20
  socialization of rising security threats and democratic hegemony 88–96
  as socializing force 72–5
Leifer, Michael 128
Lenin, V. I. 37

liberalism
  changing mechanisms of change 150
  legitimacy 88, 95
  order 39, 45–6
Louis XVI 120
Luard, Evan 37

Mahathir, Mohamed 28
Mahmud II 117
Malaya 50–1, 122, 124
Malaysia 122
  ASEAN 121, 122
  benign character 28, 124–7
  order 52, 129
  Indonesia's bid for regional hegemony 36, 37, 50–1, 52, 53
Manchuria 41, 42
Maphilindo 122
material conditions, changes in 161–4
McKinley, William 105–6, 110
Mediterranean area 155–6
Meiji government 40
Metternich, Klemens
  benign character 25, 114–15, 116
  legitimacy 77, 78, 79, 119
Mexico 164
Modelski, George 148
Monroe Doctrine
  benign character 105
  order 44, 47, 48, 109
moral values 13
Morgenthau, Hans 97n.18
multilateral age 138–46
Munchengratz, Treaty of (1833) 117
Munenori, Terashima 42
Muslim fundamentalism 152
Myanmar 121

NAFTA 148, 154
Naples revolt 114–15
Napoleon I 24, 25, 79, 112, 119
Napoleon III 79
nationalism
  Concert of Europe 76, 77–8, 79, 80
  Indonesia's bid for regional hegemony 50
  Japan's rise 42
NATO
  diplomacy 141
  security communities 148, 152, 153–4, 166–7
  Yugoslavia, former 4, 5, 142, 160

neorealism 38
Netherlands 50
New Zealand 28, 31
Nicholas I, Tzar 78–9, 116
Nixon Doctrine 125
North American Free Trade Association (NAFTA) 148, 154
North Atlantic Treaty Organization see NATO
nuclear weapons 161–2
Nye, Joseph 144

Olney, Richard 48, 49, 105, 109
openness 11
order 9, 11–12, 34–6, 61–2, 170
  Anglo-American rapprochement 44–9, 109–10
  ASEAN 128–9
  benign character 19
  China's rise 54–61
  conceptualizing international order 36–9
  Concert of Europe 118–19
  Indonesia's bid for regional hegemony 49–54
  Japan's rise 39–44
  legitimacy 89
  peaceful power transition 38–9
  status quo states 19
Organization for Security and Co-operation in Europe (OSCE) 142, 153, 154
Ottoman Empire 115–17

participation of rising challenger 12, 36, 49
Partnership for Peace 153
Pauncefote, Julian 49, 105
Philippines 122
  Anglo-American rapprochement
    benign character 23, 24, 107, 125–6
    legitimacy 82
    order 44
  ASEAN 121, 123
Pinochet, Augusto 141
pluralistic security communities 147
Poland 118
Polanyi, Karl 164
Portugal 118
power 8
  aggressor states 19
  benign character 9–10, 19, 29, 30
  legitimacy 74–5
  order 34, 37

  Indonesia's bid for regional hegemony 51
  Japan's rise 40
  regulatory conventions for power management 14–15
  systemic change 162–3
power transition theory 139
prestige, hierarchy of 35
  Indonesia's bid for regional hegemony 50
  Japan's rise 41, 42
Prussia, Concert of Europe 112
  benign character 25–6, 114, 115, 117
  legitimacy 76–7, 78, 79, 119, 120
  order 118, 119

Quadruple Alliance 76–7

racialism, Anglo-American 110–11
realism
  Anglo-American rapprochement 45, 46, 111
  benign character 9–10
  order 38, 45, 46
reconciliation 11, 13
Reform Bill (Great Britain, 1832) 110
regulatory conventions for power management 14–15
religion 13
  Islam 152
resolve of rising challenger 12, 36, 49
resources of rising challenger 12, 36, 49
revisionist states 18–19
Richelieu, Armand 76
Roosevelt, Theodore 107, 108
Rosebery, Earl of 47
Ruggie, John G. 156
rules, change management 142
Russia
  Concert of Europe 112, 113
    benign character 25–6, 113–18
    legitimacy 76–7, 78–9, 119, 120
    order 118–19
  G-8 55
  Japan's rise 39, 40, 41–2, 43
  legitimacy 92
    Anglo-American rapprochement 81
    Concert of Europe 76–7, 78–9, 119, 120
  security communities 151–2, 153–4, 166–7, 170

US hegemony 4
see also Soviet Union

Sabah 50–1, 52, 122, 124, 125
Sakhalin 43
Salisbury, Lord
　benign character 105
　order 44, 45, 47, 48, 109
Sarawak 50–1, 52, 124
Schroeder, Paul 119
security communities 7, 138, 146–8
　ASEAN 53
　multilateral age 143
　power transitions within and across 150–6
　systemic change 165–8, 169–70
Selborne, Lord 106, 108
self-binding
　ASEAN 122
　　benign character 26, 124, 127–8
　　order 53
　benign character 11, 19
　　Anglo-American rapprochement 22
　　ASEAN 26, 124, 127–8
　　attribution 20
　　Concert of Europe 24–5
　power, state 162
　USA 165, 169
self-evaluation 11
Serbs 142
Sherman Anti-trust Act 100n.33
Singapore 50–1
　ASEAN 121, 123
　　benign character 27, 28, 124, 126–7
　　legitimacy 84
　　order 52
Sino-Japanese War (1894–1895) 39, 40–1
social Darwinism 82, 100n.32, 110
social interaction 20–1
socialization 68–72
　case studies 75–6, 86–8
　　Anglo-American rapprochement 80–3
　　ASEAN 84–6
　　Concert of Europe 76–80
　legitimacy as socializing force 72–5
　of rising security threats and democratic hegemony 88–96
social learning 140, 146, 148–50, 172
　security communities 153, 154
Somalia 5
Soros, George 28

South Africa 44, 45, 81, 103, 108
Southeast Asian financial crisis 28
Southeast Asia Treaty Organization (SEATO) 123
sovereignty, state v. individual 141–2
Soviet Union
　collapse
　　legitimacy 87, 95
　　order 55
　legitimacy 75, 93
　security communities 166
　see also Russia
Spain, revolution 25, 114, 115
Spanish–American War 103
　benign character 23, 107
　legitimacy 82
　order 44, 47–8
stability 19, 70
status quo states 9–10, 18–19
Storry, Richard 41
strategic restraint *see* self-binding
structural change, sources of 3–7
Suharto, General 122, 124, 130
　benign character 125, 127
　order 51, 53
Sukarno, President 122, 124, 130
　order 50, 51, 52–3

Taiwan 59–61, 168, 171
territorial change, procedures for managing 35
　China's rise 59
　Indonesia's bid for regional hegemony 50, 51
　Japan's rise 43
terrorism 90
Thailand 121, 122, 123
　benign character 124
　order 52, 128
thick multilateralism 146–8
Thiers, Adolphe 117
thin multilateralism 146
Tiananmen Square protests 55–6, 60
trading relationships *see* economic interaction
Triple Intervention (1895) 40, 41, 42, 43
trust 151
Turkey 115–16, 117, 118, 119, 120

Union of Soviet Socialist Republics *see* Soviet Union

182 INDEX

United Kingdom *see* Great Britain
United Nations
   Corregidor Affair   125
   legitimacy   70, 74, 90, 95
   order   55
   territorial change   35
United States of America
   ASEAN   123
      benign character   27, 125, 126
      legitimacy   85
   benign character   10, 165
      Anglo-American rapprochement 21–4, 104–8
      ASEAN   27, 125, 126
      Civil War   22
      contemporary power transition   29–31
   change of change
      multilateral age   140, 144
      security communities   151, 153, 154, 155
   Civil War   22, 44, 103
   and Great Britain, rapprochement between   14, 15, 101, 102–4, 111–12
      benign character   21–4, 104–8
      legitimacy   80–3, 87, 110–11
      order   35–6, 37, 44–9, 109–10
   legitimacy   88–91, 92, 93–6
      Anglo-American rapprochement 80–3, 87, 110–11
      ASEAN   85
      as socializing force   75
   and Malaysia, confrontation between   28
   multipolarity, preparation for   1–2
   order   35
      Anglo-American rapprochement 35–6, 37, 44–9, 109–10
      China's rise   36, 54–61
      Civil War   44
      Japan's rise   43
   Sherman Anti-trust Act   100n.33
   sources of structural change   3–6
   systemic change   159–60
      future   169–70, 171–2
      policy and practice, changes in   164–5
      security communities   167–8, 170
   War of Independence   103, 104

values   73
Venezuelan border crisis   103, 111
   benign character   22, 105
   order   44–9, 109
Victoria, Queen   47
Vienna, Congress of   76, 112, 114, 119
Vietnam   121
   benign character   124
   legitimacy   85
   order   52, 129

Walt, Stephen   9
war   7, 149, 161–2
   see also named wars
warm peace   7
Weber, Max   91
Western European Union   141
Wilhelm II   45
Wilson, Woodrow   95
World Trade Organization (WTO)   35, 58–9, 141
World War I   79, 163
World War II   1, 6, 167

Yamagata, Aritomo   42
Yugoslavia, former   4, 5–6
   see also Bosnia; Kosovo

Catalogue Request

Name: _____

Address: _____

_____

Tel: _____

Fax: _____

E-mail: _____

To receive a catalogue of UNU Press publications kindly photocopy this form and send or fax it back to us with your details. You can also e-mail us this information. Please put "Mailing List" in the subject line.

United Nations University Press

53-70, Jingumae 5-chome
Shibuya-ku, Tokyo 150-8925, Japan
Tel: +81-3-3499-2811 Fax: +81-3-3406-7345
E-mail: sales@hq.unu.edu http://www.unu.edu